Good Hunting.
With

Gough Thomas's

GUN BOOK

THE CULT OF THE GUN

'In many ways it takes a man back, body and spirit, to the places where he belongs, and gives him back so many of the things of which modern commercial civilization has deprived him.'

[The gun shown above is a double flintlock 20-bore made by T. B. Heuseux of Liège about the year 1800.]

Gough Thomas's GUN BOOK

Shotgun lore
for the sportsman

G. T. GARWOOD
M.SC., F.I.C.E., F.I.E.E.,
CHARTERED ENGINEER

ADAM & CHARLES BLACK
LONDON

FIRST PUBLISHED 1969
REPRINTED 1971, 1974 (WITH CORRECTIONS)
AND 1977

A. & C. BLACK LIMITED
35 BEDFORD ROW, LONDON WC1R 4JH

ISBN 0 7136 1008 5

PRINTED IN GREAT BRITAIN BY
BUTLER & TANNER LIMITED
FROME AND LONDON

CONTENTS

PAGE

SECTION 5—SOME SPECIAL GUNS

SECTION 6—HOW MANY GUNS DO YOU NEED?

SECTION 7—BARRELS

SECTION 8—GUN-FITTING

SECTION 9—TESTS AND TESTING

(See also Section 10—'Patterns and Performance')

ILLUSTRATIONS

ACKNOWLEDGEMENTS

The author and publishers wish to thank the following for the illustrations appearing in this book: Mr. Robert Held for illustration 1; Mr. Paul Baker for illustration 2; Fabrique Nationale for illustration 4; Mr. John T. Boone for illustration 5; Churchill (Gunmakers) Ltd. for illustration 6; Mr. John Marchington for illustration 10; James Purdey and Son Ltd. for illustration 11 (*top*); W. McConnell for illustrations 11 (*centre*) and 12; *Shooting Times* for illustration 11 (*bottom*); Westley-Richards for illustrations 14 and 18; Olin for illustration 15; Major G. L. Carlisle for illustrations 19 and 21; The Kynoch Press for illustrations 24 and 26; The Birmingham Proof House for illustration 41.

PREFACE

I have been repeatedly urged to publish a collection of the weekly articles I have written over the past eight years for the 'Gun Gossip' feature of the *Shooting Times and Country Magazine*—or, to quote a distinguished American editor, 'at least, the meat from them'.

This miscellany is the result: it contains about a sixth of what I have written in my capacity as Gun Editor of our oldest shooting magazine.

In compiling it, I have kept before me the object suggested by my sub-title, 'Shotgun Lore for the Sportsman'. Shotguns are so highly variable in their performance, as well as in their adaptability to individuals and the sport they pursue, that, for the best results—sometimes for the avoidance of humiliating failure—shooters often need a better understanding of them than they possess.

This book, I hope, will help to promote such an understanding. In compiling it, I have generally avoided formal descriptions of guns, gun mechanisms and ammunition, as given in my earlier book, *Shotguns and Cartridges.* Rather, I have tried to guide the sportsman in choosing and buying a gun and critically appraising its performance, so that he may get the best out of it of which it is capable. No gun, and especially no low-priced or second-hand gun, should ever be taken on trust.

To facilitate reference, I have grouped the articles into the sections shown in the Contents, and have titled or re-titled them to the same end.

For the rest, I hope that the casual reader may find pleasure and occasional profit in browsing through these pages, many of which were written expressly for him. I hope, too, that the deliberate seeker after information may not be too often disappointed. I believe I may claim that he will find some original matter here, and some that is not readily available from any other source.

I have to acknowledge the kindness of the various firms and individuals who supplied the photographs to illustrate this book. Their names appear opposite. My cordial thanks are also due to John

T. Amber and G. L. Carlisle, who spurred me to publish, and to Joan Clifford for her generous services as amanuensis and critic. Finally, I cannot let pass this opportunity of acknowledging the kindness and encouragement I have always received from the Editor and proprietors of the *Shooting Times.*

Section 1

BACKGROUND

'My own pleasure in a good gun has thus one root but several branches . . . yet to me it has been above all the intimate, personal weapon . . . through whose instrumentality I have known many high moments, when, for a space, blood has been transmuted into ichor, and weariness, hunger and disappointment have been utterly forgotten.'

the cult of the gun

We had had a wholly delightful morning's partridge shooting within sight of Salisbury's famous spire, and now, the dogs having been watered and the beaters seen to, we were sitting with our backs to a rick, eating our lunches in the tempered, golden sunshine of a perfect September day.

Inevitably the conversation turned to the morning's sport; and then, under the mellowing influences of the occasion—solid, liquid and abstract—it took the philosophical turn of speculating on the sources of pleasure in shooting. We were all agreed that, despite our relish for roast partridge, we took no pleasure in the killing of the birds, though we certainly did in the exercise of skill, whereby we were able to kill them quickly, cleanly and expertly. Then dogs and good dog-work received their tribute, followed in due order by acknowledgements of the contributions made by the quality of the air on the Hampshire Downs, the healthful exercise, the scenery, the weather, and the pleasure of enjoying all these things in the company of congenial friends. Nobody mentioned the gun until I did. 'What about the pleasure of having a good gun in your hands?' I asked, 'and the opportunity of using it to some purpose?'

It would be untrue to say that this simple question produced a stunned silence, but it was evidently sufficiently disconcerting to the other members of the party to cause a perceptible check in the flow of conversation. The senior member recovered first. With the superiority proper to a Balliol man he dismissed the matter by saying that he never could appreciate mechanical things. But his next in order of seniority, a country sportsman of the old-fashioned school, rallied to my support. 'Oh, yes, I like a good gun!' he said; and having thus, it appeared, exhausted his enthusiasm on the subject, he lapsed into silence.

The remaining two members of the party were still, it seemed, too disconcerted by the curious vista opened up by my question to vouchsafe any response. This nettled me slightly. 'Are all you fellows so infernally civilized that you take no pleasure in owning and using a fine, personal weapon?' I asked, irritably. This produced some faint placatory murmurs, but no further response; so, seeing that the topic was not fruitful, I changed the subject.

I have often thought of that conversation since, and have wondered whether one confessed gun-lover to a party of five regular shooting men represents the normal proportion. If so, I must conclude that the majority are shut off from a source of lasting pleasure that is not altogether lacking in refinement or civilized quality. Although in my case I put the sport of shooting first, and dogs and dog-work second, I would certainly put the gun high among the delightful concomitants to which my friends had so rightly paid tribute. True, a fondness for guns has an atavistic element. Primitive man, when you come to think of it, was but a feeble, soft-skinned creature, with neither teeth and claws for attack, nor speed for flight; so that when he came to arming himself and thereby attaining mastery over the animal kingdom, his personal weapon, whether it were stone axe, spear or bow, must have been as near and precious to him as one of his own limbs. Small wonder then that little boys, the heirs to ancestral memories accumulated over such misty ages, should reach for toy weapons as they crawl from their cradles, or that the same instincts should persist in larger boys, even though they be sublimated into a civilized man's proper regard for the implements of his sport.

My own pleasure in a good gun has thus one root but several branches. As a piece of artistic hand-craftsmanship, I value it as I do an antique clock or a piece of fine, period furniture. Its ingenious mechanism gives me much joy to contemplate and care for—so does the patina of its beautiful wood and engraved metal. Its ballistic problems excite my scientific curiosity, and I have had many happy hours investigating them. And yet, if truth be told, it is in its old, atavistic relation that the gun has afforded me the greatest pleasure and satisfaction; for to me it has been, above all else, the intimate, personal weapon, the proved companion in field and flood, through whose instrumentality I have known many high moments, when, for a space, blood has been transmuted into ichor, and weariness, hunger and disappointment have been utterly forgotten.

8 September 1961

how it all began

Among the minor regrets of my life are certain conversational opportunities I have missed. One that recurs to me was when I was on my way to Cambridge to lecture to a summer school at King's. Sharing the compartment with me and my companion was a stranger, sprawling negligently in his corner and deep in one of the Greek authors. Nothing in our conversation distracted his attention until the subject arose of old-time shooting in the Cambridgeshire fens, whereat he looked up from his book and fixed me with a penetrating regard I shall not readily forget. Only then did I recognize him as G. M. Trevelyan, the distinguished Master of Trinity and social historian.

If I had known then what I learned later—that he was a keen shooting man—I think I should have been tempted to ask his views on the conversational topic that had so strongly attracted his attention. But I was too diffident or reserved to do so; and so he returned to his book and the opportunity passed.

I thought of this a year or so ago when I had occasion to look up in Trevelyan something of the social history of shooting in this country. I thought of it again when, in a recent letter which I read, a young correspondent implied that shooting was a privilege hitherto reserved for the nobility, aristocracy and landed gentry. What a curious misconception! It is almost on a par with that of certain American authors who assure their readers that only the wealthy can afford wing-shooting in England. And yet it is one that is probably shared by many here, whose view of shooting history takes in nothing beyond the jealous over-preservation of the post-Waterloo period, with its man-traps and spring guns, its desperate poaching affrays, and its lifelong friendships between landowning neighbours broken by quarrels over a few partridges.

But on a larger view it may be seen that from the earliest times, shooting was essentially a democratic sport. Before the advent of firearms the nobility pursued their 'bestes chasable' with horse and hound, and their feathered game by hawking. The lower orders of rural society confined their more legitimate operations to the latter, which they took by various traditional methods including liming and netting and the use of 'springes' and 'engines'.

The gunpowder revolution

When the first matchlock guns became available, round about 1500, they were eagerly seized on, not by the privileged classes as implements of sport, but by the peasantry as a means for filling their pinched winter bellies; so much so, indeed, as to give rise to fears that their use would menace our national superiority with the longbow, and to provoke a series of enactments designed to prohibit or limit their employment. But in the absence of effective enforcement, no admonitions, no Acts of Parliament, no threats of fines or imprisonment could deter the peasantry from using the new weapon to help themselves to the seemingly inexhaustible stocks of game and wild-

fowl that flocked field and fen. In his *Illustrations of Hunting, Fishing and Fowling*, published in Amsterdam about 1580, Hans Bols depicts a wintry landscape literally crawling with rustic matchlock-gunners in pursuit of wildfowl which they are stalking from behind river banks. No doubt the same sort of thing went on over all suitable parts of rural England.

The privileged classes, however, ignored the vulgar innovation and remained faithful to horse, hound and hawk—that is, until after 1660, when Charles II, returning from his exile in France, brought with him the new French sport of shooting birds on the wing. It quickly became fashionable, and so the era of preservation dawned. By the time of Anne, says Trevelyan, 'much of the land was strictly preserved and religiously shot by the owners, but great tracts were open to any man who could procure a net or gun'. And thus it continued, though with diminishing opportunities for the humble shooter, save in the wilder parts of the country. Yet at the height of the preservation era, Hawker writes of free shooting, presumably in southern England, and of the 'shore poppers' and 'tit shooters' who interfered with his sport. Who were these, if not the social descendants of the matchlock-gunners of Tudor times, and the social ancestors of the economically enfranchised gunners of today?

But although we are free to congratulate ourselves on the democratic basis of our modern sport, we must not regard that as anything new. Nor should we delude ourselves with the idea that we have simply returned to the conditions of our forefathers. Modern weapons, modern communications, greatly increased populations and correspondingly reduced facilities for the natural regeneration of game add up to a very different picture. In modern times good stocks of game have only existed with preservation and restrictions on the freedom to shoot. Without these latter we could easily arrive at the situation not unknown elsewhere: where everybody is free to shoot, but all game has vanished.

12 October 1962

. HOW IT ALL BEGAN A wintry sixteenth-century landscape 'crawling with rustic matchlock gunners pursuit of wildfowl'. *From* The Hunting of Birds, Beasts and Fish *by Jan van der Streat, Antwerp, 566.*

Section 2

CHOICE OF GUNS

'The gun is the essential link between the man and the kind of sport he pursues. It is not enough that it should be well adapted to one or the other. For the best success, it must be fully adapted to both.'

2. His first gun.

his first gun

To a normal boy or young man, his first proper gun provides an unforgettable occasion; and as an introduction, not only to the keen, manly delights of shooting, but also to a closely bonded fraternity embracing all grades of society, it may well prove to be a milestone of special significance in his life.

There is something unique about the glamour of that first gun—something more than mere pride of possession and the pleasurable anticipation of days afield. It seems, indeed, both to evoke and satisfy a deep instinct; and when we consider that weapons, without a doubt, were the first preoccupation of our primitive forebears, we need look no farther for the source of that satisfaction. By enabling early man to procure more nourishing food, and to defend himself more effectively against his enemies—by redressing, in short, the balance between his advanced mentality and his physical limitations, his weapons enlarged his self-confidence and freed him from one of his earliest sources of frustration. Something of this is bound to come down to the young sportsman, and to warm his heart as he regards his first gun.

A heavy responsibility

A gun is a source of power, and as such entails responsibilities, and the beginner would do well to give them some thought before he ventures afield. For all its admirable and ingenious mechanism, for all its beauty of line and decoration, a gun is designed essentially to kill living things. Carelessly or ignorantly used, it can kill a bystander as easily as it can a rabbit. What is perhaps worse, it can maim him for life and lay the careless shooter under a load of remorse from which he may never escape. Grim thoughts! Still, they should not be thrust behind, but should form the basis of an enduring resolution never to be guilty of careless gun handling. Many a young shooter has to take to the field without the supervision and guidance of an experienced elder, but nowadays he has all the essential guidance conveniently available in the *Gun Code*, published by the British Field Sports

Society and procurable from any good gunsmith. This should be studied, mastered and practised until observance of the principles it lays down becomes automatic. The fact that older and more experienced shooters may frequently be seen cutting corners should not influence the young sportsman. In this matter, if in nothing else, he may rest assured that he really does know better than his elders.

And if he has these responsibilities to his companions in the field, he has others, only one degree less weighty, to the birds and animals he pursues. Towards them, his behaviour should be in accordance with a clear ethical code, on the basis of which he is prepared at all times to defend his sport against those who would attack it. Such a code is bound to be to some extent a personal matter. For myself, I justify my shooting on a few broad considerations: that life, to endure, must unfailingly consume other life, and that death comes to all creatures—perhaps on the whole more mercifully by shooting than by any of nature's common ways. So, I say, if I avoid all wantonness in my shooting—if I shoot nothing that is not either good to eat or a member of a species on which we have deliberately declared war—my conscience is clear. There are a few riders to that. It is my duty to see that all edible creatures shot find their way safely down someone's throat ('Take, kill *and eat*,' says the biblical injunction). I take full marks on that, as anyone can. But then I must also study to shoot so as to kill cleanly, and to avoid all long shots, when a clean kill can only come about as a fluke. In this, at least, my conscience tells me when I have failed.

As for the young sportsman's broader responsibilities to wild life as a whole, the pessimists tell us that men are doomed to destroy what they most love; and it is a fact that while civilization is increasingly disposed to respect all forms of wild life, its processes tend inevitably to their destruction. In this situation, it is becoming increasingly the role of the sportsman to arrest, modify or control these processes so as to preserve to all wild creatures some part of their heritage on this planet.

Enlightened self-interest

The young shooter who takes to the field fortified in this manner with a clear code of behaviour and ethics will find every inducement to regulate his conduct accordingly. He will unfailingly come to be recognized as a good sportsman and a safe and considerate shot irrespective, to a large extent, of his standard of marksmanship. He will thus be marked for encouragement in the way of invitations and otherwise, by which he may extend his experience and acquaintance, and open up new avenues leading, perhaps, beyond the realm of sport.

Delighted and preoccupied as he is likely to be with his new gun, I would recommend him to cultivate pleasure in shooting and all its broader concomitants, and not to become what the Americans call a 'gun-bug'. Guns are fascinating things, but they are only a means to an end, and to become too wrapped up in them is looking at a grand sport—almost a way of life—through the small end of the telescope.

At the same time, the ignorance of their weapons which many Englishmen seem almost proud to display is inconsistent with the best traditions of field sport. The shooting man should know his gun, and know it well. He should know how it works, and how to give it such first-aid as it may require in the field. He should know what sort of patterns it makes, and how to load it so as to get the best results of which it is capable without straining it beyond its capacity. He should make it his business to know, before he fires the first shot out of his new gun, how to clean it and how to preserve it from rust and other harm.

Precautions

More generally, and second only to safeguarding others, the young sportsman should learn what to avoid to prevent his gun becoming a menace to his own life and limb. In the last two sections of this book, I enlarge on many of the points on which I have only been able to touch here, but there are a few words of warning which perhaps I should say now. He should beware particularly of obstructions in his gun barrels, and should recognize the ways in which they can get there—fragments of cleaning material left behind; plugs of mud or snow picked up in the muzzles; a 20-bore cartridge inadvertently loaded in front of a 12-bore; or a component left behind from a faulty cartridge. Before shooting, and on every occasion thereafter when any unusual sound is heard, or circumstances have arisen in which an obstruction could have been picked up, the bores should be inspected.

If he observes these precautions and the *Gun Code*, and confines himself to standard cartridges specifically intended for his gun, the young sportsman may look forward to many happy years of shooting.

10 November 1966

suitable guns—and others

To shoot successfully, one must point the gun in the right place—a blinding glimpse of the obvious, perhaps, yet it serves to introduce my theme.

Pointing the gun in the right place—at least, for fast work at driven game, or at other targets offering similar shots—involves the unthinking use of our amazing co-ordinative machinery, whereby sense impressions are translated with lightning speed into appropriate muscular reactions. I say, 'appropriate muscular reactions': but what are the appropriate reactions? They are the complex muscular reactions that will move *a particular gun*, of given weight, balance and proportions, in a particular way. Under otherwise identical conditions, a different gun, of different weight, etc., would require a different set of muscular reactions to point it, or swing it, in its right relation to the target; and I am a firm believer in the advantage of having only one set of reactions waiting to be triggered off by a given sense impression—in other words, the advantage of sticking to one gun, and, as Clarrie Wilson, the Olympic coach, has advised, not even handling any other.

The right gun

But there is an implied corollary here. It is, that the gun concerned shall be a suitable one—suitable, that is to say, in respect of its type, weight, fit and boring. Clearly, if the gun is unsuitable, either in relation to the kind of sport concerned, or in relation to the man using it, there is a possibility that the advantage derived from its exclusive use may be outweighed by disadvantages derived from its unsuitability.

This is a point worth the attention of several kinds of shooters. They crowd my memory. There are very young men, using ancestral guns, some of which are too heavy for them, or badly fitting, or totally wrongly bored for the class of work for which they are being chiefly used. There are others, neither young nor old, again using guns that have come down to them, and chiefly notable for being gross misfits, to which their misguided users have never succeeded in fully adapting themselves. A doubly bad case in point was that of a hefty young doctor, whose gun, inherited from an elderly relative, was a light 20-bore, instead of the 12 he could have so easily used. And this gun, instead of having the normal sort of stock its owner obviously needed, had one of those curiously cast-off stocks—neither normal, nor centre-vision nor cross-eyed—that a certain famous gunmaker was, I suspect, unduly inclined to inflict on his customers.

And then, of course, there are the middle-aged and elderly shooters still using the guns that were built for them in their youth or in their prime, and that no longer fit them, or have become too heavy in relation to their declining strength and stamina.

Why wait?

A point that Churchill used to make, when he was boosting his XXV guns before the war, is reasonable and relevant here. 'Why wait?' he used to say. 'Why leave it until it is too late before you try what a light, short-barrelled gun can do for you and your shooting?' I myself never succumbed to his persuasion, though I *did* allow dear old F. J. R. Dennison of Henry Atkin to persuade me into laying up some comfort for my declining years by going over from 30-in. barrels and $6\frac{3}{4}$ lb. to 27-in. and 6 lb. 3 oz. I am sorry he did not live long enough to know how much satisfaction I got from his recommendations.

Nowadays, the shooter who has passed his physical zenith has a double inducement for handing in his 30-in. barrelled, full-weight, old thoroughbred, and going in for something lighter and faster-handling, but in no significant degree inferior, ballistically. These same old thoroughbreds are now fetching high prices—much more, in many cases, than they cost, and more than enough to finance the purchase of a new gun. True, the new gun may not be a best English side-lock, with all the refinements of the old, but it can be a thoroughly sound English box-lock, lighter by half a pound, and, with its shorter barrels, feeling less, and much faster-handling, though still a 12-bore. Or it could be one of the better Spanish XXVs, which, so far as I can judge by superficial examination, would need a better informed or more searching critic than I am to fault in any material respect. Meanwhile, the old thoroughbred could find a new, and perhaps younger, owner, and one better qualified to derive full pleasure from it.

Perhaps I should add that these thoughts are in no way inspired by solicitude for the gun trade, but by the satisfaction I myself, and others I have known, have obtained in the way suggested.

What's in a name?

A point of some significance here is the weight carried by a famous name. I get quite a number of letters from Americans enquiring about English guns, and I cannot fail to be impressed by their frequent preoccupation with just one or two London makers, headed of course, by Purdey. I would be the last to suggest that Purdey's do not deserve the great reputation they enjoy in the U.S.A., or to underrate the value of their name there as a status-symbol, but I am sure they would be the last to claim that, in the great days of English gunmaking, they ever had any monopoly of the fine craftsmen working for the trade. To a certain extent, it would be true to say that good guns are where you find them—a natural consequence of the traditional English gunmaking practice of putting work out to specialists, working in their own little shops, or at home. By the judicious employment of these specialists, many a gunmaker, not in the topmost flight, has occasionally turned out, to special order, guns of superlative quality.

For the rest, anyone on the lookout for a best second-hand gun would be well advised not to cast his net too narrowly. It would be easy to name a score or more of London and Birmingham makers, working between the two World Wars, who regularly, not just occasionally, turned out work of a quality that even the small handful of ultra-fashionable makers would have found it hard to beat. Atkin, Baker, Beesley, Blanch, Boswell, Churchill . . . one could almost make an alphabet of them. If a gun bears the undeniable stamp of quality, the fact that it may not bear a fashionable name should not blind the prospective purchaser to a possible bargain.

Caveat emptor

One of my American correspondents, a little while ago, unwittingly cast a light into a squalid corner of the gun trade. He had a gun bearing what he thought was the name of a famous Birmingham maker. In fact, the name merely resembled that of the maker concerned, but sufficiently closely to deceive an unwary buyer. I am afraid that the practice of putting spurious, imitative names on guns must at one time have been fairly widespread; for although I have never been connected with the gun trade, and have therefore handled relatively few guns in my time compared with the professionals, I have nevertheless seen several examples of this practice. 'James Pursey', 'Wesley Richards', and more than one variant of 'W. W. Greener' come immediately to mind.

Still, it must be borne in mind that what may appear to be a deliberately deceptive name may be nothing more than an earlier trading style of a strictly honest maker. Gunmaking runs in families, and the list of gunmakers' names appearing on guns over the past couple of centuries is full of examples of such changes.

It must also be recognized that the fact of a gun bearing a name designed to deceive does not necessarily mean that it is intrinsically a bad or dishonest weapon. So far as I can recall, all the cases I have seen appear to have been in the cheap-but-honest Birmingham class—the sort of gun that used to be sold as a non-ejector for about £15 before the last war. Nevertheless, a spurious name should fully alert a prospective buyer: the trader who would deceive in one particular is not likely to be too scrupulous in others.

But the real risk in buying used guns nowadays is not associated with these masqueraders, but rather with genuine specimens that have been got up in semblance of a general condition to which, as Mr. Micawber would say, they can establish no legitimate pretensions. The best single protection against this risk is a set of plug gauges in the hands of an honest 'vetting' gunsmith.

18 November 1965

matching man, gun and sport

A London friend has come up with an interesting point in connection with recoil. He is, he says, familiar with the general rule that, in order to keep recoil within normally acceptable limits, the gun should weigh about ninety-six times the shot charge—in other words, that there should be about 6 lb. of gun for every ounce of shot; but surely, he says, this rule only applies to persons of average weight, say, 10 to

3. 'YIELDING PLIANCY'

An outstanding example of how a lightweight shooter can ride the punch of recoil. Miss Kerry Wilkinson of the Hutt Valley Gun Club, New Zealand, began shooting with her F.N. Browning 2-shot automatic 12-bore at the age of $11\frac{1}{2}$. Now, approaching 13, she weighs 6 stone 5 lb. and is 4 ft. 11 in. tall. She uses full $1\frac{1}{8}$-oz. trap loads, and makes good scores at skeet.

13 stone, and not to lightweights of perhaps only 7 to 9. He goes on to ask my opinion on what is a suitable gun for a lightweight shooter who walks long distances for a few shots at rabbits, pigeon, partridges and pheasants.

On his first point—whether the 96/1 rule needs modifying out of consideration for the weight of the shooter—I am by no means certain that it does. Indeed, both on practical and theoretical grounds, I am inclined to say not, despite the plausibility of the suggestion. When a recoiling gun is brought to rest, it means that the energy of recoil has been dissipated; and it can be dissipated by a large resisting force operating over a short distance or a small resisting force operating over a large distance, the only theoretical requirement being that the product of the force and the distance shall be the same in each case. This expresses in semi-technical language something that accords with universal experience.

'Yielding pliancy'

When a gun is fired by a big man, with muscular arms and massive shoulders, he yields relatively little to the recoil. It follows that his shoulder opposes a greater resistance to the gun than does the shoulder of a lightweight, who might be thrust backwards twice as far. In consequence the big man's shoulder could be bruised while the lightweight's could escape. We know that a blow capable of bruising the bole of a tree would have no corresponding effect on a thin and whippy sapling. This is the *reculer pour sauter* or 'yielding pliancy' principle of which the Japanese traditionally make much use in systems of self-defence, not to mention diplomacy.

Strictly *ad hoc* observation bears out these conclusions. I have known several lightweights in the shooting field in my time, including men, women and boys, but I cannot recall a single case of recoil sensitivity specifically attributable to the shooter's lack of weight. I am, of course, thinking of normal, healthy people. Obviously, any shooter whose light weight is the consequence of some unsound condition might feel recoil unduly, but such cases are not pertinent. Nor perhaps are those of an opposite kind, such as that of a 9-stone friend of my young days. There was not a pick on him, as the Irish say, but he was as tough as rawhide, and could always see me out on a long day.

Concordance

But if, as it appears, the lightweight shooter does not need any special consideration from the viewpoint of recoil, there is obviously a need to correlate weight with weight when we consider that, for overall satisfaction, most shooters need to be able to carry and manipulate the gun of their choice throughout a long day without undue fatigue. I say 'most shooters', of course, out of regard for those whose sport requires little walking or carrying, not to mention those young beginners who derive positive satisfaction from burdening themselves with guns obviously too heavy for them—presumably to demonstrate their virility.

And it is not only the weight of the gun that needs to be related to the individual shooter: if we aim at overall satisfaction, there must be a broader correlation of man, gun and the kind of sport concerned. The last time I dealt with this subject, now some years ago, I worked out a little table which was intended to act as a guide in this important matter. As the subject is one that is continually recurring, I reproduce the table below without apology. If it does nothing else, it makes a convenient summary of the things that need to be taken into account when choosing a gun and load for a particular kind of sport.

Gun guidance table

Shooter			**Gun**			**Sport**				
Resistance to fatigue	*Resistance to recoil*	*Accuracy*	*Weight*	*Charge*	*Choke*	*Game*	*Range (most shots)*	*Shots fired*	*Amount of walking*	*Value per item*
Poor	Poor	Poor	Heavy	Heavy	Full	Large	Long	Many	Much	4
Average	Average	Average	Med.	Med.	Med.	Med.	Med.	Med.	Average	7
Good	Good	Good	Light	Light	Slight	Small	Close	Few	Little	10

To use the table, note the appropriate descriptions and add up the total value, taking the individual values as 4, 7 and 10 respectively according to whether they are on the first, second or third line. The total should desirably be not less than 70. Anything less than 60 clearly indicates something wrong. By way of example, take two cases:

1. A well-equipped driven game shooter. He is a good shot, of average resistance to fatigue and recoil. He uses a light, lightly loaded, open-bored gun against medium game, at which he fires many shots mostly at fairly close range. Land-Rovers relieve him of much walking. His score from the table would be 7, 7, 10, 10, 10, 10, 7, 10, 4, 10, making a total of 85. He would be well away, with reserves in hand.

2. An inexperienced young wildfowler, of immature strength. His resistance to fatigue and recoil is no more than average. His marksmanship with his heavy, fully choked magnum is poor. He fires few shots at long range—chiefly at duck and geese—and has to do a fair amount of walking. His score would be 7, 7, 4, 4, 4, 4, 4, 4, 10, 7, adding up to 55. This is not good enough. He would probably do better if he used an ordinary game gun, moderately choked, and if he cut out the long shots and went in more for approach tactics.

So, if my friend first mentioned, who started all this, would care to apply my table to his own case, I am sure it would give him a sensible answer, though inevitably in broad terms. The indications are, of course, in favour of a light gun, but whether he would be happier with a light 12-, a 16- or a 20-bore would depend on personal factors. I myself lean towards short-barrelled 12-bores in such cases, not entirely for ballistical reasons, though I do believe that they have a better chance than the 16- and 20-bores have of throwing superior patterns with 1 oz. of shot, or even the $\frac{7}{8}$ oz. of the 2-in. cartridge.

Warning to fathers

A point comes up here of significance to parents and others seeking to enter boys properly to the sport of shooting. Arising out of the simple fact that a tube to resist a given pressure can be made lighter in proportion as the diameter is reduced, it is easier to reduce the weight of a small-calibre gun for firing a given charge than it is to do the same with one of larger bore. It is thus easy to buy 20-bore guns which, because of their lightness, seem ideal for a boy, but which, for the same reason, recoil unduly when firing the maximum charge for which they are proved. I can think of nothing more likely to put a boy off than painful recoil, particularly if the gun concerned is not a good fit. If a boy is growing fast, there is an obvious temptation to anticipate his later requirements in the way of stock measurements, with the result that he tends to mount the gun incorrectly—perhaps on his arm rather than on his shoulder. A better recipe for the fatal habit of flinching could hardly be devised. So, if he is to be fitted out with a small-calibre gun, it is most important that the charge be reduced in proportion to the weight, and preferably more so to start with.

21 July 1966

clay pigeon guns (I)

Many beginners nowadays start their shooting by joining a gun club, and their early choice of a gun is often determined by the needs of the clay pigeon shooting sport.

In my young days, clays were things you shot at for training or practice at a gunmaker's shooting school. They were essentially intended as a preparation for game shooting, and were thrown so as to imitate as closely as possible the various types of game birds commonly met with. True, there was a certain amount of competitive clay target shooting carried on then, but there was no Clay Pigeon Shooting Association (it was not formed until 1928), and I think it true to say that the average shooting man knew nothing about it. It was only when he went to the gunmaker's school for a little pre-season practice that he ever saw a clay target.

A natural consequence of all this is that there was never any question of a special gun for clay shooting, except, perhaps, among the relatively few devotees of the sport, whose choice in the matter of weapons certainly exercised no influence on the style, design or weight of game guns.

But with the great boom that took place in clay pigeon shooting after the last war, and the great wave of American influence that accompanied it, a big change came about. The over-and-under, inspired by American familiarity with single-barrelled rifles with tubular magazines, and possessing some real or imaginary virtues in relation to the inanimate target, enjoyed a remarkable upsurge of popularity—to such an extent, indeed, that beginners in this country regard this type of weapon as almost indispensable for the attainment of fair success at the clay-shooting game.

Modern clay-shooting guns

Only three kinds of clay pigeon shooting need considering here—trap or D.T.L., skeet and sporting, of which the first two have developed their own specialized weapons.

In this country, the prevailing choice for trap shooting among the best performers is undoubtedly the over-and-under. This usually takes the form of a 30-in. barrelled 12-bore weighing 7 lb. or more It is bored from half and full to full and full, and usually has a raised, ventilated rib and a selective single trigger. The stock has some distinctive features—a pistol grip or half-pistol; a high, level comb; a somewhat greater length than would be chosen for a game gun; a recoil pad; and a generous fore-end to protect the shooter's hand from the heat of the barrels.

The skeet gun favoured here is similar to the trap gun—indeed, it is often the same gun with a different set of barrels. But these barrels are shorter, probably only 26 in., and they are open-bored to ensure the largest feasible spread of shot.

4. The over-and-under is favoured by most clay pigeon shooters. The model here is M. Xantakos (Greece), European Junior Skeet Champion.

Note that M. Xantakos, like most shooters when posing for the camera, has not mounted his gun correctly. Compare illustration 21.

Sporting clays have not developed any special kind of gun, and competitors use the guns they have acquired for other purposes.

Repeaters, both recoil and gas-operated as well as the pump-gun, are used for both trap and skeet. My impression is that the pump is possibly the most popular type in the United States, and Stanbury and Carlisle, in their well-known book, *Clay Pigeon Marksmanship*, describe it as 'one of the best, if you can handle it'. It is certainly the chosen weapon of many leading American clay-shooters and, for reasons which will appear, is worth the special attention of young and adaptable beginners. At the same time, all the repeaters are inferior to double-barrelled guns on the score of safety—nothing can afford the shooter and his companions anything to compare with the assurance provided by the dropped barrels of a double gun.

General-purpose guns

If the beginner is taking up clay pigeon shooting seriously, and is in a position to provide himself with a gun or guns specially adapted to the sport; if, moreover, he is prepared to take the best obtainable advice, I have little doubt that he would end up with a trap and/or skeet gun such as I first described. But the difficulty arises with those who want general-purpose guns. I get many letters from beginners seeking that non-existent article, the all-round gun, and invariably have to reply pointing out the impossibility of meeting their specified requirements. The only thing they can do, I say, is to decide what they *chiefly* want the gun for, and to start from that. The clay pigeon gun is heavy—even the gun designed for skeet. This is to protect the shooter from the recoil of the numerous heavily charged cartridges he normally fires. The trap gun is heavily choked, so as to be able to break small targets at full range. Here, then, by way of example, is an opportunity of combining the specification of a trap gun and a gun for flighting wildfowl. Again, the skeet gun is open-bored, and a great deal of game and pigeon shooting can be done successfully with an open-bored gun, provided that long shots are not attempted.

Another approach to combining requirements is through the medium of the repeaters. Since both barrels of the trap gun are normally heavily choked, and both barrels of the skeet gun are the reverse, the versatility of the double-barrelled gun in this respect is not needed, and a pump-gun or other repeater, with its single barrel, can be made to serve the requirements of either sport if it is equipped to take replaceable choke tubes. It can also be made to serve for game, wildfowl pigeon shooting, though the lack of instant choice of open or choke boring will then operate as a disadvantage.

First things first

Since poor success at live bird shooting is more disappointing than corresponding results with clays, when neither predominates in the shooter's ambition, I usually recommend that wing-shooting requirements should come first in a double-purpose gun. It is a great mistake to imagine, as many beginners seem to do, that good work cannot be done at clays with an ordinary side-by-side gun. It is, in fact, the favoured weapon for the most difficult of all trap shooting—the trap shooting of live pigeons, as practised on the Continent; and a rough shooting side-by-side double, bored half and full, can perform admirably at inanimate targets in this kind of shooting in anything short of serious competition work.

Besides, guns can be adapted to different roles. A slip-on recoil pad can give a game gun the extra length of stock favoured for trap shooting, and some of the extra weight. An indiarubber comb-raiser, temporarily secured with sticky tape, can similarly modify the fit. And as for skeet, spreader cartridges in the choke barrel of an ordinary game gun can remove all serious disability.

24 June 1967

clay pigeon guns (II)

By the time a trap or skeet shooter has reached the stage of going in for serious competitive work, he is likely to have settled ideas on the kind of gun he requires, and to know just what he expects from it. The beginner, with his eye on the expert's choice, is inclined to think that clay targets can hardly be broken by any other means, and often sets out to acquire a corresponding specialized weapon, even though he

5. The ordinary game gun is well adapted for skeet.
American shooter, Mr. John T. Boone, Vice-president of O. F. Mossberg, using what looks like one of the famous old Parkers.

may have parallel interests in game shooting, pigeon shooting or wildfowling.

This is a mistake. There is much clay shooting, short of serious competition, that can be successfully and enjoyably undertaken with ordinary guns, as I hope to make clear, particularly if certain steps are taken, as they can be, to adapt them for work on inanimate targets.

The fully specialized gun for trapshooting in this country is usually an over-and-under 12-bore weighing 7 to $7\frac{1}{4}$ lb. and with 30-in. barrels. It has a long stock with a high, level comb to aid correct and consistent gun mounting, a pistol grip, and a generous fore-end to protect the shooter's hand from the heat of the barrels. The barrels are usually fitted with a raised, ventilated rib, and there is a single, selective trigger.

The skeet gun is often the same gun as the trap gun, but with an alternative set of barrels; for whereas the former are usually bored half to full choke in the bottom barrel and full choke in the top, the corresponding borings of the latter are usually true cylinder, and true cylinder to half choke. Moreover, the skeet barrels are shorter, 26 in. being a much favoured length.

The gun for sporting-type clays is usually a non-specialized weapon of the kind acquired by participants for other purposes.

Repeaters and recoil

Pump guns and self-loaders, both recoil and gas operated, are favoured for trap and skeet, particularly in America, where the pump gun might well prove to be the prevailing choice. They have the great advantage of cheapness over the O/U, as well as greater adaptability to other sports by the use of replaceable choke tubes. The reliable pump gun, recommended by Percy Stanbury and G. L. Carlisle as one of the best for clay pigeon shooting—'if you can handle it'—is especially worthy of the attention of young and adaptable shooters. It shares with the O/U the narrow sight-line, for what it is worth, but it lacks the virtue often attributed to the other weapon of delivering its second or top-barrel shot rather higher than its first. This does not seem to worry the American champions who remain faithful to it.

It is, of course, important that the competitive clay pigeon shooter, firing, as he does, considerable numbers of cartridges carrying a full shot load, should not be put off by recoil. It is for this reason that the regular trap and skeet gun is of full weight—half to three-quarters of a pound more than a regular game gun of the same bore. The self-loaders claim, and need, special attention in this respect, because shooters vary in their reactions to the recoil of these weapons, even though it is fairly claimed by the manufacturers that they recoil less than fixed-breech guns. Yet the long-recoil type of repeater has a recoil which is developed in two phases, the latter of which can be shown to have a vibratory aspect which some shooters find distressing. Others find the metallic ring from the receivers of some short-recoil repeaters objectionable, and quickly productive of headache.

On the other hand, the recoil from the bottom barrel of an O/U is generally found to be even less than the generous weight of the weapon would imply, because of the directness of the thrust to the butt.

Muzzle-brakes, effective in reducing recoil, and easily applicable to single-barrelled weapons, unfortunately give rise to blast effect, which can be highly objectionable to shooters on the flank, and are therefore barred in competitive trapshooting under C.P.S.A. rules.

Adapting the beginner's gun

The newcomer who comes to clay pigeon shooting from game shooting or wildfowling should recognize that he can often gain some advantage by adapting his existing gun to the special requirements of trap and skeet. For trapshooting, extra stock length can be provided by a slip-on recoil pad, which has the further advantage of adding something to weight and thus taking something away from recoil, apart from its cushioning effect. A raised, level comb can be achieved by the means recommended at the end of the previous article. Comb-raisers come in a range of heights and are obtainable from most good gunsmiths.

If the existing gun does not carry enough choke in the right barrel for best results, something can be done by reducing the shot size. No. 8 shot, at 450 pellets to the ounce, makes considerably denser patterns than the No. 7 so often favoured in this country, which only runs to 340. *Assuming that the gun shoots the two sizes equally well, a quarter-choke will throw as dense a pattern with No. 8 as will a full choke with No. 7.* Practical results are likely to fall somewhat short of this, whilst still leaving the smaller shot with a useful margin of superiority, to which the greater spread will duly contribute.

Another useful addition to the normal gun is a slip-on hand-guard. These devices are effective in protecting the hand from hot barrels, but if inadvertently drawn back against the fore-end push-button, can cause the fore-end to fall off—a disconcerting thing. A very little ingenuity can forestall this.

As for skeet, the ordinary game gun is quite well adapted to the sport in its normal state, though it will usually carry more choke in the left barrel than is desirable. Scatter cartridges—barred, incidentally, in competitions under I.S.U. rules—and No. 9 shot are the answers here. We have no British scatter cartridges, but they are made by American and Continental firms, and the Hull Cartridge Company assure me that they are prepared to import supplies of the Remington scatter loads on demand.

Refinements

There are aspects of the performance of the specialized clay pigeon shooting guns which are worthy of the attention of newcomers and old hands alike.

The first of these is the relation between the charge centre and the line of sight. Some O/Us print their top and bottom barrel patterns at substantially different elevations, but not others. There are unconventional possibilities of rectification here in the event of the difference being disadvantageous, though I have not the space to pursue the subject any further now.

Over-and-unders with cast-off stocks can, and theoretically should, tend to shoot to the left, as I have previously pointed out. The divergence can be sufficient to prejudice performance. These guns should preferably be made with straight stocks, and adjusted for fit on the comb height.

Some ready-made trap guns carry excessive choke, perhaps 50 mils or thereabouts. I believe the Italians are especially inclined to over-choke their guns, and two Merkels have recently come to my notice in a similar state. It should be recognized that, with ordinary trap cartridges, an over-choked gun may make patterns that are actually inferior to those thrown by one more moderately choked, both in respect of quality and density.

Keen competitive trap shooters sometimes praise a gun as being good for 'holding its patterns'. This, I suspect, is nothing more than an indication that some guns, as they heat up, throw their patterns more or less off the mark, owing to unequal expansion of the barrels. The successful American Ljutic trap gun bases its claim to superiority on the avoidance of this very thing; and it is clearly a subject worthy of more attention in the design and construction of trap guns than it has so far received.

9 December 1967

twelve or twenty?

It is perhaps just as well to re-examine settled preferences and convictions from time to time, against the changing background of circumstance; so the challenge of the smaller bores to the ubiquitous 12 should now and then be taken up, if only for the benefit of the newer entry.

Such a challenge has been fairly thrown down by a correspondent from Glossop, who argues the case for the 20-bore magnum for general mixed shooting, 'barring wildfowling'. I quote from his letter:

'I have yet to see an article in *Shooting Times*,' he says, 'in defence of the smaller bores, especially the 20, which, in my opinion, is a grand weapon, if used with discretion.

'The general idea appears to be that any weapon smaller than the 16-bore is a toy. This, of course, is far from true. Without involving myself in the mysteries of ballistics, I can safely say that the 20-bore can kill outright . . . at ranges of forty to fifty yards. This is, of course, when using the $2\frac{3}{4}$-in. cartridge.

'An average shot, using a 20-bore, can compete most favourably with anyone of the same standard using a normal $2\frac{1}{2}$-in. 12-bore.'

An unrealistic aspect

This is a familiar presentation of the case, and one which I always consider unrealistic, to the extent that it implies that the gun kills the bird. As I often say, birds are not killed by guns: they are killed by charges of shot, 'and then only by those pellets, travelling with adequate velocity, which the regularity and density of the pattern, combined with the skill of the shooter, are together capable of bringing to bear'.

The effectiveness of a particular charge of shot—say, an ounce, such as might be thrown by a $2\frac{3}{4}$-in. 20-bore or a lightly loaded 12—against a particular target, will thus be determined by the velocity of the pellets and by the pattern, and not at all by whether the charge originally came from one gun or the other. As for the influence of the gun on these essential factors, both 20-bores and 12s can be loaded to give a high, medium or low velocity, and neither has any exclusive attribute here; though, for reasons I shall come to in a moment, the likelihood is that standard 20-bore cartridges will be loaded to a somewhat lower velocity than those of larger gauge.

As for pattern, the overall density, as defined by the percentage of the total charge thrown into the standard 30-in. circle at 40 yards, will be the same, if the guns are bored alike. It will *not* be denser in the case of the 20-bore, because, contrary to widespread belief, the spread of the charge is not influenced by the calibre, but only by the degree of choke. But though the pattern density will thus be the same for the same charge thrown by similarly bored guns, it remains for consideration whether either is likely to have an advantage over the other in the quality of the patterns thrown—that is to say, in the uniformity of distribution of the pellets. There is scope here for significant superiority: a well-bored 20 might indeed throw a pattern of superior quality to that thrown by an indifferently bored 12, but the likelihood is once again the other way.

Loaded dice

It would seem therefore that although, *for equal charges*, the $2\frac{3}{4}$-in. 20 *might* be capable of outshooting the 12, the dice are loaded against its doing so. The explanation of this state of affairs is to be found chiefly in the longer shot column of the smaller gun.

Practical experience going back over several generations has shown that guns normally perform best with a 'square charge', that is to say, a charge that occupies a length in the barrel about equal to the bore diameter. Heavier charges entail longer shot columns, requiring higher or more sustained pressures for the attainment of a given muzzle velocity. They also entail a higher proportion of distorted and abraded pellets, and thus bring about a longer shot-string in flight, with a greater proportion of pellets travelling with less than average velocity and energy, and on more irregular courses, giving inferior patterns. Something can be recouped here, and usually is, by loading the small-bore cartridge to give a somewhat lower pressure than that needed for the attainment of equal velocity; but it is still only *something*: there is no general prospect of converting the disadvantage into an advantage. If there were, the 20-bore would long since have been recognized as the best gauge for firing light 12-bore charges.

There is the further fact, true, at least, of this country, that the experience gained by gunmakers in boring gun barrels has been related chiefly to the 12-bore, and there is no gun out of which they are so well qualified to get the best results as they are with this gauge. And, of course, it must not be forgotten that although many of our most experienced users of 12-bore game guns prefer the light, 1-oz. load we have been discussing, the standard charge, and the most popular, is $1\frac{1}{16}$ oz., or $1\frac{1}{8}$, with its greater potential.

The gun and the shooter

But there is another factor in the effectiveness of a given charge of shot, which I have mentioned but have not considered, namely skill—the ability of the shooter to centre his pattern on the target; and if the smaller-bore gun makes for greater accuracy, it might yet recoup its disadvantages.

Owing fundamentally to the fact that, for equal strength, a smaller-bore tube is lighter than a large one, 20-bore guns can be, and usually are, made lighter than 12s. So far as this lightness reduces fatigue, it could well promote more accurate shooting, though the measure of it would depend on the shooter and the kind of sport he chiefly follows. If he has to walk long distances for few shots, the lightness of the 20-bore could be advantageous, even though he inevitably has to submit to more recoil for a given charge. But with driven game, little walking and more shooting, the lightness of his gun might fail to make up for the extra punishment he has to take.

This point, if followed up, leads to the broad proposition I have previously dealt with here at some length—namely, that for the best overall results in shooting for sport, it is necessary to correlate man, gun, load and the kind of sport concerned, including under this last head whether much or little walking is involved, and many or few shots. Such a process of correlation would undoubtedly lead to the conclusion in some cases that the 20-bore is the right weapon; but the conclusion would not be reached solely on the ground of ballistics.

No change

Coming afresh to the matter, I find myself reaching the same broad conclusion as I reached some years ago, when I took up the challenge of the small-bore magnum to the conventional $2\frac{1}{2}$-in. 12-bore gun, as the established weapon for general mixed shooting in this country. On that occasion, I took the views and evidence of many leading gun-makers, ammunition manufacturers and ballistics experts, both in this country and on the Continent. But notwithstanding the impressive case made out for the small-bore magnum by the French gunmaker and magnum specialist Kerné, there was no doubt that the balance of evidence was against him; and, as I said in *Shotguns and Cartridges*, 'the verdict must go to the $2\frac{1}{2}$-in. 12-bore as being still the supremely effective weapon, in the hands of the average shooter, for firing the standard game charges favoured in this country. . . . The small-bore magnums do not, in general, throw such good patterns, and their lighter weight has to be purchased by some loss of velocity or increase of recoil, or both.'

Still, in expressing that conclusion, I made due reservations on behalf of the greater overall suitability of the smaller gun in certain circumstances, which every man must judge for himself. If a man likes a 20-bore and thinks he shoots better with it—more especially, if he is satisfied that he gets more overall pleasure and satisfaction with a gun of that gauge—he is above and beyond all argument. But if he asserts that his 20-bore kills as well as, or better than, a similarly bored 12, the onus of proof rests heavily upon him.

16 December 1965

the XXV gun—craze or conquest?

When Robert Churchill introduced the distinctive type of short-barrelled game gun now generally known as a 'XXV', he alienated much potential support by his sweeping claims and combative publicity. Opposition to his ideas rallied at first to the criticism that, whatever other merits these guns might possess, they did not shoot so hard as those with barrels of 28 or 30 in., as then generally favoured. The opening battle of the campaign was thus fought on this issue. The leader of the opposition to Churchill was the *Field*, and it is a matter of history that it was roundly defeated. A rigorous course of practical experiments showed beyond doubt that, although the shorter-barrelled gun had a slightly lower velocity than its longer-barrelled counterpart, the difference was not of any practical significance. That one battle decided the campaign. The opposition having been routed on their chosen ground, they were reduced to guerrilla tactics. The gun looked odd; it was less pointable; its reduced forward weight was actually a disadvantage, inasmuch as it caused the shooter to check his swing; there was an offensive muzzle blast; and the reduced weight produced an objectionable increase in recoil.

Churchill fought back on all these points. The gun did not look odd—it looked just right; with its distinctive rib, it was more, rather than less, pointable; its reduced forward weight and improved speed of handling, by enabling the shooter to get on to his bird more quickly, more than made up for any loss of velocity; etc. etc.

A spurious suggestion

But I have no intention of going over all the early struggles of the XXV gun. After all, that was forty years ago, and we know now that the gun *did* get itself established, and became the favoured weapon of a substantial minority of game shooters. Indeed, so substantial was the minority that most gunmakers of any consequence came to offering 25-in. barrelled guns with Churchill-style ribs. The XXV, in short, established a new orthodoxy in shotguns; and now that all the controversy has died down, it competes on equal terms with other guns for the favour of shooting men.

Nevertheless, there was one thing that was spurious in all this, and that was the implication—fostered by Churchill's use of 'XXV' as a distinctive symbol—that there was some exclusive merit in this particular barrel length. I see much evidence of this in my correspondence with shooters, who, when they are thinking of trying shorter barrels, fly at once to the idea of 25 in., even if they have been used to 30 in. all their lives. They might well do better with shorter barrels, but it by no means follows that 25 in. would be the best length. But the XXV was the archetype, and it is now a rooted tradition—the very symbol of all short-barrelled guns; so that in considering where these guns are now going, and what their progress may mean, I must confine myself to the Churchill-style XXV.

Fashion or trend?

What has aroused my curiosity, and prompted this article, is the fact that these guns are undoubtedly enjoying a new wave of interest and popularity. My correspondence alone testifies to the interest, and one supplier tells me that orders for this type are three or four times what

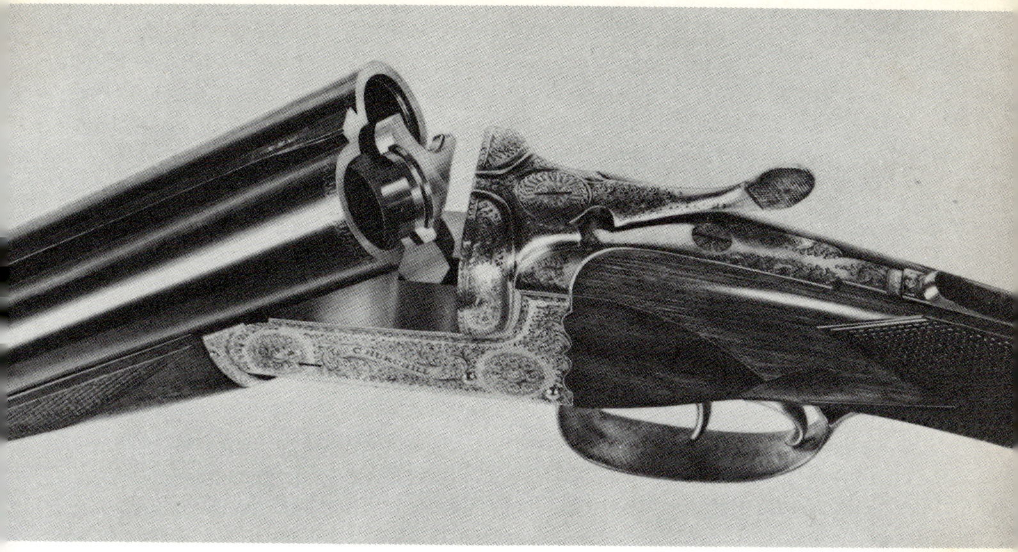

6. THE CHURCHILL 'REGAL' XXV
The archetype of the modern 25-in. barrelled gun. Note the high, tapered rib.

they were only a few years ago. What is happening here? Is the XXV, after forty-odd years, undergoing something like a population explosion, as sometimes happens in the biological field, when, after a long struggle, a species suddenly romps ahead? Or is it simply that attractive Continental XXVs have recently become available on the medium-price market? Whatever the cause, there can be no doubt about the fact: the XXV gun is, *at the moment*, on the up-and-up.

There are, of course, fashions in sporting guns, as in other things. Sometimes the fashion proves disadvantageous in the long term, and goes into reverse, as did the choke-bore craze of the 1870s. But gun fashions are by no means so erratic or capricious as most, and I am inclined to think that what we are witnessing is a permanent move towards the short-barrelled 12-bore for game shooting in this country—encouraged and facilitated, no doubt, by recent importations.

One can see good reasons for such a trend. The majority of men still using 30-in. barrelled guns nowadays—guns, that is to say, of the kind evolved in the black-powder era—are doing so for no better reason than that they inherited them, or acquired them on advantageous terms. At least, they do not represent a deliberate choice of barrel length. To a far lesser extent, this may also be true of 28-in. barrels.

I am sure that if all shooters in the British Isles were offered an opportunity of exchanging their guns for others of similar quality and condition, there would be an impressive swing towards 27, 26 and the spell-binding 'XXV' ins.

So far as rough shooters are concerned, it would be a logical choice. Much walking and little actual shooting put a premium on a light, handy gun, even at the expense of some increase in recoil. And if we take a broader view, embracing all shooters and all the characteristics of the short-barrelled gun, we might well see this present trend as being no more than the final step in a long evolutionary process—the process of delivering the sporting gun from the burden of all barrel weight and barrel length in excess of that necessary for ballistics and for the proper handling and direction of the weapon. The arms historian of the future will undoubtedly recognize this process as having been started by Henry Nock's patent breech of the 1780s; and he may come to recognize it as having been completed by Robert Churchill's 25-in. barrelled gun of the 1920s.

Repercussions

The steady supersession of long barrels by short—if it continues—would have some interesting repercussions in this country and abroad. Converts to the XXV gun—even the modestly priced Continental sort—receive a heady draught of those qualities of lightness, balance and speed in action which have hitherto been found only in best guns of any greater barrel length, and never in those of 30 in. The bullish second-hand market in these latter guns would accordingly become increasingly easier, though trade as a whole would benefit from the popularity of a newer style.

At the same time, the ideological gap between conventional guns and the repeaters would be widened. Manufacturers of these latter weapons would be stirred to new efforts to maintain their position, and aluminium alloy barrels would receive a fresh impetus.

Cartridge manufacturers, too, would feel the impact of the changing fashion. I always regard the Eley 'Impax' cartridge, with its 1-oz. load in 12-bore, as a sign of the times, and if guns of the XXV type continued to maintain their progress, we could expect to see the ammunition manufacturers devoting still more of their energy and skill to developing cartridges especially suited to them. Rough shooters, pinning their faith to full loads, but fully susceptible to the seductions of a light gun, would increasingly demand the impossible from the cartridge manufacturers—and possibly get it.

Misfits

In all this, there would be some regrets. Just as the modern low-roofed motor car is grossly unsuited to a really tall or long-bodied man, so is the short-barrelled gun to certain shooters. True, a long-armed man of large physique looks under-gunned with a XXV gun, but the incompatibility may go beyond appearances. Precise muscular control seems easiest with a certain muscular load, and the kind of man I have in mind may need rather more length and weight in his gun barrels, and the steadying influence of a larger moment of inertia, to achieve the best results of which he is capable. It would be regrettable if such a man succumbed to the lure of lightness and fast-handling quality to the detriment of his shooting. This, of course, is a consideration that may arise on the kind of shooting rather than on the kind of man. It is generally recognized that most men find a slow, long-barrelled gun least disadvantageous, or even positively advantageous, for flight shooting and the like. As ever, the stronger the fashionable trend, the more independence of mind and judgment is needed to assess its true worth in individual cases, and to resist it if need be.

22 December 1966

the importance of balance

Two cases have recently cropped up which go to strengthen my belief that a generation of shooters is growing up with far less appreciation than their fathers had of what balance means in a gun. In one case, from all the proprietary English and foreign guns on the market, a reader had to choose what was probably the worst balanced of the lot, by a considerable margin! I am not referring to repeaters, but to conventional double guns, among which even cheap specimens can be found that are unexpectedly well balanced.

After shooting qualities, good balance is the grand merit in a gun, and for very good reasons. The active manipulation of a gun involves a considerable expenditure of energy, and it can be shown that less—perhaps far less—energy is required to manipulate a well-balanced gun than is involved in putting a badly balanced one through the same motions.

Balance cannot be determined merely by poising the gun on the edge of the forefinger, as is often done, and noting whether the point of equipoise falls at about the knuckle of the action. It certainly should do—say, within $4\frac{1}{2}$ in. of the trigger—but that is only part of the story. Good balance requires that the weight of the gun shall be concentrated as much as possible between the hands. If this condition is fulfilled, it will make the least demand on the energies of the shooter for one of its weight. It will in consequence feel responsive, eager and co-operative in action, and may well leave the shooter at the end of the day with reserves of energy—and accuracy—that he would otherwise not possess. But if the gun has its weight more dispersed fore and aft, it will feel leaden and sluggish, and will not only take more out of the shooter, but will deprive him of the positive pleasure to be derived from using a well-balanced weapon.

Facts and figures

I have gone into these matters elsewhere in some detail, and have shown that the things determining good balance can be measured, and expressed in figures that afford a reliable indication of handling quality and the amount of energy involved in shooting with various guns. (Strictly for technical readers, I may say that the quantities measured are the weight, point of static balance, least transverse moment of inertia and radius of gyration.) I make a point of measuring as many as possible of the guns passing through my hands, and have accumulated a useful amount of balance data concerning guns of all types.

A few things in particular strike me about this information. First, is that the figures go absolutely in step with the practical appraisal of balance, as determined by handling. This justifies my approach. Secondly is the large gap between the best and worst balanced guns for a given duty; and thirdly is the indication of a decline in standards—the indication that many of the guns accepted without question by modern shooters are well below the balance standards established by English makers before the war.

A few examples will serve to bring out these points. If we take as a standard a best London 12-bore game gun weighing a scant $6\frac{1}{4}$ lb., and having 27-in. barrels, we can represent the measured balance data by a 'figure of inertia' of 100, representing the energy demanded from the shooter for its active manipulation. Compared with this, a sound and popular Belgian gun rates 141, and a famous Italian O/U, 151—fully half as much more energy for what may be exactly the same shooting.

Declining standards are witnessed even by old and new guns from the same stable. For example, a typical 30-in. barrelled double gun produced in quantity by a famous Birmingham firm before the war weighed 6 lb. 15 oz. and had a figure of inertia of 145, which was a respectable figure, all things considered. But the modern equivalent, bearing the same name, though with shorter (28-in.) barrels and weighing a trifle less (6 lb. $13\frac{1}{2}$ oz.), has gone up to 152. It should have gone down to about 135.

I have no doubt that the current popularity of the shorter-barrelled guns springs from an intuitive appreciation of these things, particularly on the part of those shooters who are no longer prodigal of their energy. For example, the figure of inertia for a Spanish 25-in., weighing 6 lb. net is only 112—little more than our best London standard costing far more.

But it should not be necessary to cut barrels down to 25 in. to attain the balance standards of the past. The danger is that if shooters do not appreciate and demand well-balanced guns, the trade will not bother to produce them.

3 June 1967

TESTING A GUN FOR BALANCE By timing the horizontal oscillations of the gun in its wire-spended cradle, the inertia ('moment of inertia') can be calculated. This is the factor that chiefly termines the liveliness and handling quality of a gun.

Section 3

CHOKE

'It lengthens your reach, but may lighten your bag.'

(Old Hampshire sportsman)

'The best degree of choke for filling the game bag is always the least degree consistent with the requirements of the class of sport concerned.'

(the author—*Shotguns and Cartridges*)

fallacy of choke

Last season, something happened to an acquaintance of mine which I have seen several times over the years. He had a gun with which he shot confidently and well. It was a plain weapon and not of very good quality; and so one day he decided he deserved something better. Accordingly, he placed an order with a celebrated maker for a new gun to be built to his carefully thought-out specification. In due course, it was delivered, and appeared to embody all his requirements.

At first, he gained much satisfaction from handling a weapon so much superior to its predecessor. But as the months went by, the horrid conclusion could not be denied—his standard of shooting had fallen off considerably. Yet the gun survived every check: fit, balance, patterns, trigger pulls—so what could be wrong?

Old campaigners will already have the answer: the new gun carried considerable choke in both barrels, whereas the right barrel of the old gun was a cylinder.

It seems that every generation is determined to learn the hard way some of the things that previous generations have fully mastered and duly left on record. Thus, according to the 1906 edition of the Badminton Library volume on *Shooting*, the celebrated *Field* trials of Chokes v. Cylinders, held in 1875, established that 'the choke was very superior to the cylinder gun. The former averaged from 180 to 200 pellets in a 30 inch target at 40 yards; the best of the latter only from 130 to 140 . . . But though there was a rush for the new guns at first, they are not now so popular as they were, as it has been found that they are not so well adapted for an ordinary marksman as is a gun which makes a larger killing circle . . . It is not therefore incorrect to say that . . . the greater majority of shooting men . . . content themselves with having the left barrel slightly choked.'

There indeed speaks the voice of experience—the experience of a generation of shooting men who, it seems, had eagerly given the close-boring principle an extended trial, only to find it disappointing in practice.

Burrard's Recommendation

Even our modern authority, Burrard, whose great experience in plating guns led him to adopt a very critical attitude towards open boring, was prepared to recommend as little as a quarter choke for the right barrel of a gun intended for general rough shooting in this country.

Having quoted such eminent authorities, I am diffident about adding anything on my own account. But I did at least have a 6-ft. pattern plate permanently mounted in the grounds of my old house, and can let it speak for me. It proved to me that, although open-bored barrels cannot be relied on to hold together the patterns from ordinary high-velocity loads, yet with standard velocity cartridges of good quality, they are capable of throwing superlatively good game-getting patterns. And so they would be, no doubt, with many cartridges whose 'high velocity' label is not meant to be taken too seriously, or even with really high-velocity cartridges, if specially loaded to avoid high pressures.

Why then the modern craze for choke? The popularity of clay pigeon shooting and wildfowling; the psychological appeal to the new entry; certain manufacturing considerations and other reasons all suggest themselves. But I cannot help thinking that we shall have to learn all over again what our fathers and grandfathers learned more than half a century ago: that the less choke we can do with the better.

When I was a young man, and found myself in a good wildfowling country, I got one of the heavy artillery specialists to build me a heavily choked, 3-in. case 12-bore for duck shooting ashore and afloat. It took me two seasons to realize the implied fallacy underlying my choice of that formidable weapon. The fallacy was, that whereas game is shot at ranges of from, say, 20 to 40 yds., wildfowl have to be taken at ranges of from 40 yds. up to the limit of reach. In cold print, the proposition seems absurd, and in practice it is absurd. I have shot many wild grouse and partridges to which the long-range argument could perfectly well have been applied; and I have equally shot plenty of duck between 20 and 40 yds. In any case, I did not do well with my big gun; but when I reverted to my ordinary game gun, with its improved cylinder right, I shot my duck far better, notwithstanding its less powerful punch, and certainly with far greater ease.

In a word, the case for heavily choked guns, whether it be for game, pigeon or wildfowl, appears to rest simply and solely on the answer to the question, at what range is it *necessary* for you to take *most* of your shots? If the answer is, without a doubt, over 40 yds., then you probably need lots of choke. But unless you are an expert on the mark, you will certainly have to pay for it with many missed chances at closer range.

16 June 1961

choke *versus* cylinder—permissible aiming errors

There is no doubt at all that in recent years there has been a sharp revival of interest in the question of gun borings, and the relative merits of the different degrees of choke for various classes of shooting. One can point to several good reasons for this. The large new entry of shooters are generally of a more enquiring turn of mind on technical points than their fathers were. Then again, the increased popularity of pigeon shooting and wildfowling has focused attention on the merits of choke, and the same could be said for clay pigeon shooting and D.T.L. On the other hand, skeet has done much to restore the reputation of true cylinder boring in its proper sphere, being helped in this by the crimp-closed cartridge. Last come the many instances of shooters who have abandoned old, open-bored guns, with which they shot well, for new, heavily choked Continental ones, with which they have shot badly. Some of these, who have acted on my advice to have most of the choke removed from their right barrels, have come back to me with a much-heightened perception of the harm choke can do to the game tally when misapplied.

In these circumstances, a question that was recently put to me is probably one that has occurred to many readers. 'Why,' I was asked, 'do you always say, when you are speaking about choke, that the open borings give the shooter a better chance, *particularly at the shorter ranges at which most game is shot.* What has range got to do with it? I should have thought that everything maintained a certain proportion, and that the open boring would stand in the same relation to the choke at 40 yds. as it does at 20.' This is a good question: it reveals that the man who asked it imagined the shot from a gun as spreading from the muzzle in a true cone—a sharp cone in the case of a choke barrel, and a broader one with a cylinder. If this were so, range would indeed have nothing to do with the question: the open-bored barrel would permit the same *angular* aiming error, in excess of that permissible with a choke, at all ranges. In fact, however, shot charges do not behave quite in this orderly, geometrical manner.

Trumpets, not cones

If the bulk of the charge from a gun could be contrived to leave a visible envelope in the air, just large enough to contain it, we should see, on regarding the envelope from the flank, that it was not a cone, but slightly flared, like a trumpet. Further, the choke-trumpet would not only be smaller in diameter at the mouth than the cylinder-trumpet, it would also have more curvature, so that at the mid-region the relative disparity would be even more pronounced, as shown in my diagram.

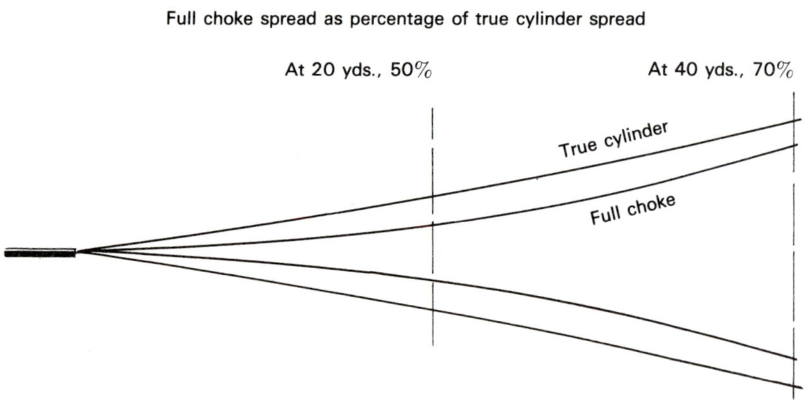

8. Proportionately smaller spread of choke patterns makes missing easier at short range.

It will be seen that the choke makes more demand on aiming accuracy at the shorter ranges than it does farther out.

For those who prefer to think in terms of figures, the matter may be put another way.

The spread of the bulk of the charge (which, incidentally, is the *same for all calibres*) is given in *The Shooter's Year Book*, published by

I.M.I. For improved cylinder and full choke, the figures are as follows.

Range	— 10	15	20	25	30	35	40 yds.
Imp. cyl.	— 15	20	26	32	38	44	51 in.
Full choke	— 9	12	16	21	27	33	40 in.

Because of this spread of shot, every gun permits of a certain aiming error, measurable as an angle. If we take as a basis the aiming error permitted by a full choke, we can very quickly work out from the above data what increase in this error would be permitted by an improved cylinder. Thus—

Range (yds.)	*Permissible increase in aiming error*
10	66 per cent
20	62 ,, ,,
30	41 ,, ,,
40	28 ,, ,,

These figures bring out the essential point admirably. At 25 yds. or so—a common game-shooting range—a man armed with an improved cylinder may commit far greater aiming errors than his companion using a full choke, without falling below the latter's standard of performance, as measured in terms of game bagged for equal chances. They also show the full-choke man the need for allowing his birds plenty of law, whereby he may show to less disadvantage.

Overdoing it

The physical fact underlying these observations is, of course, that the control exercised by choke over pattern weakens with range. At the excessive ranges quoted in some shotgun sagas, it would make little difference whether the gun was a true cylinder or the tightest choke ever bored, as witness the case of the man who wrote to one of our leading cartridge manufacturers complaining, 'There must be something wrong with these cartridges of yours. I shot at a paddling of duck on the water at 200 yds., *and not one of them was touched.*'

16 April 1964

choke—a neglected aspect

It is a common thing for shooting writers (myself included) to warn beginners and others of the disadvantages of having too much choke in guns required for ordinary mixed shooting, as opposed to those specifically intended for long-range work. Most game, according to the familiar argument, is shot at moderate ranges—say, 25 to 35 yds.; and at such ranges open-bored guns are well capable of delivering killing patterns. By using heavily choked guns for such work, therefore, the tendency, taking one shot with another, is to put an unnecessary amount of lead into birds killed with accurately aimed shots, and to miss others which might have been killed by the wider-spreading pattern of an open-bored barrel.

I have no desire to go back on that: it remains one of the fundamental truths of shotgun shooting. Indeed, having just helped to eat a pheasant which was taken at closer range than it should have been, I heartily endorse the cooks' views on this important point. French cooks have a saying: '*Vive le braconnier!*'—hurrah for the poacher!—because his methods, however nefarious, often produce game for the table without a shot mark. I am not to be taken as commending poachers, but I do commend avoiding the unnecessary mangling of game.

But there is another aspect of this choke *versus* open boring question where game guns are concerned. It is one that is hardly ever mentioned, yet it is important and pays for consideration.

Two flaws

Shotgun patterns are nearly always compared on the basis of average density. This gun, we say, is a full choke. It puts (we believe, or hope, or blindly trust) 70 per cent of its shot into a 30-in. circle at 40 yds. But this other gun, we say, is an improved cylinder, and it puts only 50 per cent of its charge into the same circle. If our charge in each case is $1\frac{1}{16}$ oz. of No. 5, this means that the choke barrel might put 164 pellets into the circle, whereas the cylinder would only put 117. Put as simply as that, the case for the choke barrel, as the better guarantor of success, seems unanswerable. It was this presentation that deceived our grandfathers when choke boring was first introduced a hundred years ago. It took them a little time to find out the flaws in the argument. The main flaw is the one I referred to in my opening remarks. The other one is concealed by over-simplification.

What we ought to have said, as cross-examiners, on the first presentation of the case is: 'Very good; but *where* does the choke barrel put its extra pellets?' The answer is that it tends to put its extra pellets into the central parts of the pattern. *There is, indeed, a greater degree of equivalence in the outer zone of patterns than the overall percentage would imply.* The significance of this can best be pointed out by considering a *reductio ad absurdum.* Let us imagine that the extra 47 pellets in the choke pattern previously mentioned were concentrated in a circle the size of an orange. It would still be a 70 per cent pattern, as against the other's 50; but what use would it be to an ordinary shooter? He could not rely on placing those extra pellets on his target—it would be like trying to shoot flying game with a rifle. And it would not even be an accurate rifle. John Brindle described some interesting experiments several years ago which indicated that shotguns make but poor groups with the dense central parts of choke patterns; so even a super-shot would, for the most part, be dependent on those parts of his pattern which had no more than improved cylinder density.

Objection considered

'But,' the choke enthusiast would say, 'you cannot argue from an absurd supposition. The extra pellets in choke patterns are *not* concentrated in the way you have been imagining: they are quite widely distributed over the pattern.' That, of course, is true . . . but *how* widely? It is time we considered.

There is plenty of experimental evidence on this point, showing some very significant results. In round figures, it indicates that a normal full choke might be expected to put 60 per cent of its 164 pellets into a 20-in. circle, leaving 66 in the outer 10-in. ring, whereas a normal improved cylinder might put only 50 per cent of its 117 pellets in the 20-in. circle, leaving 59 in the outer ring.

So far as the outer ring is concerned, therefore, the full choke would give, not 20 per cent more of the total charge than the improved cylinder, *but only 3 per cent*; and as the average shot would make a great deal of use of that outer ring, he would not get anything like the extra pellets from a full choke that the normally quoted percentages would imply. *With a particular gun and load he might even get less.*

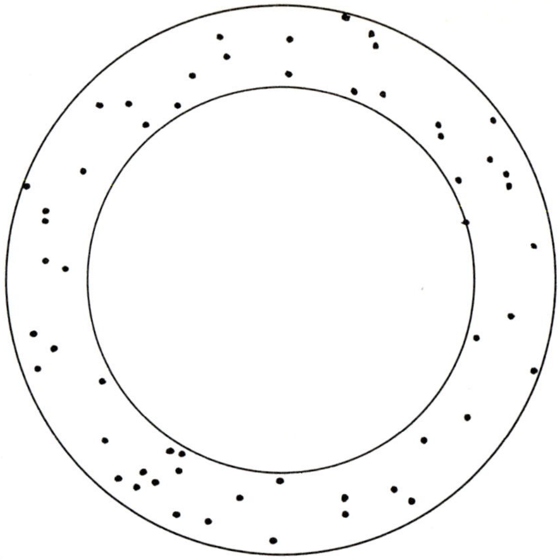

A. Improved cylinder

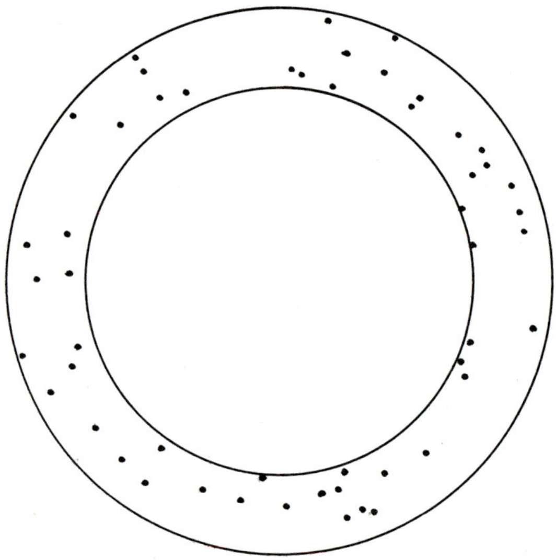

B. Full choke

9. At normal shooting distances, the outer zone of an improved cylinder pattern will often contain more pellets than that thrown by a full choke.
Above are the outer zones of two typical good 30-yd. patterns of $1\frac{1}{16}$ oz. of No. 6 shot, *A* made by an improved cylinder and *B* by a full choke. Total pellets in the circle were 176 for *A* and 252 for *B*, but the outer zone of *A* contains 55 against *B*'s 52. The outer zone comprises half the total area in each case.

Conditional advantage

The greater proportionate concentration of choke patterns towards the centre can be, and indeed is, represented as an advantage. Articles occasionally appear in the shooting press explaining tricks whereby home loaders can increase this concentration, as a means whereby duck, for example, can be killed at ranges of 60 to 70 yds. This is all very well provided the shooter is a sufficiently good shot to take advantage of the technique, and provided his gun is sufficiently consistent as to where it places the dense pattern-centres in relation to the line of aim. But neither of these conditions is normally fulfilled—far from it, so far as the man is concerned. We may be sure that if there were any advantage ordinarily to be had from the use of ultra-dense-centred patterns, even for long-range wildfowl shooting, the technique, which goes back to the muzzle-loading days, would long since have been standardized. The perfect dense-centred pattern, if anybody wants it, is a solid ball.

But returning to ordinary mixed shooting, the basic argument against an undue degree of choke remains as set out in my first paragraph. It is reinforced by the consideration that, over the greater part of the pattern circle, the performance of the open-bored barrel at full range approaches that of the choke much more nearly than the commonly quoted pattern percentages suggest.

23 February 1967

Section 4

OLD AND SECOND-HAND GUNS

'Who buyeth hath need of a hundred eyes: who selleth hath enough of one.'

(Old proverb)

those 'immaculate' old guns

Hardly a post goes by but I receive an enquiry about an old hammer gun: some posts bring me two or three. The general pattern of these letters is so similar that it is sometimes hard to realize that they have not been concerted. Almost invariably, the writer gives me the name engraved on the gun, which he not unreasonably—though more often than not incorrectly—assumes to be that of the maker; and he asks me to tell him something about this maker, and if he is still in business. Then he describes the gun and its proof marks, and asks me to state its age, whether it is nitro-proof and what is its value. Sometimes he encloses a stamped addressed envelope.

In my reply, I usually have to state that the name engraved on the gun is quite unfamiliar to me, and that I can find no trace of it in any of my records. By way of extenuation for this instant betrayal of the oracular character with which some readers undoubtedly, but quite unjustifiably, invest me, I explain that the name engraved on English guns is traditionally that of the vendor rather than that of the actual maker, so that the unknown name concerned is probably that of some country gunsmith, long since vanished without trace, save in the parish registers. I add that the maker was almost certainly one of the Birmingham firms regularly working for the trade; or, if the proof marks are Belgian, one of the busy makers of Liège, who, before the last war, supplied the great bulk of our imported guns.

For the rest, I tell my enquirer what I can from the proof marks; and if, as is so often the case, the gun bears no indication of having been nitro-proved, I point out, as a matter of duty, that it must be considered unsuitable and potentially unsafe for use with modern smokeless ammunition. I often do this with compunction, conscious as I am that I am probably instilling doubt and distrust in place of what may previously have been unswerving loyalty to some faithful but superannuated old warrior. Lastly, I say that *I cannot, in any circumstances, undertake to value guns.* Sometimes I add that, even if I were prepared to do so, I could not value them unseen.

The 'immaculate' ones

But there is a particular sub-division of this class of enquiries to which I wish to draw attention—that is, the considerable number of these old stagers stated by their owners to be in 'immaculate' condition. This is a description that always arouses vehement suspicion in my mind. There is an inherent improbability about an old hammer gun being in immaculate condition which the user or, more particularly, the prospective buyer of such a gun would do well to contemplate. Consider: the central-fire hammer gun with rebounding locks and top-lever snap action, as made in this country up to the outbreak of the last war, attained what may be considered for present purposes to be its final state of development fully ninety years ago. It was rendered obsolete by the perfecting of the hammerless gun in the 1880s; and although it retained its popularity with the older and more conservative sportsmen for long after that, the number of manufactured in good and medium quality must have declined greatly by the turn of the century. Thereafter, the hammer system, because of its simplicity, became increasingly the preserve of makers of the cheapest, not to mention the nastiest, kind of weapon. The chances are, therefore, that a good quality hammer gun is really an old one —probably seventy or more years of age. Over such a long period, it is likely to have been through several hands and to have known many vicissitudes, including times when it will have been neglected or abused; and an immaculate *appearance* may mean no more than that the superficial signs of these adventures have been removed. But what effect they may have had on the constitution of the weapon —on its continuing capacity for safe and satisfactory service—may well remain a question. It is one that all owners and prospective purchasers of such guns should ask themselves.

A case in point

I raise this matter, not only because it arises so frequently from my correspondence, but because I have just been studying one of these 'immaculate' old guns, with what may be typical results. This particular specimen bears the name of a celebrated London maker, and was in its day a best-quality weapon. It is still a beautiful one. It is a double 12-bore with three-stripe damascus barrels, rebounding locks and top lever, and was probably made between 1872 and 1875. The bores, if not too closely scrutinized, appear flawless. The locks are mirror-bright and are as good as new, with no sideways movement of the hammers. The stock is a particularly handsome one of dark, richly figured walnut. The minor features, too, all bespeak the thoroughbred: the beautifully carved shell fences, with their delicate evolute curve merging into the line of the bar; the elegant hammers, matched to a hair—a masterpiece of filing and tastefully engraved all over; and the accurately executed fine scroll covering the action, lock-plates and furniture.

This gun is notable for several indications of having seen very little active service. The chequering is unmarked, and yet I cannot persuade myself that it is other than the original. The face of the standing breech is absolutely free from pitting around the striker holes. The muzzle ends of the barrels, so often in these old guns reduced to paper thickness, show no trace of wear. The engraving on the under-side of the trigger guard, sometimes almost worn away, is as sharp and clear as if it were new, as is the engraving on the heads of the screws securing the horn butt-plate. The maker's name engraved on the top rib is equally sharp and clear, and not, as might be expected, almost erased in the process of successive rebrownings. Surely, one would say, a genuine 'widow's gun'—a find, and perhaps an out-standing bargain for someone.

A puzzle

And yet it has the puzzling and inconsistent features of barrels lapped out to within a whisper of proof, and of faint but unmistakable traces of the action having been tightened. The hinge pin has at some time been removed and the action bar squeezed, so that the upper part of the forward slot is some thousandths of an inch narrower than the lower. The enlargement of the bores could, of course, have come about from the removal of pitting resulting from a period of neglect; but the indications that the action has been tightened are so much at variance with the other features I have described as to constitute a puzzle that I have been unable to solve. But it is perfectly clear that the gun has had a 'past', though perhaps a far less lurid and debilitating one than that of some of the other allegedly immaculate specimens brought to my notice.

24 February 1966

second-hand guns (I)

There has always been an active market in second-hand, good-quality guns, and, for reasons that are not far to seek, really good specimens are becoming increasingly rare and expensive. Concurrently, gun-coping is on the increase, and much care is necessary when buying from strangers, and particularly from a certain kind of private gun dealer who has been forced into growth by present conditions.

The question that has been put to me by a reader is therefore timely. 'Will you please tell me,' he asks, 'what faults to look for when buying a second-hand, best-quality, English, d.b., h.e., side-lock 12-bore.' I am tempted to reply that the best thing the would-be buyer can do is to take the gun to the original maker, or to some other first-class maker whom he knows and can trust, and be guided by his findings and advice. But that, perhaps, would be evading the question; and so I will assume that the buyer is anxious to exercise his own judgement, so far as possible.

The chief things to look out for when buying such a gun as my enquirer specifies are as follows.

1. Has the gun been nitro-proved, and if so, is it still in proof? If it is not, do not touch it. (This is likely to need the services of a gun-maker and his gauges straight away.)

2. Is it a modern or outdated type? If it has 28-in. or shorter barrels, and weighs $6\frac{1}{2}$ lb. or less, it can be regarded as a modern type . . . but see (5) below. If, however, the barrels are 30 in. and the weight $6\frac{3}{4}$ lb. or more, it strictly belongs to the black-powder era, even if nitro-proved and cannot command so high a price. Such a gun is likely to be *at least* forty years old. Nevertheless, at the right figure, it might be an admirable weapon for the man who wants a gun for firing full game charges, and does not object to the weight.

Pitting and pitfalls

3. Are the barrels pitted? (Wipe the bores quite clean and dry and make sure.) Slight pitting is an aesthetic rather than a practical draw-back; nevertheless, it ranks high as a defect, and should be reflected in the price. If there is no pitting, the barrels may have been lapped out

without practical detriment. But they may possibly have been lapped out to the verge of proof limits without quite clearing the pitting, which an unscrupulous vendor might then dismiss as a trifling blemish that could easily be removed at any time. So it might appear until the gun is gauged, when it would become apparent that any further lapping would involve re-proof, with all its attendant bother, risk and expense.

4. Have the bores been enlarged? Though the barrels may be sound, so that they ring like a bell when suspended and flicked with the finger nail, and entirely free from pitting and also in proof, the proof marks may reveal a story of past neglect and significant loss of substance. For example, the marks 12 *and* 12/1 (or ·740 in.), together with an *R* surmounted by a crown, would mean that the gun was originally proved as a 12-bore and subsequently re-proved as a 12/1, the successive nominal bore diameters being ·729 in. and ·740 in. To effect this transition, the gun is almost certain to have been heavily lapped or even fine-bored. Even so, it might still be a good gun, with an indefinite expectation of life, but it could *not* be honestly described as 'in mint condition' or 'equal to new', though it might be got up to look like it. Here again the price should acknowledge the facts.

5. Are the barrels originals? If they bear no name on the top rib or elsewhere, they are certainly not, nor are they likely to be of the highest quality. Sleeved barrels are stamped as such; and although likely to be in every way satisfactory, they do not command so high a price as original ones in good condition.

6. Have the barrels been shortened? If so, there will be no choke, save possibly a recess. There will also be a reduction in the muzzle flare, which it would need a micrometer to reveal.

Last, if the barrels have survived this inquisition and are free from dents, which should be carefully checked, and from lifted rib(s), which the ringing test should prove, there remains the large question whether their shooting has been impaired by the vicissitudes they may have undergone. This is the last thing a certain type of vendor would bother about, but it should be the first concern of the buyer. A best-quality gun should make best-quality patterns with a suitable cartridge, and performance should not be taken for granted. Nor with renewed, sleeved or shortened barrels should it be assumed that the charge is still correctly delivered to the point of aim. The gun, in short, should be tested.

3 May 1963

second-hand guns (II)

I started in my previous article to list the faults to look for when buying a second-hand, good-quality English game gun. By the time my space had run out, I had only dealt broadly with the question of dating the gun and with possible defects in the barrels. So now I pick up, and turn to the action.

7. Is the gun tight? To test for tightness, wipe the lumps, slots, flats, breech-ends and standing breech clean and dry. Remove the fore-end, also the locks if the gun is a self-opener. Now hold it horizontally, triggers downwards, with the breech-ends of the barrels resting in the left hand. Then, with the right fist, strike little sharp blows on the upper part of the stock, varying the position up and down until it can be felt that the stock is undergoing maximum vibration about the grip. At this stage, if the gun is at all loose or 'off the face' it will rattle impressively.

8. If the gun appears tight, is it honestly tight? Guns can be tightened, not only by the honest methods of the gunmaker, but by dishonest practices whereby they shoot loose again after little service. Examine the lumps, slots, action bar and standing breech for any signs of hammering or punch-marks, and consult a gunmaker on anything that looks at all suspicious.

9. Is the action sound? Examine the action bar with a magnifying glass, particularly at the foot of the standing breech. I once spotted a hair-crack this way, much to the embarrassment of the good and honest dealer who had failed to notice it when he himself had bought the gun.

10. Are the locks free from rust? Apart from broken springs and the possible need for some adjustment of the trigger pulls, this is the only thing likely to be at fault with best-quality locks. Otherwise, examples such as those made by Brazier, Chilton and Stanton seem everlasting—indeed, I do not believe their working life has ever been determined.

11. Is the stock sound, and free from cracks or glued repairs? The small or grip and the head are the vulnerable parts.

12. Is the stock the original? A best gun will have a stock of corresponding quality and figure. If, in fact, the stock is of plain quality, it is obviously a replacement—a fact that should be reflected in the price asked.

Caveat emptor

13. Has the gun been converted or 'doctored'? This is a large subject, and one that would need a wily old gunsmith, and not a private individual like myself, to do justice to it. But I have already dealt with the commonest conversion, namely, barrel-shortening. Other conversions, such as double to single trigger, are routine operations and in no way dishonest. But then things start shading off. For example, a country dealer once offered me a Purdey gun which, though of no recent vintage, as I could tell from the number, had been elaborately done-up. My suspicions were aroused by the fact that the action and lock-plates were freshly marbled, as in a new gun. A brief inspection satisfied me that the gun had been converted from full cross-eye to normal cast-off. The action had been heated and the strap and the lock-plates bent, so that these parts were now soft that should have been hard. What had been done internally to bring everything back into line was a matter for conjecture—I did not stop to enquire. This might, of course, have been a highly competent and honest conversion job; but it was not honest of the dealer to leave it to me to find out what had happened.

Cases of this sort have given me a strong dislike for done-up guns; unless, indeed, they are offered by an undeniable gunmaker as being fully reconditioned and guaranteed—a very different thing. I am particularly suspicious of any indications of recent heat-treatment, as in the case above mentioned.

But all said and done, there is so much of the past history and condition of a gun that cannot be inferred or determined without a micrometer and barrel gauges, that the best course for the ordinary shooter who is thinking of buying an expensive second-hand gun is to take it to the original maker, or one of comparable standing, for a thorough vetting. Such a gunmaker will be able to tell him everything he needs to know—except, possibly, what the gun is worth.

On that subject, he will have the natural bias of a contingent buyer —a bias that may be increased by trade jealousy if he is not the actual maker. I could tell some amusing stories in this connection.

As I have already stressed the importance of testing the gun, I will only add that in the case of a best gun it is not age that counts; it is not even the amount of fair wear it has had; rather it is the amount of neglect and ill-treatment it may have suffered that determine its condition and value.

10 May 1963

Section 5

SOME SPECIAL GUNS

'De gustibus . . .'

(Latin tag)

10. A beautiful old hammer gun of 1878 by Cogswell & Harrison, London. Note the damascus barrels, graceful hammers and shell fences. This gun, suitably loaded, makes splendid patterns, and despite its lack of choke is a wonderful game-getter.

hammer guns

It is a lazy summer day as I sit down to write these notes. The distant tors of Dartmoor, normally visible from my study window, have vanished in a heat haze, along with much of the intervening country, which elsewhere has taken on the pastel tints for which these parts are well known. Even the martins from under the thatch are chasing flies with less than their usual energy, and there is a hypnotic quality in the leisurely clink of the smith's hammer up the road and in the rhythmic thud-thud of a baler in the valley. In these circumstances, I am not sorry to have been called on to deal with such a pleasant, old-fashioned subject as hammer guns.

Four questions have come up, more or less together. How many of these guns are there still in use in this country? Answer: I estimate *at least* 50,000. How much does one have to pay for a first-class specimen? Answer: I understand that there is a lively and possibly an increasing demand for undeniable old thoroughbreds in good condition, which may fetch £80 to £90. Are they dangerous, even if nitro-proved? Answer: They are prone to inadvertent discharge by faulty manipulation, but not otherwise, if of good quality. And that brings me to a more pointed aspect of these guns, which needs a longer answer.

Ministerial mystery

A young reader has come to me with a copy of the *Farm Safety* leaflet, *Guns*, issued by the Ministry of Agriculture, and has asked me to clarify for his guidance the instructions on the use of hammer guns therein. In the course of advice on what to do when first handling a gun, the leaflet says, 'with a hammer gun, make certain that the hammers are right down and not even at half-cock'.

I must confess that this makes no sense to me. I take it that the author's intention was to warn readers against handling hammer guns with the hammers cocked; but the words used imply a complete misunderstanding of the nature of the ordinary hammer mechanism, and of the requirements of safe manipulation, so perhaps we had better start from the beginning.

Two types of hammer mechanism need considering—the earlier or non-rebounding kind, and the more modern rebounding variety, which was invented by the well-known lockmaker Stanton in 1869, and which rapidly superseded the other.

The non-rebounding lock had three positions: cocked, half-cocked, and fired or 'down'. When the hammer was cocked, the gun was ready to fire at the pressing of the trigger. When it was down, the hammer rested on the striker, which in turn rested on the cartridge cap. Both these were danger positions with a live cartridge in the chamber—the first for obvious reasons, and the second because the slightest tap or blow on the back of the hammer could cause the gun to go off. So a third or intermediate position was provided for safety—the half-cock position. In this, the sear nose engaged in a deep slot in the tumbler, so that the trigger could not be pulled; nor could the gun be discharged accidentally by a blow on the hammer, because the latter was held firmly out of contact with the striker. A gun with this kind of lock could only 'go off at half-cock' by some obstruction or breakage of the mechanism.

Automatic safety

Stanton's lock, as still made, also has three positions: cocked, half-cocked and down; but it has the grand advantage that the down position is only attained momentarily in the act of firing, after which the hammer rebounds instantly and automatically to the safe, half-cock position. As in the previous case, it is then impossible to discharge the gun accidentally by an external blow on the hammer, which is positively restrained from moving. But there is a difference in that the trigger can be pulled with the hammer at half-cock. No movement of the hammer ensues, however, because the lock, in this position, is in a state of equilibrium.

A gun with a rebounding lock, or, as we might now call it, an ordinary hammer gun, because the earlier type of non-rebounding lock is hardly ever seen nowadays, except on muzzle-loaders, is thus always cocked or half-cocked when it is picked up. The hammers will never be 'right down' as the Ministry's leaflet enjoins, and they would not be safe if they were.

A great improvement

The rebounding lock represented a great gain in safety and convenience. The sportsman never had to remember to put his gun into the safe or half-cock position when it was not cocked and ready to fire—it went there of its own accord. And not only was the gun freed from the possibility of accidental discharge by a tap or blow on the hammer when it was inadvertently left down on a live cartridge, but there was far less risk in the process of cocking. In one of the older locks, if the hammer slipped from the thumb at any stage in the process, the gun almost certainly went off. But with a rebounding lock, the hammer has to be back to something very near the fully cocked position before accidental release is likely to fire the cartridge.

Even so, I have heard an elderly sportsman deplore the passing of the non-rebounding lock on the grounds that the newer kind 'has no half-cock position'. But it has, as I have explained, and one to which it unfailingly gravitates whenever possible.

Manipulation

I ought not to leave this subject without a word on the manipulation of hammer guns, because the special dangers associated with them can be greatly diminished if they are handled correctly.

The dangers are, of course, of a hammer slipping from the thumb in the course of cocking or uncocking; and, more remotely, of pulling the wrong trigger when uncocking. Cocking or uncocking a hammer gun with the barrels pointed to the ground, as usually advised, is *dangerous*. The posture involved is most awkward, and there is a constant tendency to avoid it by raising the muzzles. Further, with this method one is too largely dependent on friction between the thumb and the ear of the hammer to prevent it from slipping. By far the safer way to handle the hammers is to do so with the gun pointed straight up to the sky, and held firmly by the left hand around the barrels. Then, if it goes off, nobody will be hurt. But it is far less likely to go off, for then the thumb will no longer tend to slip over the ear of the hammer. On the contrary, it will tend to slip ever more securely into the crutch between the ear and the head.

If anyone has any doubts about this, let him slip two short lengths of thin rubber tube over the ears of the hammers to cover the knurling, and then try cocking and uncocking the gun *with a well-greased thumb* in the alternative ways described. He will find it a convincing experiment!

An alternative way of safely uncocking the gun, arguably better with a sound, well-adjusted weapon, as being free from danger due to faulty trigger manipulation, is to open the breech first, with the gun, of course, pointed to the ground, and the fingers well clear of the triggers in the process.

Light from the past

I find it hard to imagine that anybody shoots nowadays with a pair of hammer guns, but it is well to recall that many of the legendary performers of the past used nothing else on their big days. If only a film could have been preserved, say, of Lord Walsingham and Lord de Grey shooting, and shooting safely, side by side at Croxteth or Elveden, on one of the days when they shot over a thousand pheasants, I have no doubt that we should see some pretty work in the way of accurate drill as well as shooting. The rule then was that no *cocked* gun should ever be passed from loader to shooter or vice versa. Even if the shooter had only discharged one barrel, he had to uncock the other before returning it to the loader; and as throughout these proceedings, the guns were pointed skywards when changing or shooting, we may be sure that they were not lowered to the ground for cocking and uncocking. Speed as well as safety would have suffered if they had been.

A nostalgic subject indeed! Sometimes I wish that progress, so called, had stopped at that point.

12 August 1967

black-powder guns

The efforts that have been made by the Proof Authorities and the Gun Trade Association in recent years to educate the public in the importance and significance of proof have undoubtedly borne fruit. Clear evidence of this is provided by the press of visitors to the proof-house stands at successive Game Fairs, while I myself receive a steady stream of letters from readers on the subject.

In consequence, it is now widely known that 'no small arm may be sold, exchanged or exported, exposed or kept for sale or exchanged or pawned' (I quote from the *Notes on the Proof of Shot Guns* published by the Proof Authorities) 'unless and until it has been fully proved and duly marked'. Also that 'arms previously proved and bearing apparently valid proof marks are deemed unproved if the barrels have been enlarged in the bore beyond defined limits or if the barrel or action has been materially weakened in other respect'.

As this extract implies, there is nothing in the relevant statutes—the Gun Barrel Proof Acts of 1868 and 1950—which debars the sale, etc., of arms duly proved and still 'in proof', whatever the class or scale of proof to which they may have been originally submitted. In particular it is still perfectly legal, so far as the Proof Acts are concerned, to sell guns proved for black powder only, provided that they have not become out of proof for any such reason as those indicated above.

In view, however, of the risk incurred by the user when smokeless cartridges are used in a black-powder gun—one, that is to say, which has never been nitro-proved—many of our more responsible gunmakers not only refuse to deal in such guns, but will not accept them for repair, except for the purpose of preparing them for re-proof. Others, not unreasonably, consider that there is still a legitimate market in black-powder guns, provided that the limitation of these weapons are made quite clear to the buyer. A third class of vendors, in which may be included certain innocent private individuals as well as the less scrupulous vendors who work on the *caveat emptor* principle, sell these guns without mention of proof to uninformed buyers, who proceed to use them with modern smokeless ammunition in complete ignorance of the danger involved.

An unintended situation

This situation, in which a vendor can sell a gun in a dangerous or potentially dangerous state, without violating the law, is precisely that which the Gun Barrel Proof Acts were designed to prevent. It is a situation that has come about for historical reasons. For centuries, the only powder in existence was black powder. Then, when smokeless powder was introduced, the two kinds ran side by side for many years, black remaining the 'ordinary' powder and smokeless a 'special' powder, for which a special proof was in due course introduced, though it was not made compulsory until 1925. So long as a gun was suitable for use with ordinary powder, it could reasonably be regarded as a fair article of trade, requiring no warning. But now the situation is completely changed. What was the special powder of 1900 has become very much the ordinary powder of 1963 ; while the ordinary powder of the earlier period has now become so extra-ordinary that those who still desire to use it have difficulty in obtaining supplies.

In these circumstances, *I suggest that every gun sold without express reservation carries the implied warranty that it is suitable for use with ordinary—that is, smokeless—ammunition.* If I am right in this (and I must emphasize that I write as a layman without special legal knowledge), two things follow: first, that anyone wishing to sell a black-powder gun, whether privately or otherwise, should not only avoid a direct breach of the law by ensuring that the gun is still in proof, but should protect himself from any possible charge of breach of implied warranty by warning the buyer of the limitations of the weapon, in a manner beyond any possibility of subsequent dispute; and secondly, that anyone who has innocently bought such a gun under the impression that it is suitable for use with ordinary cartridges, only to discover to his dismay that the gun is potentially dangerous when so used, may find, if he takes legal advice, that he is not without the means of redress under the Sale of Goods Act or otherwise. Better still, he may find the vendor responsive to reasonable representations made on the lines suggested in this article.

29 August 1963

the over-and-under

Often, a correspondent has vigorously asserted the merits of the over-and-under shotgun against what he has wrongly considered to be my prejudice against that weapon. Recently, I have received an unusually large number of letters expressing this view. I think, therefore, that it might be opportune if I were to attempt a broad review of the over-and-under principle in the light of the opinions expressed and of its history and progress.

The O/U has had a curious history, which, rightly interpreted, should throw a true light upon it. It appears that most of the early double-barrelled guns and pistols were of this kind. Why, it cannot be said with certainty; but it is at least certain, as well as significant, that with all the early ignition systems—matchlock, wheel-lock, flint and percussion—it was as easy to arrange the barrels one way as the other. The reason for the superposed system being preferred was probably that men everywhere were used to single-barrelled guns, and to the appearance they presented to the eye when aiming; so that the obvious thing to do with a second barrel was to tuck it out of sight under the first.

But when Henry Nock's patent breech of the 1780s so far improved the ignition of the flint gun as to enable it to be made with far shorter, and therefore lighter, barrels than hitherto, whereby the double gun became firmly established as the normal sporting type, the O/U system was decisively dropped, and stayed dropped, for well over a century.

A curious reversal

It is not easy, at this distance in time, to understand the reason for this curious reversal in gunmaking practice, unless, indeed, the side-by-side principle, apart from making a less clumsy-looking gun, was found to possess—or was *believed* to possess—some shooting merit. It may have been found easier to make both barrels of an S/S gun deliver their charges truly to the point of aim. And the visible double barrel may have been regarded as more 'pointable', or as providing a better aiming facility. This, I know, is contrary to modern O/U doctrine, but not entirely so to modern O/U practice, as exemplified by the Browning 'Broadway'.

But one thing is certain. Men knew just how well they could shoot before the S/S double gun came into favour, and if its visual or other characteristics had been such as to cause any falling off in their performance, its popularity would have been short-lived. As we know, it was not short-lived. It survived, most significantly, that hiatus between the perfecting of the flintlock in the early 1800s and the arrival of the percussion system, when gunmakers were desperate for novelties, and were patenting every kind of sensible and stupid device they could think of to gain a pull over their rivals. I have no doubt at all that if any gunmaker at that period had thought he stood the slightest chance of staging a revival of the O/U system, he would have done so, and would have attributed to it more merits than its present-day champions have ever dreamed of.

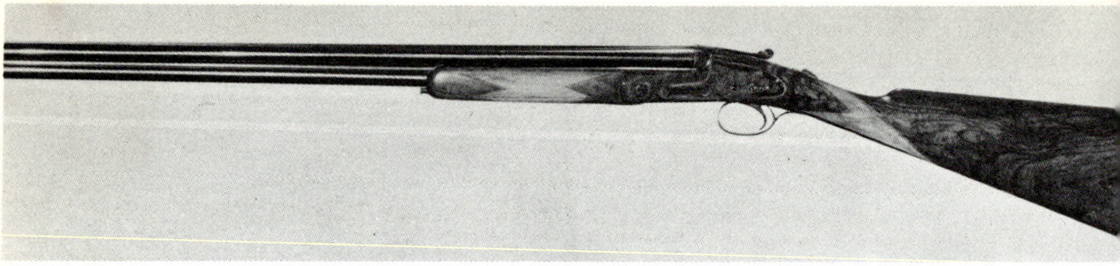

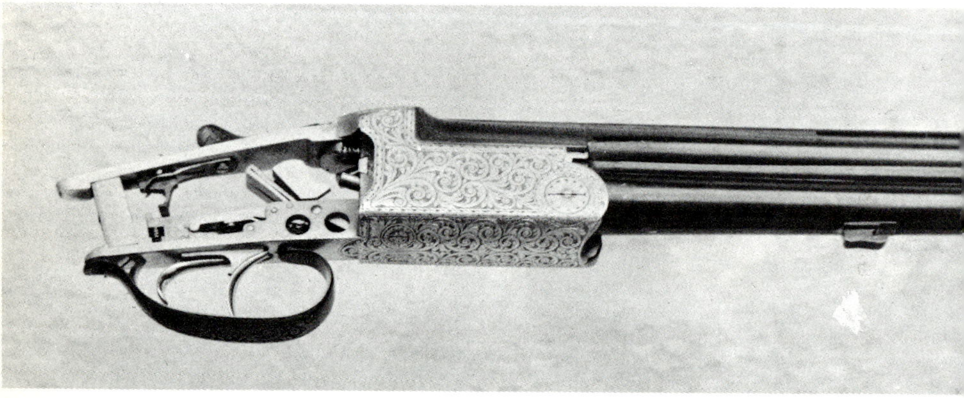

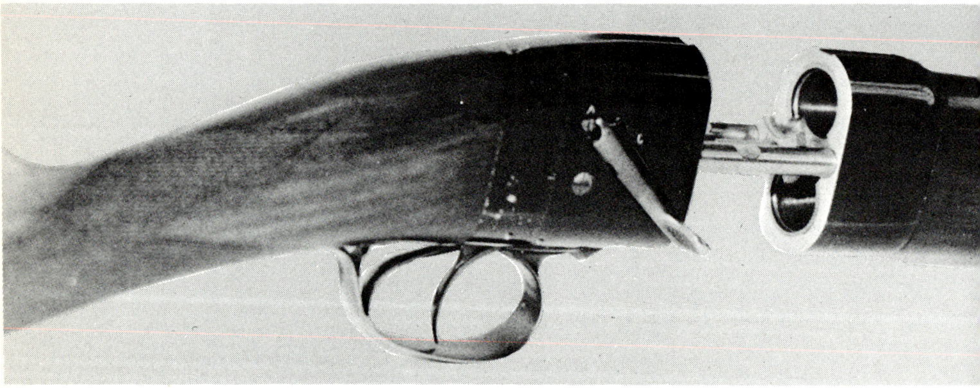

11. THE DESIGN OF THE OVER-AND-UNDER GUN IS STILL EVOLVING

Examples of special interest are shown on this page and on page 74. *Top* The elegant Purdey-Woodward. *Middle* An Italian Rizzini (?) with German 'Blitz' action. *Bottom* The ultra-lightweight French Bretton.

The S/S double survived another significant phase during the trap shooting of live pigeons in the latter half of the century. The betting on these matches was very heavy. The celebrated Capt. Horatio Ross, as great a performer at the traps as he was in the field, has recorded that on one occasion, as he was about to take a particular shot in a match, he realized that his personal stake of £10,000 (worth fully £50,000 today) depended on whether he hit or missed. Yet, during this period, when muzzle-loaders were still much used, and when it would still have been technically quite easy to produce an O/U pigeon gun if it had been thought in any way advantageous, the principle was never revived.

One can well understand it. The performance of the crack pigeon shots of the day—men like Ross, Elliott, Fulford and Brewer—was such as to leave no room for the suggestion that their S/S guns were in any way ill-adapted to their task. In 1891, Fulford, in a match with Brewer, scored 100 straight at 30 yds. rise—and this at a living bird which the new ZZ target is said to imitate. The pages of Gladstone's *Record Bags* contain numerous accounts of similar shooting at both live and inanimate targets, practically every one of which we are entitled to assume was made with an S/S gun. Perhaps the most conspicuous of these accounts, from the 'pointability' angle, is that of a Mr H. Cornish, an Indian Superintendent of Police, who shot 50 snipe straight, and finished with 96 for 100 cartridges.

The O/U revival

Seen against this background, the reason for the revival of the O/U in the first quarter of the present century is sufficiently clear. Burrard has expressed it plainly. 'The primary object', he says, in *The Modern Shotgun*, 'was the search for something new. A degree of finality having apparently been reached in ordinary hammerless ejectors, the makers of best guns very naturally wished to bring in some improvement, as otherwise their businesses would suffer owing to the extraordinary longevity of the weapons they built.' But O/Us were not only revived: they survived, and with the advent of cheaper models and the upsurge of clay pigeon shooting, have much increased in popularity.

Burrard points to American influence here—part of that general influence, I have no doubt, that the Americans have exerted on clay pigeon shooting. Confirmation comes from eminent commentators on the other side of the Atlantic. The Americans are traditionally and predominately riflemen. For generations they have been accustomed to

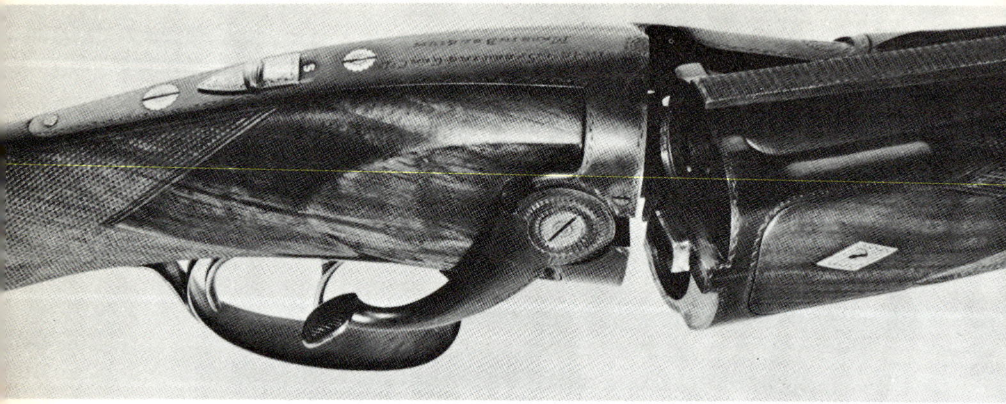

12. MORE OVER-AND-UNDERS OF SPECIAL INTEREST

Above The Lebeau-Courally side-opener. *Below* A nameless French example with drop-down action locked by a sliding false breech as in the Finnish Valmet.

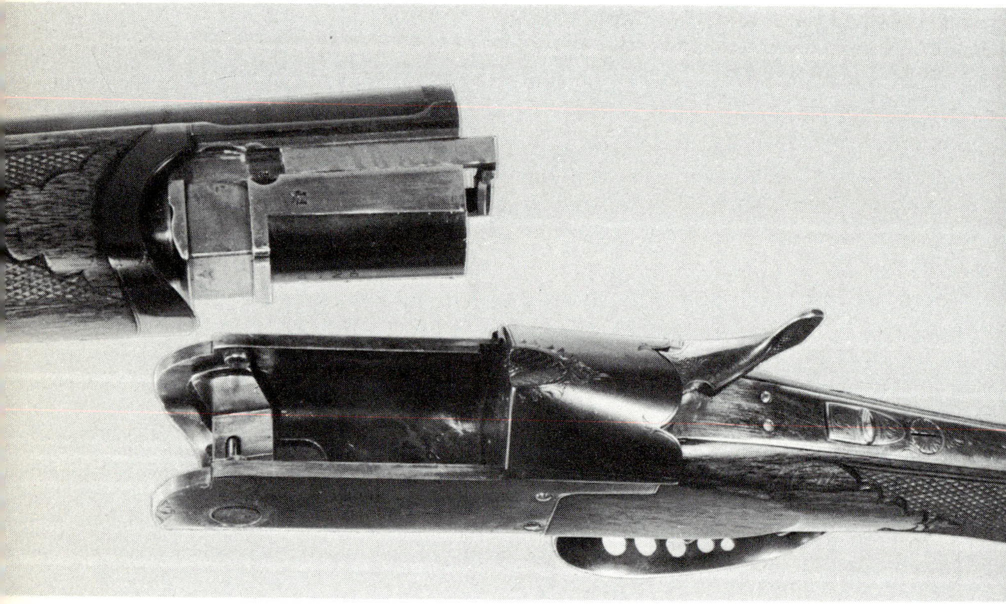

repeating rifles with tubular magazines beneath the barrels and large, deep fore-ends, and the O/U shotgun would make an obvious appeal to them as a weapon that both looked and felt familiar. J. O'Connor, the gun editor of the New York *Outdoor Life*, evidently holds this belief. He says that he would 'make a guess that this [the new-found popularity of the O/U] is due to the rifle-mindedness of the American shooting public'. He cites as advantages the 'single sighting plane, recoil that goes back in a straight line, and no crossfiring with slugs'. As disadvantages, he mentions its being more expensive to make and its greater resistance to a side-wind.

Significant opinions

These American opinions are significant as not being weighted by any overriding loyalty to the English type of gun. Elmer Keith, now probably the doyen of American writers on the shotgun, and a man of vast practical experience, gives much the same reason as J. O'Connor's for the popularity of the O/U in America. The advantages he quotes are the single sighting plane 'for those who must have it', reduced recoil *from the lower barrel*, and the difference in charge elevation between the two barrels, which can be advantageous to the trap shooter, as I myself have pointed out. The disadvantages he lists include its reduced ease of loading, arising from the much wider opening angle, its usually more complicated mechanism, its susceptibility to heat mirage and cross-winds, and its clumsy appearance. He adds that it is 'the most costly of all shotguns', quality for quality being understood.

Summing up

The facts and opinions given in this brief review present a consistent and intelligible picture. After its early start, we see the O/U principle decisively superseded by the side-by-side, probably for one or more of the reasons I have given. We see the Golden Age of shooting pass without giving rise to any suggestion of inadequacy on the part of the latter weapon. But as this attained its final development, we see the O/U revived on a commercial motive, and in 'best' quality. After a pause (and two world wars) we witness a great expansion in clay pigeon shooting, accompanied by a wave of American influence, fostering a demand for O/U guns, which could now be satisfied by the availability of new and improved models at popular prices.

But in view of their history, O/U guns certainly cannot be upheld as representing a radical improvement on the more popular weapon, though some users of them, particularly recent converts, with the zeal of their kind, do not hesitate to make the attempt. The experts are more lukewarm. Percy Stanbury, in *Clay Pigeon Marksmanship*, is conspicuously lacking in enthusiasm; while the famous American exhibition shot Herb Parsons, when he was a member of J. Robinson's All-American trap team, used a side-by-side.

Nevertheless, most trap shooters, and a few game shooters, prefer the O/U, and consider that they shoot better with it, which, for them, puts it above all argument.

The outlook for the superposed weapon at the moment is bright. Trapshooters being a fraternity, engaged in a competitive sport, the members naturally show a strongly imitative tendency in their choice of equipment; and as clay pigeon shooting extends its appeal, their increasing adoption of the O/U is bound to have a marginal influence on game shooters—often one and the same individuals.

The only cloud visible on the O/U horizon is the pump-gun, described by Percy Stanbury as 'one of the best, if you can handle it', for clay target shooting, and the choice of many leading American exponents. Its cost is but a fraction of that of the most popular of the O/Us.

22 April 1965

single-trigger guns

A reader whose reasoned contentment and satisfaction with his double-triggered gun was being undermined by a single-trigger enthusiast came to me a little while ago for moral support. I was pleased to afford him what I could, for I have long regarded the single trigger as having failed to establish any general superiority over the normal arrangement.

There is, of course, nothing new about this contrivance, which was known in the flintlock days; and if it had been one of undeniable utility, the inducement to perfect it in those highly competitive times would have been too powerful for gunmakers to resist. Indeed, towards the end of the flintlock era, they seemed to be at their wits' end to find novelties to attract custom, and were prepared to try anything likely to find favour with the sporting public. It is, I think, significant that in this highly fertile soil the single trigger never took root. The admitted imperfections of the early specimens, especially their proneness to double discharge, hardly provide sufficient reason, for if there had been obvious utility and consequent demand, these imperfections would have been remedied. As it was, apart from sporadic appearances, the single trigger lay dormant for the best part of a century, when the bringing to perfection of the hammerless ejector stimulated gunmakers once again to seek for novelties to attract custom.

This competitive revival in the early 1900s quickly focused attention on the defects of the earlier models and brought about a recognition of the need for providing for the involuntary pull which takes place between the two deliberate pulls. A number of single-trigger mechanisms were accordingly introduced in which the involuntary pull was rendered ineffective, either by a blocking device or by a delaying action. A few of these ingenious contrivances have become thoroughly established as being both efficient and reliable. Some are non-selective, the order of firing the barrels being invariable, while others are selective, and admit of choice, according to whether a selector device is set to fire the right or left barrel first.

The modern picture

In its modern form, the single trigger commands a much wider acceptance. In America, I believe, it is usually regarded as a *sine qua non* in a good double gun; and in this country, the serious clay pigeon shooter, if I may trust my impression, would regard himself as gravely handicapped without his over-and-under, his raised ventilated rib and his single selective trigger. I have no doubt at all that gadget-appeal is a powerful factor in the American attitude (which, incidentally, is showing signs of change), and fashion a corresponding factor in ours. The utility factor, which undoubtedly exists alongside these others, is most difficult to evaluate. It is significant that there is no corresponding demand for single triggers among game shooters. Some prefer them: others do not—choice seems to be freely regulated by personal preference.

The advantages commonly claimed for single triggers are that they avoid the bruising of fingers and increase the speed and accuracy with which the second shot can be placed. My personal belief is that they add nothing to speed, for if I can trust the evidence of my own reactions, the finger can always beat the eye. In other words, I find that by the time my brain is ready to say 'pull' for the second shot, my finger is always ready and waiting on the second trigger. Accuracy is another matter. Second-barrel shots are undoubtedly less accurate than first-barrel, and it can hardly be denied that the need for shifting the trigger finger is likely to be a contributory factor. Nevertheless, the dominant factor is, I believe, the interruption of swing by the first shot, for the relative inaccuracy of second-barrel shots may still be observed when a single trigger is being used, though perhaps to a lesser degree.

Neglecting the arguments on behalf of bruised-finger sufferers, it would accordingly appear that the case for the single-trigger rests on some marginal gain in second-barrel accuracy. A man would need to fire a very large number of cartridges with both single and double triggers before he could attempt to evaluate this gain. Even then, his conclusion would only be valid for himself. The price that has to be paid, on the other hand, is in no way conjectural. Single triggers, whether selective or otherwise, deprive the double gun of its great advantage of *instant* availability of open or choke boring; they add materially to the cost and complexity of a gun, and are prone to get out of adjustment or to fail unless carefully maintained. An important incidental objection is that they habituate the user to a minority system, and thus throw him out of perfect accord with any double-trigger guns he may possess or subsequently acquire. This perfect accord, which I believe to be indispensable to the attainment of the highest proficiency in shooting, would, I am sure, never survive switching back and forth from single to double trigger.

19 September 1963

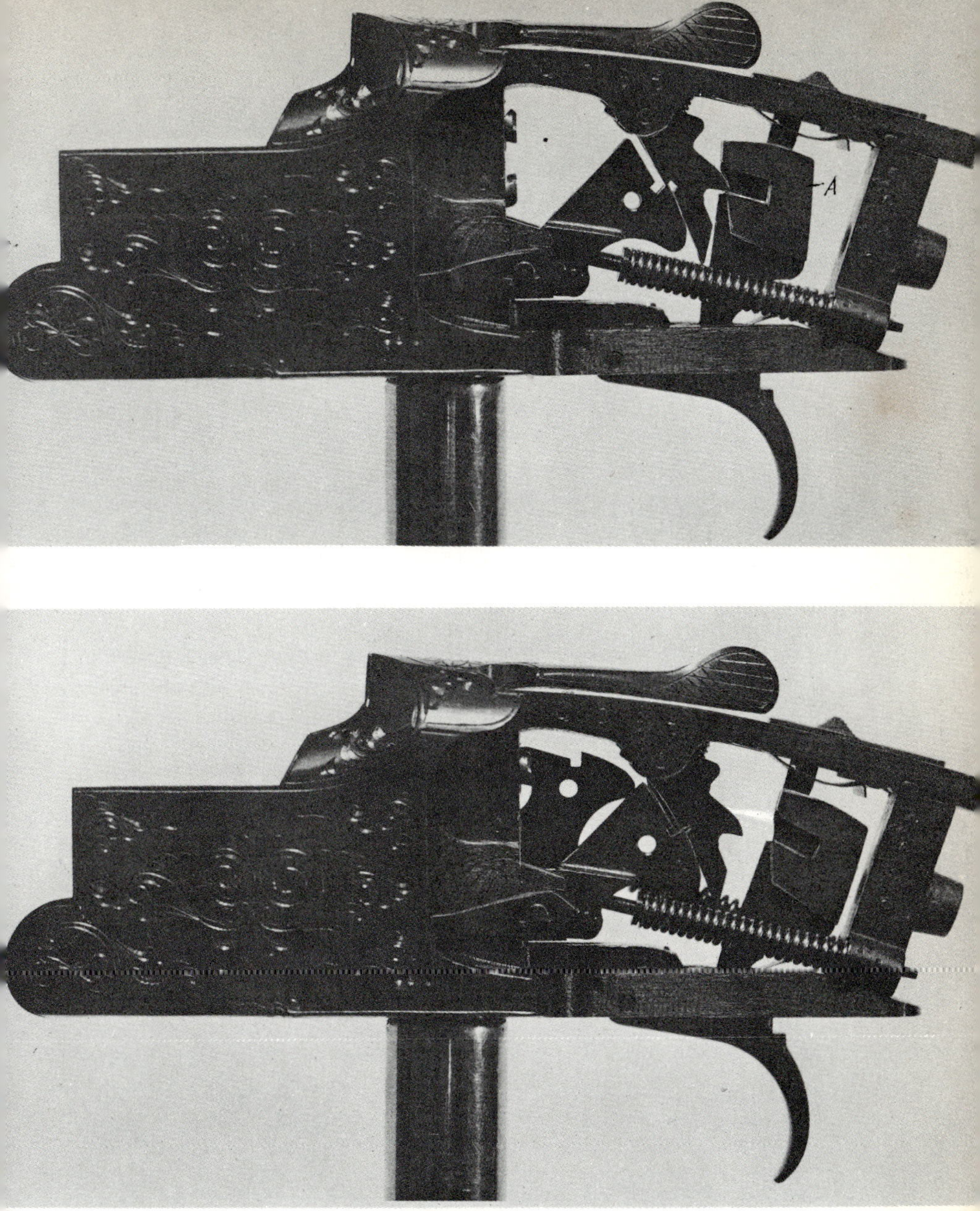

13. MODERN INERTIA-TYPE SINGLE-TRIGGER MECHANISM

.s fitted to the Winchester M 101 over-and-under. *Top* Ready to fire the first shot. Pulling the trigger lifts the /eighted sear-lifter *A* which disengages the sear of the far-side hammer. This then falls and fires the lower arrel. *Bottom* The sear-lifter is then thrown back by recoil to the position shown. When it is returned by its ontrolling spring, it engages the near side sear, ready to fire the upper barrel. (The involuntary second pull takes place when the lifter is right back and out of engagement with the sear.)

self-opening guns

I have sometimes wondered why no enterprising gunmaker, so far as I am aware, has ever tried to create a demand for a self-opening gun in the popular-price class.

There can be no doubt about the merit of the self-opening principle. In a hot corner it gives a non-ejector something like the fire-power of an ejector, and puts an ejector on the way to parity with a pair. And it is not only that: it undoubtedly makes a gun much more pleasant to use. There is a principle at work here which I believe everybody intuitively understands and appreciates. Certain manually operated mechanisms have to be pushed and pulled through all their evolutions. They are inert, uncooperative, and manifestly dead. Others are endowed with a sort of life: they are alert, expectant and eager to be off. Give them the cue for action, and they will do all the rest for themselves.

A hammer gun with the old under-guard lever was a perfect example of the inert kind of mechanism. The lever had to be pulled sideways; the gun had to be opened; the spent cases had to be pulled out one by one and the new cartridges inserted; the gun had to be closed; and the lever had to be pushed back. Finally, each lock had to be separately and manually cocked . . . eight deliberate operations, not counting the reloading. The self-opening hammerless ejector provides the perfect contrast: with it, these eight operations are reduced to two. All one has to do is to press the top lever. The gun then opens by itself, ejects the fired case or cases, and remains firmly open until it is deliberately closed, whereupon the locking bolt snaps home and the gun is ready for action. In a high-class specimen, nicely adjusted, there is an aesthetic pleasure as well as practical advantage in all this.

Modern self-openers

Although the Needham hammerless ejector of some ninety years ago came near to anticipating the self-opening principle, the Purdey gun of 1880, based on F. Beesley's celebrated invention, is generally regarded as the archetype of modern self-openers. It was an invention that has contributed notably to the pre-eminence widely accorded to the weapons produced by this famous house. Even now, eighty-three years later, it still has strong claims to be regarded as the best of the self-opening actions. It is certainly the most ingenious and the least well understood: indeed such eminent authorities as Greener and Burrard have both given explanations of its method of working which are quite incorrect and imply basic misconceptions. The action makes ingenious use of one and the same mainspring to fire the lock, cock it, and open the gun.

14. Self-opening guns are usually found in the top price-bracket. This 'Connaught' easy-opener with the Smith action by Westley-Richards is a notable example in the medium price range.

In the Holland & Holland self-opener, a coil spring is accom modated in the fore-end, and kicks against the upper part of the knuckle joint of the action, to the same effect. The Lancaster Twelve-Twenty action also uses an auxiliary spring, but it is a vee-spring, carried on the lockplate. The Smith action, as used in the Westley Richards 'Connaught', is an adaptation of the Anson & Deeley action, and uses the mainspring; but both this and the Lancaster are not true self-openers, but rather easy openers.

A neglected development?

If the state of the gun trade in this country were such that gunmakers were eager to introduce novelties, I could only regard the absence of a popular-priced self-opener as a neglected development. The Holland action gives a clue to what might be done, for I cannot imagine that it would be difficult or costly to adapt their simple principle to a cheaper type of weapon. If I remember correctly, it was Mr. G. T. Cox of Patstone & Son, Southampton, who pointed out to me many years ago that it is the non-ejector that would stand to benefit most from the addition of a self-opening feature, and that this could be achieved by the simple addition of a coil-spring between the barrels, so that it bore on the extractor leg. My old Purdey—my favourite gun for many years—was a self-opening non-ejector, and I often thought that I preferred it to an ejector which was not self-opening. Its fire-power was little inferior, and it was certainly more pleasant to use.

There is admittedly one thing which would tend to reduce the initial effectiveness of the self-opening principle in a cheap gun, and that is the stiff condition in which many, but by no means all of them, are sent out. But this is only a passing state of affairs: guns last a long time, and the full benefit of the self-opening feature would soon accrue. The alleged general disadvantage of the self-opener—the effort required to close it—may be greatly minimized by correct design, and in any case disappears with the acquisition of a little knack.

1 August 1963

Section 6

HOW MANY GUNS DO YOU NEED?

'How happy could I be with either were t'other dear charmer away . . .'

(*The Beggars' Opera*, II, i)

the happy gunner

I was about to clean my gun when I noticed the following gossip paragraph on the fragment of a Sunday newspaper which I was tearing up for this purpose.

> Guns at £1,306 5s. a Pair.
>
> 'When I open my guncase, I want everybody to gasp,' an American recently instructed Purdey's the gunsmiths. At their factory near Paddington last week, I spent a couple of hours watching how they are carrying out his wishes.

The paragraph was accompanied by a photograph of a lock-plate on which bob-white quail were inlaid in different shades of gold, *à la Fabergé.*

I suppose this should have been enough to make any shooting man's mouth water. To be quite honest, mine did not. I have found by experience that a gun which is too much of a cabinet specimen—too unmistakably an *objet de vitrine*—is a very mixed blessing to one to whom shooting is first and foremost a field sport. If a sportsman, as opposed to a gun collector, has a very beautiful gun, he will inevitably want to use it. But when he takes the precious thing into the field every shower of rain becomes a menace and every trifling scratch and bruise on the beautiful stock an agony. He is afraid to stand it up for fear someone may knock it down, and he is afraid to lay it down for fear that moisture or grit may penetrate its delicate interior. When he travels with it he is afraid to let it out of his sight; and in short, his joy of possession is completely soured by care.

Nor is the man entirely happy who owns too many guns. Not only can he be bedevilled by indecision as to which of them to take out on a given day, or by temporary hoodoos affecting one or other of them, but his shooting form is bound to suffer from inevitable differences in their weight, balance, fit and trigger pulls.

If I were asked to name the man who, in my experience, got most satisfaction out of a gun, I should unhesitatingly name David W., who, when I knew him many years ago, was a sort of part-time handyman at a remote Welsh inn, where they had good fishing and shooting. David also acted as guide and gillie to those guests who needed his services—and of whom he duly approved. If they failed to come up to his private standards, he invariably had other occupations that pressingly demanded his attention. A true Celt!

Instead of a wife

The twin passions of David's life were undoubtedly shooting and a certain much-cherished gun of his; and since he was a confirmed bachelor, I always considered that this gun stood him roughly in lieu of a wife. It was a 12-bore hammerless non-ejector of indeterminate age which bore the name of an alleged English maker, but which obviously hailed from Belgium. It was a good gun of its class and had been well cared for, and from muzzle to butt-plate it had acquired a fine patina that could only have come by fair wear and tear combined with much rubbing, oiling and loving attention. It carried a fearsome degree of choke in both barrels, and, as David knew well where to point it, he not infrequently brought off some remarkably long shots, even though, by the same token, he missed nearer ones that should have been his.

But for the innate breeding of his race, David would, I am sure, have boasted inordinately of this gun. As it was, he never spoke of it: perhaps he thought its merits too rare for common mention. But when he brought off one of his brilliant shots, his eyes would flash, and he would give a quick double pat to his gunstock, as it were in secret, which was far more eloquent than any boasting could have been. I firmly believe that he took no credit to himself on any of these occasions, but transferred it all to his gun; and that in the depths of his Celtic imagination he invested it, if only subconsciously, with some of the attributes of the legendary weapons of folk lore.

And the moral of all this? It is surely that the happiest state of a shooting man is that of one who owns but a single gun—a good one indeed, but not too new, or rare, or beautiful—in which he has complete confidence and which he uses exclusively, so that it is of necessity the agent and instrument of all his successes and a well-remembered feature of his best shooting days. Given such a gun, he need feel no envy of the owner of the largest and most opulent battery, even though it were composed entirely of Purdey's $2,500 gold-inlaid gasp-producers.

17 November 1961

the one-gun doctrine

Easily the most earnest and prolonged gun consultation I have ever been drawn into was one I held with a friend with whom I used to share rooms when, long ago, we were both struggling young men, trying to mount the first rungs of the ladders of our respective professions. In those days, university graduates were not courted and flattered and pursued with tempting offers of wonderful jobs, but were considered lucky if they could persuade some distinguished professional man to engage them at a nominal salary while they fed on the scraps of wisdom and experience that fell from his table. In a word, we were both hard up—not, in retrospect, an unhealthy state for a young man to be in, but an embarrassing condition for one, like my friend, who wanted to buy a gun.

His uttermost limit, I remember, was £10, and our confabulations were concerned with the best way of laying out this princely sum, or such lesser amount as could be made to suffice. In those days, one could go to Vaughan's or Whistler's in the Strand and choose from a bewildering stock of warranted second-hand weapons, ranging from Purdey hammerless ejectors in unblemished condition for as little as £60 to hammerless non-ejectors by reputable Birmingham makers for upwards of about £7 10s. There were usually some excellent bargains to be had by anyone willing to accept a gun with a less-popular feature, such as a side-lever, or some oddity in the way of engraving or the like. There was one, I remember, engraved with a design representing the theme of wine, women and song—bottles, cards, dancing girls and the rest—for which something considerable was knocked off, doubtless out of recognition of the fact that the worship of Bacchus and Venus is not compatible with the successful propitiation of Diana.

In the end, my friend and I decided that this was the best line to pursue—I mean, that of a gun in the less popular class; and so he bought from Whistler's a Henry Atkin hammer gun.

A bargain and a lesson

This was a really beautiful little 12-bore, of the highest possible quality, with Joseph Brazier locks and a lovely figured walnut stock with a fine fiddle pattern. It had two pairs of steel barrels, one game-bored and the other choked, and was fitted in a top-quality leather case, complete with cleaning implements. The whole outfit, which was entirely without blemish, cost £8—I repeat, £8.

My friend used this gun for two sorts of shooting—for wildfowling and for general mixed shooting inland. On his wildfowling days, he used his 30-in. choke barrels: at other times he used the 28-in. game-bored pair. Oddly enough, despite the balance and handling quality of this gun, its unexceptionable patterns, its beautiful trigger pulls, and the fact that it fitted him to a nicety, my friend did not do so well with it as he had every right to expect. It was not long before we found out the reason: it was the switching to and fro between two sets of barrels of different weight and length, with their different effect on the balance and responsiveness of the gun, that was responsible. In consequence, my friend never had the chance of developing any single, self-consistent co-ordination complex in his use of the weapon. But when he abandoned chopping and changing and stuck to one set of barrels only, he found a great improvement in his performance. This case, and similar or related experiences over the years, have made me a strong believer in the 'one man, one gun' principle—in the advantage, that is to say, capable of being derived from total and exclusive familiarity with a single weapon. I recognize, of course, that not every man can satisfy his shooting needs with just one gun (or a matched pair), but I am sure that, if he can, he stands to gain from it. Clarrie Wilson, the Olympic coach, may be quoted as an outstanding supporter of this principle, and has gone so far as to say, 'Stick to one gun, and don't on any account *handle* any others.'

'Co-ordination complex'

I might reasonably be content to rest on such an authority, but in fact I feel bound to try to explain what I meant just now when I referred to a single, self-consistent co-ordination complex.

When we handle a familiar tool or instrument or implement of sport, which has to be directed or used in some precise way in response to sensory stimuli, usually by what we see, we appear to build up in the brain and muscles and nervous system a set of *memories*. These memories serve as a system of reference data, whereby a given sensory stimulus is translated subconsciously into appropriate muscular action—in just the same way that an engineer, on receiving information about a weight to be lifted, can look up in a table the right size of wire rope to use.

Somehow, somewhere in our brains, we have the capacity to tie up these sets of memories into neat little bundles, each appropriate to a particular case, and to file them away for use, as and when required. These little bundles of memories are really what I mean by co-ordination complexes.

When we pick up a particular implement, we cannot use it properly until we have dug out of the file the right bundle of memories, and stuck them up in the place where they become the operative set for the occasion. The selection of the right set—and this is important—is determined by some preliminary signal. The clearer and more unmistakable that signal is, the better for the avoidance of error. If, for example, I select a hammer from the rack in my workshop, I can see before I touch it that it is the light, instrument-maker's hammer, and not the heavy, engineer's hammer, and I can at once proceed to use it accurately. But if in some way they could be disguised so that they were indistinguishable by inspection, I should fumble for a moment until I had decided by weight and feel which one I had picked up. I might fumble much longer if, instead of being such very different hammers, they were closely alike in weight and shape.

If, on the other hand, I only possessed one hammer, there would be no possibility of error: there would be only one set of memories available, and their invariable exercise would have engraved deep channels of habit in my mental, nervous and muscular machinery.

An anomaly explained

To complete these analogies by which I have tried to underpin the 'one man, one gun' philosophy, I should add that, having selected the right co-ordination complex for the occasion, we still seem to have the others in sight, for we can occasionally take a piece of data from the wrong sheet. Even now, five years after having got rid of a motor car with an overdrive, I notice that, when the wind is behind me or I am going down a long, slight gradient, I still occasionally feel for the overdrive control that is not there.

In these terms, I believe it is possible to understand my friend's difficulty with his Henry Atkin gun, and to reconcile that with what might appear to be a first-class anomaly presented by Clarrie Wilson. In the very same article as that containing the advice quoted, he explains that he owns a gun with three sets of barrels—26, 28 and 30 in. Surely, this is effectively three guns, not one, and Mr Wilson ought to be put off form pretty thoroughly by switching from one to the other, as he says he does, for skeet, game and trap shooting respectively. But, he explains, 'through use, the minute I pick up the gun with the appropriate set of barrels, it feels at home, and handles as I expect it to'.

Mr. Wilson's gun, I understand, is a Brno over-and-under. With the 30-in. barrels, this gun handles, to me, unaccustomed to such tools, like a weaver's beam. With the 26-in. barrels, it is transformed; and the explanation of his adaptability (apart from his exceptional gifts) lies in the strength and decisiveness of the signal conveyed to his brain when he picks up a particular gun-barrel combination. It is the instrument maker's hammer and the engineer's hammer over again. But my friend with his Henry Atkin received no such decisive signal. His two sets of barrels, though of different length, were obviously adjusted to be otherwise as nearly alike as possible, and in using them, I believe he was constantly switching over to the wrong co-ordination complex, and applying to the one situation the muscular reaction appropriate to the other.

If there is a lesson to be learned from all this, it is that the man whose shooting form is most likely to suffer from using several guns is the one who uses, say, two or more game guns which are *approximately* the same as to weight, fit, balance, and trigger pulls, but which are nevertheless just that little bit different. He is the man whose co-ordination complexes are likely to get mixed up. But the man who uses one gun, and one gun only, for game, and another of totally different weight, form, balance, etc., for wildfowl or trap or whatever it may be, may, like Mr. Wilson, get away with it. Men like one of my American correspondents, with whom I expostulated for harbouring *eighteen* guns, appear to seek their main satisfaction in gun-collecting rather than in shooting, and are little affected by these considerations. But they cannot enjoy that degree of intimacy and affection capable of growing up between a man and a favourite implement or weapon, which in time can acquire something of the character of an old friend.

29 April 1965

Section 7

BARRELS

'Barrels are widely variable. They vary much in their material, their mode of construction, their standards of workmanship, the skill and care with which they are bored, chambered and rimmed, and more particularly their performance, which can be very different from their nominal rating.'

barrels first

When the young cornet of hussars who was with Wellington in the Peninsula wanted to take home one of the famous Spanish guns of the period, he did not bother about the lock or the stock: he simply brought back the barrel, and had it fitted up here. True, the Spanish guns of the Napoleonic era had a reputation which the great English makers had hardly overtaken, but it was on their barrels that their reputation chiefly rested—their hard-shooting quality, and their unequalled strength. It was widely held that there was no charge capable of being stuffed into a high-class Spanish barrel that could be relied upon to burst it.

I have often thought that, in their judgement of a gun, our forebears had an advantage over us. To them, more especially in the days of the percussion muzzle-loader, a gun was nine-tenths barrel. The stock was a piece of plain wood necessary for handling: the lock was a mere adjunct. For reasons probably arising out of the shooting characteristics of the flintlock, and the predominance of the low-flying, walked-up partridge in the English shooting man's calendar, they appear to have attached relatively little importance to the fit or the balance of a gun. But the barrel—that was a different matter! How it shot with various charges, what grain and brand of powder went best, what weight and size of shot, what kind of wadding—these, and the resulting 'garnish' and penetration, as measured by the perforation of paper pads, were all-important.

Distractions

They still are, but the modern sportsman, particularly if he does not fire many cartridges on many days throughout the season, has had his attention diverted from these essentials, and more especially from that vital, fixed element among them—the barrel. The use of steel which,

BARRELS OF GLASS!
steel liner of the Winchester M 59 automatic shotgun is reinforced by 500 miles of glass fibre, shown being applied. The glass reinforcement is bonded to the liner, and the resulting composite l is stronger than a steel one of the same dimensions. *See page 101.*

unlike its damascus predecessor, bears no outward evidence of its quality, the general use of factory-loaded ammunition, and the distraction afforded by the various competing mechanical arrangements of the modern gun—not to mention such things as the figure of the stock and the engraving—have relegated the barrel to a relatively minor place in the regard of all too many modern shooters.

If we look back, we can see that this regrettable process was much aided by the invention of choke boring and the use of the micrometer, whereby certain degrees of muzzle constriction came to be associated with certain standards of patterning performance. This gun, we credulously say, has a constriction of 20 thousandths of an inch, therefore it ranks as a half choke, and since a half choke is down in the book as a boring which gives a 60 per cent pattern in a 30-in. circle at 40 yds, this gun will behave accordingly.

So, for the majority of shooters buying the less expensive guns straight off the shelf, it is true to say that the barrel is taken on trust, not only for what it is, but for what it does. It is also probably true of the majority of those who sell them.

Variables

But barrels are widely variable. They vary much in their material, their mode of construction, their standards of workmanship, the skill and care with which they are bored, chambered and rimmed, and more particularly their performance, which can be very different from the nominal rating. The makers of the better-class ready-made guns presumably check their performance, but, even so, the load, a vital factor, is never stated. Some Continental makers mark their barrels distinctively according to the degree of choke, but the marks, I understand, are made at the time of proof, and are based solely on the amount of constriction. One maker—I believe it is Beretta—recognizing that such marking conveys no guarantee of patterning performance, adds a certificate, certifying that the performance is in accordance with the dimensional indication. But, again, the load is not specified.

Only in the better top-grade guns, made to order, is the shooter relieved of doubt. Such guns can be and usually are built to give a specified performance with a specified load, and the shooter can personally witness the final testing of the gun before accepting delivery. As for the quality of the barrels, the maker is invariably prepared to say what is the make and grade of steel employed. That, and his reputation, give the shooter all the assurance he needs.

Modern barrels

Modern barrels, we say, are made of steel. But steel is merely a generic name for a large family of iron alloys, of widely different composition and physical characteristics. Steels used for gun barrels range from ordinary low-carbon or mild steel, as used in structural engineering, to high-class chromium-nickel-molybdenum alloys made in electric furnaces. Strength may range from 25 tons per square inch to more than twice that figure. I believe that the steel most favoured for gun barrels in this country at the present time is what is known as a 3 per cent nickel steel, designated as En.21 in British Standard Specification No. 970/55. This has a strength of 45 to 50 tons.

Commercially, steels are known by all sorts of names which give the shooter little information. Sometimes they are makers' grade names (Vickers A, Bellota Urko-1); sometimes they are fancy names (Hercule, Boehler-Blitz); and sometimes they are merely indicative of a process (Whitworth's fluid-pressed, Siemens). This is a matter in which the shooter is much in the hands of the gunmaker; as the gunmaker himself, indeed, is much in the hands of the steel manufacturer. It is a vastly specialized subject, in which the only guiding principle that can be offered to the buyer of a gun is that he is likely to get about what he pays for. There are some happy exceptions to that, inasmuch as some makers of inexpensive guns, because of the large number of tubes they buy from the steelworks, can afford to use a higher grade metal than one would expect. The old B.S.A. double gun of the pre-war days, for example, used Jessop's fluid-pressed steel; the AYA people use a high-quality Bellota electric alloy steel; and I believe that the great Manufrance organization, even in their cheap 'Robust' gun, use Hercule triple-palme.

Making-up

Barrels are made up in several ways—with an independent lump, brazed; with chopper lumps, brazed; with chopper lumps, dovetailed; and with integral lumps on the monobloc system. The method favoured in this country for best guns is that of the brazed chopper lump, though the brazed independent lump is quite satisfactory for normal service. My personal opinion is that the best system of all is the monobloc system, favoured on the Continent, but not here, in which the tubes are forced and soft-soldered into a solid breech-piece, incorporating the lumps. I have found this system to have several merits.

The quality and strength of all barrels subjected to brazing can be impaired by over-heating, though there is little excuse for that with the modern facilities available for heat control. Conversely, the primitive quality of the steel can be improved by the barrel maker. The old Spanish makers did this by prolonged cold-hammering, and Manufrance stoutly claim to make the best barrels in the world by a modern application of the same process, allied with localized heat-treatment for the benefit of the lumps, which, in their case, are double-dovetailed. They further claim that, at any position along the barrel, the wall-thickness is rigorously the same around the whole circumference—a point on which gunmakers have, for centuries past, tended to fall down.

Here, again, the shooter is much in the hands of the gunmaker, but he is entitled to a preference for chopper lumps, and he should not make the mistake of looking askance at the Continental monobloc barrels merely because they *look* as if they had been sleeved. There is a big difference.

Performance

But, safety assumed, it is performance that matters most. If a shooter is satisfied with his gun's performance, well and good. If not, and if he is quite sure he knows how to test it, he should do so with normal cartridges. If performance is sub-standard, it may pay handsomely to have the barrel or barrels checked and, if necessary, re-regulated. Any of the established repairers who advertise in the shooting press would undertake the work.

11 March 1967

damascus barrels

Even if I were otherwise unaware of it, my correspondence would leave me in no doubt of the substantial numbers of the old damascus-barrelled guns still in circulation. Owing to their age and condition, and to the fact that many of them are hammer guns, they do not command high prices; and so they seem to be falling increasingly into the hands of beginners, who are continually writing to me about them. A notable feature of their letters is the lack of awareness they often display of the real nature and, what is more important, the limitations of these weapons, so perhaps a general note on the subject may be helpful.

Damascus barrels were the final development of an ancient method of forging a gun tube. Broadly, this method consisted of taking a strip of suitable iron, wrapping it round a mandrel after the manner of a bandage, and welding the helical seam by 'jumping'. This had the merit of making a tube which was seamless in the plane of greatest stress. The method was retained in the damascus barrels when they were introduced over a century and a half ago; they still employed the principle of welding-up a strip of metal that had been wrapped round a mandrel, but the strip itself had become an elaborately composite thing of iron and steel. My sketches will make the manufacturing process clear.

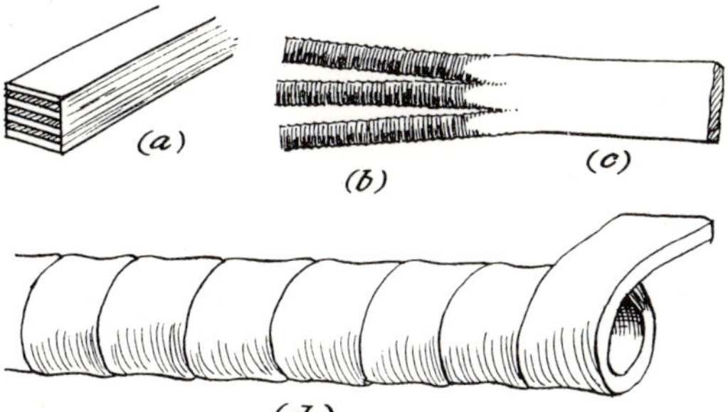

10. Stages in the forging of damascus barrels.

First, a number of strips, alternately of iron and steel, were welded together into a solid bar, which was then rolled out into square rods, as at (*a*). These rods were then heated and twisted—twisted so tightly, indeed, that when finished they looked like screws, as at (*b*). Two, three or more such rods were then welded together to make a flat bar or strip (*c*), and this was finally wrapped around a mandrel, as at (*d*), and welded into a tube. When this tube was bored and turned and finished, it was browned by a chemical process which attacked the iron and steel differently, thus revealing the beautiful pattern which has given damascus barrels their name, from a resemblance to the swords, etc., for which the ancient Syrian town was so long celebrated. Different methods of construction yielded different patterns, more prized on the Continent than here, and known by various fancy names, such as crolle, rose, bernard, laminette, moiré, horseshoe, etc.

What exactly the originators had in mind when they developed damascus barrels I frankly do not know and have never succeeded in finding out. Obviously, they wanted to make barrels with a beautiful 'figure', as it is called; but I am sure they also wanted to improve their strength and safety. In the days when it was not possible to produce considerable masses of steel of predetermined composition, the knitting together of iron and steel in the manner described was probably considered the best way of making a tube which combined the ductility of the one with the tenacity of the other. Further, the intricate pattern of welds eliminated the possibility of extensive flaws, such as those capable of being produced in a solid billet of steel by an inclusion of slag that has become elongated by rolling along with the metal. Nevertheless, weight for weight and section for section, damascus barrels are inferior in strength to steel; for although their steel component might have an ultimate tensile strength of 50 tons per square inch (Greener says 60), their iron component might have only 20 to 25. Against this, a good steel barrel will have a uniform strength throughout of 35 to 40. For this reason *damascus barrels must always be considered unsafe for use with smokeless powder cartridges unless they have been nitro-proved and stamped accordingly.*

But one cannot contemplate the obsolescence of these lovely barrels without regret. Made, as they were, on the anvil, they were a superlative expression of the smith's craft; and since the best welders only worked on the best materials, it was possible to tell the quality of the barrels by the regularity and perfection of the figure on one of 'the old brown guns'.

29 March 1963

barrels—past, present and future

It is odd to think that steel, as the material *par excellence* for gun barrels, has had but a short reign, historically speaking, and that its old challengers were active within the memory of men still shooting. And if those same challengers are now dead, they will by no means lie down, as witness the large numbers of damascus-barrelled guns remaining in service—some of them nitro-proved—and thriving on a diet of smokeless cartridges. Besides, new challengers have reared their heads in recent years, so that steel may well shift uneasily on its throne.

The requirements of a gun-barrel material are complex, and it is doubtful if an international panel of experts could agree on an ideal specification, particularly if £ s. d. were brought into account. Over the years, there seem to have been two opposing principles at work, namely ductility and tensile strength, both under the banner of safety. A barrel made of a material of high ductility but low tensile strength, such as more-or-less pure wrought iron, would bulge at a relatively low excess pressure. But by bulging it would relieve the pressure, and thereby protect the shooter. A material of high tensile strength but low ductility, on the other hand, such as a high-carbon steel, would not be capable of finding relief in this manner, or to the same extent, and might burst with a charge that the other might accommodate, subject to some deformation. As I have implied, tensile strength and ductility tend to be incompatible.

The typical representatives of these two principles are, of course, the familiar, beautiful and sentimentally regarded damascus barrels, wrought with great skill from twisted rods of laminated steel and iron; and the modern alloy steels, such as the Austrian Boehler 'Superblitz', to quote an example of rather extreme properties in the opposite direction. Yet, from the limited viewpoint of safety, a barrel of this latter material would not have such an overwhelming superiority over one of the former as a study of its physical characteristics might suggest.

A forgotten trial

In 1888, the Guardians of the Birmingham Proof House, by formal resolution, carried out an elaborate trial designed 'to test the strength of the various kinds of English and foreign barrels employed in sporting guns'. They procured three specimens each of thirty-nine different kinds of 12-bore barrels in the form of rough tubes; and, having machined them all to uniform size and thickness of wall, they tested them with progressively increasing proof charges until they bulged. The barrels in each of the groups were then averaged and placed in order of merit according to the charges they had withstood. At the top of the list came a barrel of 'English machine-forged laminated steel in three rods'. According to the definitions in Greener's *The Breech Loader*, published shortly afterwards, I gather that this was what we would call a three-stripe damascus barrel. Second came one of Whitworth steel. Third came a best English two-stripe damascus; and then the also-rans. In these, English and foreign, steel and damascus, were so mixed up that analysis here is impossible, though in fairness it must be said that the English barrels tended towards the top of the list and the foreigners towards the bottom.

The report of this trial, dated 1 December 1890, and signed by Samuel B. Allport, then Chairman of the Guardians, included the results of supplementary tests, as well as some suspect conclusions on pressures; but the main results quoted no doubt yield the fair comparison that the trial was intended to make, and reveal why many gunmakers and shooters long remained faithful to damascus barrels.

Today, the trial is forgotten, if only for the good reason that most of the barrels tested are no longer made. Even their descriptions would probably not be fully intelligible to a modern gunmaker. And, of course, there was no chemical analysis of the substance of any of the barrels, so that we cannot judge why, for example, Whitworth had to yield the palm to damascus. ('Whitworth steel', it should be noted, implies a process for eliminating inclusions of slag in the ingots from which gun barrels are made, and not steel of a particular composition. But it ought to have been a very good steel, for the report gives the price at 90s. per pair of tubes, as against 29s. for the winner.)

Demand for lightness

A major factor in the steady supersession of damascus by steel was undoubtedly the availability (perhaps it would be true to say *increasing* availability, following on the results of the trial) of higher tensile steel tubes, whereby gunmakers were able to lighten their guns forward and so meet the demand for improved balance and fast-handling quality. Once these better-balanced, steel-barrelled guns had appeared, there was no going back. Few things in a gun have such an appeal as that wonderful liveliness—that sense of eagerness—that steel barrels alone seemed capable of giving—at least, until the appearance of the new challengers I mentioned.

Some comments in the 1890 Birmingham report contained an adumbration of the future. Speaking of the composite barrels, it said, 'The elasticity and tenacity are affected . . . by the mechanical structure set up in the compound irons by the various modes of twisting and laying them together.' This contains the essence of the idea underlying both the wire-bound barrel of an Asiatic *jezail* and the fibre-glass-bound barrel of the Winchester Model 59. It is the idea—a very ancient one—of co-orientating strength and stress. What it contains for the future of the shotgun, it would be hard to say. Certainly the Winchester barrel is a clever and courageous development, which combines strength and lightness in a remarkable degree. It is stated to have *two or three times* the strength of conventional steel barrels, and to withstand plugging tests that no steel barrel would survive. It is constructed basically by winding 500 miles of spun glass filament on a thin (0·02 in.) steel liner and bonding the whole in polymer resin, and is possibly adaptable to double barrels constructed on the *canon fretté* principle referred to below.

But I believe that the large wire-wound naval gun—another example of the same idea—became obsolete because of its lack of transverse rigidity, whereby its accuracy was probably unduly sensitive to variations in the strength through ageing of the cordite charge. Here, I am guessing: but I wonder if the Winchester glass-wound barrel varies abnormally in its mean point of impact with changes of load?

Another lightweight

There is, of course, no law of god or man decreeing that a firearm shall have at least a liner of ferrous material, accustomed as we may be to the idea. We had brass-barrelled artillery, brass-barrelled blunderbusses and brass-barrelled pistols quite recently; and now we have high-duty aluminium-alloy barrels in the extra-lightweight version of the F.N. Browning two-shot automatic, and in the more recent weapon of the same kind brought out by the Armalite Company of America.

Here again are undeniable potentialities for strength and lightness in previously unknown combinations. Weight for weight these alloys (R.R.56, for example) can have *three times* the strength of 30-ton steel. Mr. B. T. Miller, vice-president of the Armalite concern, writes to me impressively on this point in describing tests on the new gun. With a 20-bore cartridge lodged in the chamber ahead of a 'short magnum' 12-bore, firing of the latter produced 'no measurable effect whatsoever' on a new barrel. Three successive tests, in which normal loads were used, stepping up from $2\frac{3}{4}$ to $3\frac{3}{4}$ dram-equivalent, produced only a 'slight swell'. Mr. Miller does not say whether the 20-bore cartridge was set off in any or all of these tests, but the results were striking enough in any case. I doubt if any steel barrel could have put up such a performance. Bearing in mind the lightness and handling quality that can be built into a gun with barrels of this sort, and the anodic coating of near-diamond hardness that can be formed in the bores, it is hard to think that we shall not be hearing more of them.

Fretted barrels

With sleeving now thoroughly established, it seems remarkable that no British firm has adopted the fretted barrel, with its possibilities for combining greater strength with a reduction in the cost of producing double guns. Superficially similar to the sleeving idea, the fretted barrel can be much superior. The monobloc breech end, or *tonnere*, into which the tubes are soft-soldered, is designed and machined *de novo*. It avoids any join at the weak spot just ahead of the chamber cone; it requires no chopper-lump tubes; it eliminates all possibility of impairing the molecular structure of the metal by overheating; and it enables the breech end of the barrel to be given an initial degree of compression by the shrink-fitting of the *tonnere*, with a significant gain of strength. Some Continental makers of the highest reputation use this system in their top-quality guns; and Régis Darne, who claims to have invented it, is on record as having protested at the abolition of the old St. Étienne triple proof—presumably because of the demonstration it afforded of the strength of his *canons frettés*. Here, surely, is something else for the future.

20 May 1965

long barrels or short?

The subject of barrel lengths, long since tidied up and filed away—or so I should have thought—shows some signs of revival.

Towards the turn of the century, when the black-powder era was drawing to a close, the orthodox barrel length for a 12-bore game gun was 30 in. A few decades later, when smokeless powder had fairly ousted the older kind, 28 in. became equally well established; and so things remained until just after the Kaiser's war, when the late Robert Churchill threw down the gauntlet of his 25-in. barrels to the gun trade and the public. Churchill was an all too highly vocal advocate of his opinions, and aroused violent opposition both inside and outside the trade by his sweeping claims and exaggerations ('Handles like a 20 and shoots as hard as a 10'). The ensuing controversy is a lively memory of the 1920s. It ended with a victory for Churchill, when it was established that the loss of velocity incurred in reducing barrels from 28 in. to 25 was not material from a practical point of view—only about 30 f/s of observed velocity; a loss which, as Churchill did not fail to point out, was likely to be compensated by the shorter gun's fast-handling quality, and therefore the greater speed with which the shooter could get on to his bird and the shorter range at which he could frequently take it.

But Churchill did not win quite the victory that has been conceded to him. All he really established was that there are good practical arguments for barrels shorter than 28 in., subject always to personal preferences. What has been conceded to him, however, is a kind of tacit acknowledgement that there is some exclusive merit attaching to 25-in. barrels. This, of course, is absurd; and yet Churchill has undoubtedly endowed this particular length with a vertiginous attraction for most men when they come to dallying with the idea of shorter barrels. I see clear traces of this in my correspondence; and it is significant that the A.Y.A people, in developing a shorter-barrelled gun for the British market, have gone straight for 25 in., as a bird to its nest. But perhaps they may be wise in following closely in Churchill's footsteps, for he not only established a tradition, he also made the best 25-in. barrelled guns, and thus left behind a legacy of goodwill for the Churchill-type 'XXV' which may be shared by any conscientious imitator.

For those who missed the fun

For the benefit of those who missed the ding-dong contest between Churchill and the *Field* in 1925 and the evidence that finally emerged, or who, for one reason or another, are unsettled in their confidence or convictions on the subject, I would like to summarize one of the good practical arguments mentioned above.

The practical shooter is concerned with four aspects of barrel length, namely (1) weight, balance and handling; (2) aiming and pointing; (3) confidence; and (4) ballistics. Here, I am solely concerned with the aspect last mentioned, for if only a man is confident that he shoots better with barrels that are shorter or longer than the common choice, or even if he merely prefers them, he is beyond the reach or need of argument. For the rest, the effect of barrel length on ballistics was investigated thoroughly by W. D. Borland at the time of the Churchill controversy, and the results of his experiments were published as an appendix to Burrard's *Modern Shotgun* in 1931. Borland gives his results in terms of the average or 'observed' velocity over the first 20 yds. of flight for barrels of various lengths, and from these I have worked out what more nearly concern the ordinary shooter, namely, the velocity, and more particularly the energy, with which the shot strike the target at full range.

Inappreciable gain

Taking a 28-in. barrelled 12-bore as the standard, and firing a normal game charge of smokeless powder and No. 6 shot, the effect of longer or shorter barrels, expressed as the percentage gain or loss of striking velocity and energy at 40 yds., is as follows.

Barrel length	25	26	27	28	29	30	31	32	33	34
	(	% losses	)		(		% gains			)
Velocity	2·6	1·4	0·5	—	0·3	0·5	0·7	0·8	1·0	1·2
Energy	5·0	2·3	0·9	—	0·5	1·0	1·4	1·8	2·1	2·4

These figures confirm that, *from the limited viewpoint chosen*, the gain due to barrel length in excess of 28 in. is inappreciable in a 12-bore gun. As for the shorter barrels, even the 5 per cent. loss of striking energy associated with a length of 25 in. is submerged in the variations from round to round of the cartridges giving the average

17. LONG BARRELS OR SHORT?

Evidently the shooter is a factor. This tall, long-armed sportsman can nearly reach the muzzle of a 25-in. barrelled gun . . .

. . . but looks thoroughly at home with a 30-in.

results quoted, and in the field would be at least partly compensated by the faster-handling quality of the shorter gun.

31 October 1963

sleeved barrels

I am often approached by gun-owners who are contemplating having the barrels of their guns sleeved, and they regularly ask me one or more of the following questions:

1. Is sleeving, in the circumstances explained, a good idea?
2. Must the sleeved barrels be of the same length as the originals?
3. Will sleeving reduce the value of the gun?
4. Will the sleeved barrels shoot as well as the originals?
5. Are sleeved barrels really safe?

This is evidently one of those subjects that need ventilating from time to time, and it would be advantageous to deal with it now.

Is sleeving a good idea? Speaking generally, it is undoubtedly a very good idea, but there are some important qualifications. The work must not be attempted in unsuitable cases; and when it is done, it must be done expertly.

The proof authorities afford the shooter a large measure of protection here, and I will return to the point later. But in the meantime I must point out that their protection, of necessity, is limited to the basic safety of the job, and in no way safeguards the shooter from the error or errors into which he can easily fall in specifying the details of the work.

Is it necessary?

But although sleeving, broadly regarded as a means for rejuvenating old guns on economical terms, may be a good idea, it may be bad tactics in individual cases.

Some shooters owning high-quality guns are much irked by the presence of moderate pitting in the barrels, and conceive the idea of sleeving as a way of removing a blemish which they cannot learn to tolerate. Two points come up immediately here. First is that the pitting may be insignificant, both from the safety and from the performance points of view. All it may need is ignoring. And even if the shooter cannot bring himself to ignore it, there is still no case for sleeving while any possibility remains of removing the pitting by lapping out the bores. Any practical gunsmith would advise on the possibilities; and although the barrels may not stand the necessary amount of lapping without becoming out of proof, it may still be possible to have the work done and the barrel or barrels re-proved without material risk of failure.

If the barrels are past further service, and the gun concerned is of sufficiently good quality and condition to justify the expense, the best course is undoubtedly to have a new pair of barrels *and* to have the old ones sleeved, either as a spare pair or as a pair with alternative boring. For example, the new barrels could have game boring, and the sleeved pair more choke. But there is a potential snag in this procedure which arises on my next point.

Care needed

Must the sleeved barrels be of the same length as the originals? The direct answer, of course, is no. Still, much care is needed in making a radical change. Several readers have come to me with proposals for having 30-in. barrels sleeved as 25s. This might well turn out successfully, but is perhaps more likely to prove unsatisfactory. Ordinarily, weight, balance and possibly the mean point of impact of the shot charge would be much altered; and although the change might seem advantageous when the gun is first handled indoors, it might prove different in the field. The lighter gun would recoil more. For comfortable use, it might need some reduction in the user's familiar load. This could lead to loss of confidence, with irrational but none the less serious effect. The alteration in balance and handling quality, too, might prove a mixed blessing. Some men, less deliberate in their movements than others, and more prone to bad gun-mounting habits, do not shoot so well with short barrels as they do with those having more forward weight. Time and trial alone will reveal the facts, and the extent of any indiscretion in the choice of length for the sleeved barrels.

I myself would play for safety. Unless I were in desperate need of a lighter gun, I would not contemplate more, say, than a 2-in. reduction. And, in any case, I would discuss the matter with the gunmaker.

18. NEW BARRELS FOR OLD

The three stages of the sleeving process as carried out by Westley-Richards. *Right* New tubes ready machined. *Centre* The old breech ends cut off and ready for machining preparatory to receiving the new tubes. *Left* The new tubes finally in place.

I would tell him exactly what I was hoping to achieve by having my gun sleeved and would give him an opportunity of saying just how far he could meet my requirements.

The money side

Will sleeving reduce the value of a gun? It depends entirely on the circumstances of the case. Gun dealers use sleeving as a means for restoring old, neglected guns to life, whereby their value is obviously greatly enhanced. On the other hand, a really high-class gun with nothing worse than slight pitting in one or both barrels might well be reduced, both in intrinsic and market values, by sleeving.

The only circumstances in which sleeving provides an absolutely unequivocal answer to the shooter's problem are when his barrels are beyond further service, whether through age, accident or neglect, and when he cannot afford new barrels, or cannot justify the expenditure. The economic appeal of sleeving is then overwhelming. In saying this, I have deliberately excluded the complications arising out of the possibility that the shooter may be wanting to do up his gun with a view to selling it, or trading it in for another. I can only leave him to work out any such problem in the light of his own genius for such things.

Performance

Will sleeved barrels shoot as well as the originals? Ballistically, there is no reason why they should not shoot better. It is all a matter of the relative merit of the boring. But, as I have already indicated, whether or not the shooter will shoot better with his sleeved gun involves questions other than ballistics. Every single respect in which it differs from the original weapon may be significant from the standpoint of performance, or of the confidence on which performance so largely depends. Weight, balance and speed of handling, equally with the density and quality of the patterns thrown, come into the picture, as I have already indicated in connection with barrel length. If the shooter is thoroughly satisfied with the original gun, except for the state of the barrels, and shoots well with it, there would be a good case for trying to preserve all its characteristics intact in the sleeved weapon.

Safety

The proof authorities, in their memorandum of January 1960, deliberately refrain from expressing any opinion on the soundness or otherwise of sleeving. Yet the shotgun user who is concerned about the safety of this process when properly carried out is not left entirely without official guidance, for, as the lawyers say, *res ipsa loquitur*—the thing speaks for itself. If the proof authorities, charged as they are with securing the safety of the public in their particular field, and approaching the subject of sleeving, as they have done, with the utmost circumspection, are nevertheless prepared to stamp sleeved barrels which pass their test with the appropriate proof marks, even the most apprehensive shooter may surely rest content. Guns are dangerous things, anyhow, and even the best of barrels are subject to accident and deterioration, so that any increased hazard due to competently sleeved barrels is unlikely to be significant. I myself would use them with confidence.

18 May 1968

Section 8

GUN-FITTING

'A man . . . is a flexible, adjustable and educable form of gun-carriage, and any process of gun fitting that assumes . . . that he is rigid, and transfers to the gun the whole of the onus of arriving at a mutual accommodation, fails to recognize their respective natures.'

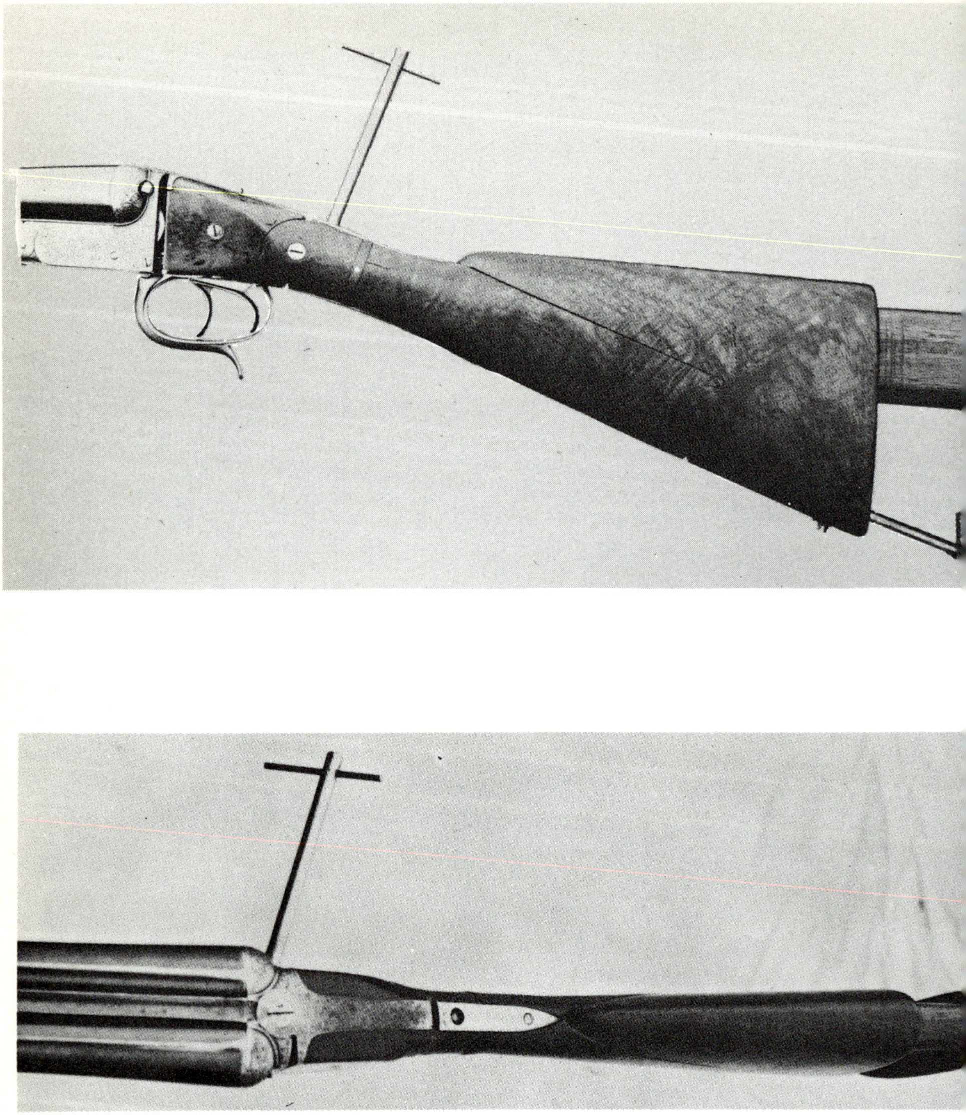

19. A TYPICAL TRY-GUN
Side and top views showing adjustments for length, bend and cast-off.

the try-gun—a dubious oracle

It is generally considered that the man who has to put up with a ready-made stock to his gun is bound to be at a disadvantage as compared with one whose stock is made to his individual requirements, as determined by a try-gun fitting. So he may be, but it does not always follow; and in some cases I can recall, the shooter would almost certainly have been better off with a standard, off-the-shelf article, than he was with his hand-tailored affair.

Perhaps I should say, for the benefit of those readers who may never have seen a try-gun, and are unfamiliar with these ingenious tools of the gun-fitter, that a try-gun resembles an ordinary shotgun in appearance and functioning, but it has a system of joints and extensible portions built into the stock, whereby the length, bend, comb-height and cast can be adjusted over a wide range of values. Roughly speaking, its mode of use is for the gun-fitter to set it to what appears to be about the right dimensions for the particular customer being fitted, and to make subsequent adjustments according to observations of where his shot pattern strikes the gunmaker's plate in relation to an aiming mark, which may take the form of a suddenly appearing bird.

Not infallible

As I say, the try-gun is an ingenious tool, but it is also a dangerous one in the hands of anyone other than a highly skilled fitter. Its great shortcoming, and a potential source of faulty diagnoses, is that it does not, and cannot in the nature of things, make any allowance for the extent to which a man's shooting errors are determined by the inappropriate shape of his gunstock, and by his idiosyncrasies of gun-mounting and posture respectively. Some of these idiosyncrasies may be undesirable and correctable, and should, in fact, be corrected rather than compensated by some modification of the stock.

A man, after all, is a flexible, adjustable and educable form of gun-carriage, and any process of gun-fitting that assumes, by implication, that he is rigid, and transfers to the gun the whole of the onus of arriving at a mutual accommodation, fails to recognize their respective natures. Far better that the gun-fitter should do what some of the most experienced gunmakers still prefer to do, and that is, to take careful note of all the leading particulars of the shooter's physique, and then to prescribe the form of stock out of their large experience of what such a man should require. In effect they say, 'This is the right stock for you: go and get used to it.'

Personal demonstration

If I may be allowed to use myself as a demonstration model, I think I can make my point. I stand a scant 6 ft. in my shoes, and from a lathy youth, have since become a stock-size man of medium build. The scientifically cut, ready-made clothing of these times (40-in. chest) fits me to perfection, except that it reveals my arms as being $\frac{1}{2}$ in. shorter than the average. I have a strong neck ($16\frac{1}{2}$), traditionally a sign of obstinacy, but fully up to average length. My shoulders, divested of the minimal padding I permit my tailor, are of medium width, and neither sloping nor square. Not a handsome specimen, nor one of Lysippan proportions, but obviously one providing a pretty average gun-carriage for a sporting 12-bore. I should add that I am right-handed and right-eyed, and shoot from my right shoulder, with both eyes open.

What sort of stock ought I to have for general mixed shooting? Obviously an average or standard stock; and indeed the one I have got is just that. It has been arrived at over the years by a process of trial and error, with the assistance of various gunmakers, and it enables my gun to come up sweetly and snugly, with the rib in line with my eye, and with the foresight on the mark every time, provided I do my preliminary mounting deliberately, and do not fluster. It equally enables me to take the quickest of snap-shots successfully, at which, indeed, I seem to be rather better than my average form would imply. I find it impossible to imagine that I am not correctly fitted.

Odd variations

And yet, if my shooting posture were other than it is, my gun could be a gross misfit. If, for example, by choice or natural predisposition, I shot with my head upright, in what, it might reasonably be argued, is a good and natural position, I should need a gun with a drop at the heel of 3 in. instead of my familiar $2\frac{3}{8}$ in., and a cast-off of over 1 in. instead of my present $\frac{5}{16}$ in. And since my jaw rather than my cheek would then be snugged into the stock, it might be thought that I should have, in addition, a high Monte Carlo comb. The curious thing is that, if an inexpert gun-fitter, in consequence of his having adapted his try-gun to an upright head-posture, had persuaded me to accept such a preposterous stock, I could possibly have got used to it, and could even have persuaded myself that I had been well fitted.

I have, of course, taken an extreme example, and no competent gun-fitter would be likely to prescribe such an abnormal stock for such a normal man. Nevertheless, I have seen some very odd variations from the normal form prescribed for men without any demonstrable peculiarity of physique or vision, and I vehemently suspect that they were no more than the result of such misconceived gun-fitting as I have described.

The voice of authority

I must confess that, having written the last preceding paragraph, I turned up Churchill's *Game Shooting*, to see in what way an expert coach and gun-fitter might shoot me down. Somewhat to my surprise, he endorses what I have said. 'Never,' he says, 'have the stock of a gun bent or cast off to compensate for faults in gun mounting. These should be corrected, not by deforming the gun, but by improving your style.'

The practical conclusion emerging from all this is that the try-gun is very much the tool of the expert. It is not by itself an oracle on gun-fit, but is, in fact, capable of yielding erroneous conclusions if relied upon too exclusively. It may well enable a man to shoot well at a gunmaker's plate or at clay targets thrown on the testing ground, but it may do so at the expense of endorsing and perpetuating idiosyncrasies that would be better corrected, and could be corrected, by a little time and practice. Perhaps the best form of practice in such circumstances would be for the shooter to adapt himself, by 'dry shooting' and practice in the field, to a gun stocked according to the prescription of the kind of expert who does *not* use a try-gun, but who relies on observation of the shooter's physique, etc. I myself, if I were ordered an abnormal stock without being conscious of any corresponding abnormality, would always go to such an expert for a check-opinion. I should recall to mind that there is at least one case on record where a man was diagnosed by try-gun fitting as having a left master eye, when in fact the eye in question was made of glass!

11 November 1965

fixing the shotgun's backsight

If by aiming we mean the pointing of a gun in a determinate direction in relation to where the shooter is looking, then, in that broad sense, all shooters aim. It is equally true of the man shooting from the hip at rabbits bolting in covert; of the practised driven game shot who says that he is totally unconscious of his gun at the instant of firing; and of the trapshooter drawing a conscious bead on his flying target.

For the correlation of line of sight and direction of gun-pointing, the hip-shooter is entirely dependent on his innate powers of co-ordination, whereby, on a jet-black night, he can still point his finger accurately at a faint and solitary star. The driven-game shooter, however, is not so dependent, whatever he may say. As his gun comes into position for firing, the barrels, rib and foresight necessarily come into his field of vision, and are perceived by him, whether consciously or not. Further, by what he thus perceives, he is capable of determining (and, if necessary, adjusting or correcting) his direction of pointing. To this extent he has an advantage over the hip-shooter, who, if his instinctive co-ordination fails him, has no means of telling what has gone wrong. The trapshooter presses this advantage to the limit. Dealing as he does with targets having but a low transverse velocity, and using something more nearly approaching a rifle-shooting technique, he is at pains to maintain a constant relationship between where he is looking and where his gun is pointing. For this purpose, he makes use of all available aids, namely, a high conspicuous rib, perhaps fitted with a supplementary bead to act as a kind of backsight to the ordinary bead at the muzzle, and, what is more important to my present theme, a high level comb to his stock, which, he claims, preserves his eye in a constant position in relation to his barrels, and therefore to the line of flight of his shot charge.

The true backsight

Rifle shooters who use and understand the peep-sight know that it is less of a sight than a device for locating the optical axis of the eye, and that this axis, or the eye appertaining to it, is the true backsight.

I remember that many old infantrymen in the last war, who had been trained with the SMLE, were shocked by the size of the landscape visible through the aperture sight of the P14, and quite failed to see how it would be possible to do decent shooting with it. Yet if only the eye could be preserved in the right relation to the breech, even an aperture backsight would be unnecessary. To do this, however, with the degree of accuracy necessary for rifle shooting, would involve putting the shooter's head in some kind of rigid support—say, a plaster cast—securely attached to the rifle. This is not an idea that I would feel justified in submitting to the Ordnance Board.

But the combat rifleman in war needs to shoot to an accuracy of—what? Say, five minutes of angle, whereas the shotgun shooter can get by with fifteen or twenty. These figures may be challenged, but what remains is the fact that the eye—the backsight of the shotgun—can be located with sufficient accuracy by correct fitting and correct mounting. The trapshooter, above all others, points the way.

Osteology

The dominant factor in this problem would appear to be that conspicuous feature of human anatomy, or, rather, osteology, known as the cheekbone. If you place your hand horizontally on your cheek, with the fingers straight and rigid, and then move the hand sharply up towards the eye, you will find that your forefinger comes hard up against a projecting bony shelf, which, unless your face is a good deal fatter than mine (and I am by no means lantern-jawed), has comparatively little fleshy cover. Beneath this shelf, the jaw forms a more or less vertical wall. The accompanying photograph, which will appear a trifle less macabre if I explain that it is of a 100-year-old skull prepared for study by medical students, shows these two features admirably. Indeed, it will be apparent that, if it were not for the covering of yielding tissue, they would be capable of accommodating a gunstock in accurate relationship to the eye socket above, always provided that this relationship were not impaired by the changes of posture involved when taking shots at different elevations.

My own experiments endorse practical experience in showing that the necessary conditions can be complied with. First, on the point about the effect of the intervening tissue, I find that when

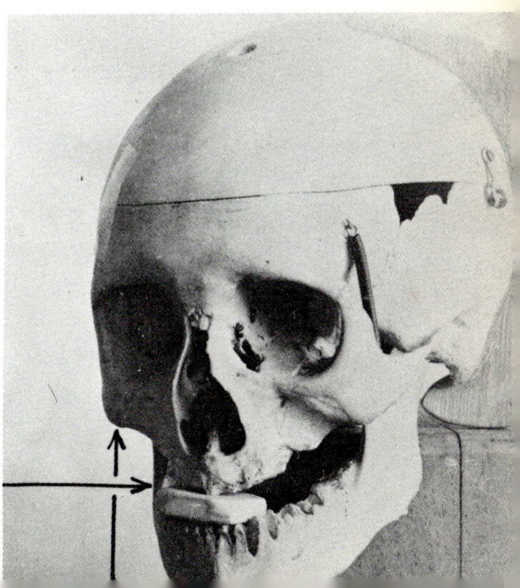

20. The vertical and horizontal bases of the shotgun's backsight.

an experienced shooter with a normally full face has mounted his carefully fitted gun, the stock fits well into the space between his cheekbone and his jaw—so well, indeed, that a vertical line from his temple falls outside the flank of the stock. His cheekbone, in other words, overlaps the stock.

21. The comb of the stock of a correctly mounted gun fits snugly into the bony angle shown in the previous photograph (see page 117).

On the other point, concerning changes of posture, I find that with the gun pointed at a slight elevation, his cheekbone is centred at a point about $2\frac{1}{2}$ in. from the forward end of the comb and that this undergoes very little change with changes in elevation. My 'model', I should say, leans his head but slightly forward, and turns it about 25 degrees towards his gun, and I am satisfied that his head movement in relation to the gun is very slight, in whatever direction he may be shooting. I myself seem to conform to every one of these particulars, though I do not shoot anything like so well as my model.

Neck length irrelevant?

I note, incidentally, that the bend of the comb of my friend's gunstock (I cannot go on calling him my model), at the point where his cheekbone so nicely fits, is $1\frac{9}{16}$ in. So is mine—exactly; and it would appear that this dimension is, or should be, determined by the height of the centre of the eye-socket above the cheekbone, give or take a trifle for the thinness or fatness of the shooter's chaps. Moreover, I am informed that there is little variation in this dimension in normal skulls. If that is the case, neck length should be irrelevant in determining the bend of the stock at the point in question. Yet there is no doubt that a long-necked man needs more bend than a short-necked one.

Where, then, have we arrived? Bearing in mind, as I said just now, that there appears to be very little shift of the cheekbone along the comb when taking shots at different elevations, there would seem to be no justification for the long, straight (and I might add, ugly) Monte Carlo comb. All that is needed is that that part of the comb over which the cheekbone may require to range—a very limited length—should be at a constant height, about $1\frac{9}{16}$ in. below the line of sight for normal men, and that the bend at heel and therefore the depth to toe should be determined by the length of the shooter's neck and the slope of his shoulders. So what we have arrived at in this excursion is nothing more or less than the Greener 'Rational' stock. We might have done worse.

Two points remain. The first is that reducing the thickness of the comb or varying its height can reduce or do away with the need for cast. The second is that since our leading coaches and gun-fitters cannot always agree on what constitutes the correct stock for a given man, I beg to be acquitted of any intention of laying down the law on the subject.

2 September 1967

English and American ideas on gun-fitting

One or two points have cropped up on my previous article, 'Fixing the Shotgun's Backsight', in which I made the point that the eye is the backsight of the gun, and that it should be fixed in relation to the aiming line of the barrels by arranging the height of the comb so that it fits into the right-angled recess between the malar or cheekbone and the flank of the jaw. I drew attention incidentally to what I am assured is a fact, namely, that in normal skulls—by which I mean normal, adult, male skulls as worn by the inhabitants of these islands

—there is little variation in the distance between the cheekbone and the centre of the eye-socket, from which it would appear that, however much the stock might require to be bent to accommodate a man's neck length and the slope of his shoulders, the comb-height at the spot where his cheek rests should be about the same. This works out to give a bend of about $1\frac{9}{16}$ in. at a point about $2\frac{1}{2}$ in. from the front end of the comb

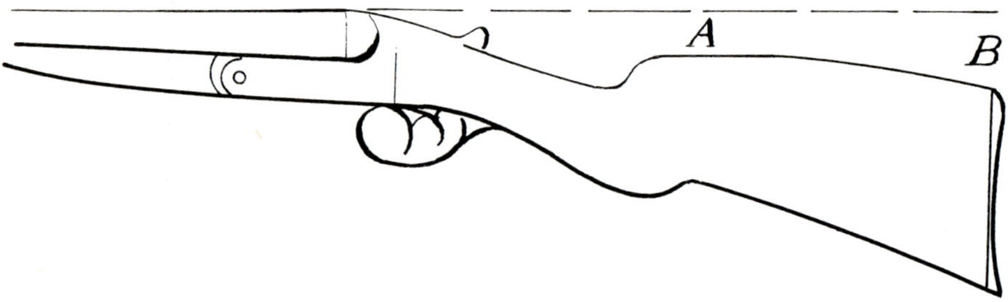

22. THE GREENER 'RATIONAL' STOCK

The high, level comb at *A* maintains the shooter's cheekbone, and therefore his eye, in the right position in relation to the aiming line above the rib. The bend at *B* is independently determined by the length of the shooter's neck and the slope of his shoulders, so as to ensure full-length bedding of the butt. This is substantially a Monte Carlo stock with fully faired-off comb, and was not ill-named.

The Greener 'Rational' stock

This line of reasoning, as I duly observed, leads straight to the Greener 'Rational' stock, and I have been asked to say just what was this form of stock. It is described fully in the fourth edition of Greener's book, *The Breech-loader and How to Use It*, as a half pistol-gripped stock with an arched form of comb, which can be seen in the light of the foregoing remarks to be nothing more than a stock with a comb running straight and level to the point of face-contact, after which it dips gradually down to give whatever bend at the heel is necessary to ensure a full bedding of the butt in the shoulder.

The Greener stock never came into general favour, chiefly, I suppose, because of its somewhat odd and unfamiliar appearance, and because it does little that cannot normally be done by a conventional stock correctly adapted at the vital point in question, where the cheekbone rests. But for the man with a long neck and sloping shoulders it would appear to afford the best way of providing full butt contact with the shoulder and correct face contact at the comb. If, in such a case, the comb is carried in a straight line down to the heel, there is a gap left between the cheekbone and the stock, and the lack of a firm bedding here accounts for the tendency possessed by many strongly

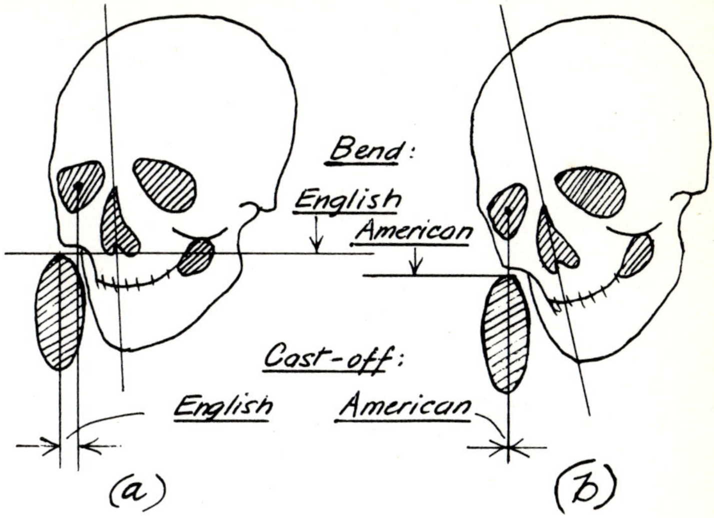

3. Diagrams show how, y slightly leaning the ead, the cheekbone can naintain its correct posi-on on the comb of the tock, even when the end is substantially in-reased. At the same me, the need for cast-ff is reduced or elimi-ated. This gives the tock-form favoured by merican gunmakers.

bent stocks to bruise the face. The tendency is increased by the greater upward jump on firing of guns stocked in this manner.

Bend and cast

Towards the close of my article mentioned above, I made a brief reference, just as I was running out of space, to the interchangeability, within limits, of comb-height, comb-thickness and cast-off in the correct fitting of a gun. The point is well brought out by the comment of a Kenya reader, to whom I am indebted for many instructive observations on shotguns and their ways. He writes, 'In the latest *Shooting Times* received here you discuss cast-off. This is a very British idea, and does allow the use of a straight stock. Percy Stanbury fitted me with a stock bent $1\frac{3}{8}$ in. at the comb and $1\frac{7}{8}$ in. at the heel, with $\frac{7}{16}$ in. cast-off. This suits me very well, though it has a tendency to shoot high; but I can change to a standard American auto or pump—$1\frac{1}{2}$ in. and $2\frac{1}{2}$ in. and no cast-off—and shoot almost as well. Both guns come up directly on to the mark.'

My drawings above show clearly, I believe, how this interchangeability comes about. At (*a*) we have a cast-off stock tucked correctly into the space between the jaw and the cheekbone, with the eye in the right position over the rib between the barrels. At (*b*) we have a stock without cast-off, but with greater bend. For correct alignment, this requires that the eye shall come over further to the left (regarded from the viewpoint of the drawing), which it does. The head, tilting over from the neck, leans over the comb, which is now of reduced height, until it rests with the cheekbone and jaw in roughly the same positions as in the previous case. It is not difficult to see from these drawings how comb-thickness can be introduced as a further factor modifying fit. They are, of course, exaggerated for clarity, and help to explain why it is that even the best and most experienced gun-fitters cannot always agree on what is the right stock for a given shooter. It is unlikely that any two of them would assign precisely the same values to the indeterminate factors that go to make up adaptability.

21 September 1967

Section 9

TESTS AND TESTING

Confidence is the key to good shooting: testing is the key to confidence.

the right way to test a gun (I)

It is not unusual for a boy to pick up a gun for the first time and, after a little preliminary instruction and practice in handling and mounting it, to start right off and shoot well—at least, at the simpler flying targets. This early promise is seldom sustained: as soon as the boy realizes how well he is doing he begins to think, and so begins to miss. Introspection in the act of shooting is, indeed, fatal to success, and for this reason I should be sorry to start any young shooter on the evil course of worrying unduly about the performance of his gun. It has to be a very bad gun-cartridge combination that will not cope satisfactorily with shots at moderate range, and the cause of consistently bad performance under easy conditions must almost invariably be sought elsewhere. Still, there are situations in which the gun itself comes fairly under suspicion, and for this reason every shooter should know how to test his weapon.

In the course of the many conversations I had at the Game Fair with friends and strangers, the subject of testing guns for pattern came up twice, and in each case it emerged that the man concerned did not know the right way to perform such a test, and had thereby failed to learn the significant facts it might have taught him. If you are going to test a gun, it is essential to do it properly: otherwise you are not only wasting cartridges, but quite probably deluding yourself.

Shotguns are normally tested by firing them at a suitable target at a distance of 40 yds., and observing how many pellets they put into a 30-in. diameter circle, and with what degree of regularity. But this simple statement by no means contains all necessary guidance for the carrying out of a valid and useful test.

First, there is the question of a suitable target. The best is undoubtedly a sheet of plain iron, not less than 4 ft. square, and coated with a very thin coat of whitewash between shots. If a sheet of iron is not available, paper will serve, and old paper sacks, opened up and stuck together as necessary, will do quite well.

Then there comes the question of the 30-in. circle. This must not—I repeat, *not*—be drawn on the target before the shot. I am prepared

24. Testing a gun for pattern under ideal conditions at the I.M.I. factory. The targets are 5-ft. steel plates and are changed automatically by the impact of the shot.

to be told, and told again, that a well-known writer, in a recent book, has described a contrary procedure; but it is not only wrong to draw the circle first, and contrary to the practice of gun and ammunition makers, but it may vitiate the test and conceal the very information it could most usefully yield, as I hope to show. The correct procedure is to make an aiming mark in the middle of the target, and to aim carefully at this mark as with a rifle when taking the shot. The pattern is then examined, and the centre of the charge estimated by eye, ignoring the aiming mark, and the 30-in. circle drawn about the centre so estimated. (I shall be dealing with the interpretation of the pattern later.)

Next comes the fact that it is necessary to fire *at least* six shots at six separate targets for each barrel. It seems almost impossible to avoid getting a poor round every ten or a dozen shots—I mean a round with a pellet count conspicuously below the average—and if one fires less than six shots, including such a round, the average result so obtained will not fairly represent the performance of the gun. If one fires only one shot, it is only too likely that that one shot will be the poor round!

The last point on procedure is that the distance of 40yds. should be measured (and I mean *measured*: not paced) using a tape measure or its equivalent, and should be taken from the target to the point on which the shooter stands, not to the muzzle of the gun. The importance of measuring the range arises from the fact that a small error can have a disproportionate effect on the result.

Now we come to the study and interpretation of the patterns. Undoubtedly the most convenient thing to do, which I do myself whenever possible, is to use an iron plate, as described, and to photograph the pattern after drawing the 30-in. circle and making some conspicuous identifying mark in the top right-hand corner or other fixed position. Such photographs, if enlarged to about 4 in. in diameter, are admirable for study and record. Otherwise the total pellets striking within the circle must be counted and noted down for each shot. Also the position of the charge centre must be noted, and each pattern studied and judged for uniformity and comparative freedom from empty patches before re-washing the plate.

If the patterns are paper ones, they should be identifiably marked, taken home, spread out on the floor, and the individual pellet holes marked with a dab of black ink or the like. I myself use a miniature cork stuck into a holder and a common ink pad. It may sound a bore to have to mark up half a dozen patterns in this way; but after you have done one, it will seem a rewarding task, because you will realize that you have never really seen the pattern before. When they have all been done, they should be individually inspected, the pattern centre estimated by the eye, and the 30-in. circle drawn. The pellets within the circle may then be counted and noted down, as before; also the position of the charge centre in relation to the aiming mark.

You should then make a neat summary of the results, and since you may be glad to refer to this later, it should be carefully preserved.

The following table is an actual record, and apart from one poor round per barrel (bracketed) is very satisfactory indeed, so far as pellet count is concerned. The average figures of 69 and 48 per cent are quite close enough to the nominal figures for full choke and improved cylinder of 70 and 50 per cent respectively, and, with the exceptions noted, there is little individual variation from the average figure.

But we have so far taken no note of the quality of the patterns, as distinguished from the mere pellet count. Nor have we considered the implications of the fact that the gun shoots about 10 in. low with this

Test on 12-bore D.B. gun No. 12345 by A. B. Smith & Co. Date:
Cartridges: Eley Grand Prix; $1\frac{1}{16}$-oz. No. 6 (287 pellets). Crimp.

	Left Barrel (nominal boring: full choke)	*Charge centre*	*Right Barrel (nominal boring: imp. cyl.)*	*Charge centre*
	207	8 in. low	146	10 in. low
	212	9	155	10
	(165)	8	143	10
	201	10	(108)	9
	205	9	139	11
	200	11	141	9
	198	8	135	10
	203	8	139	9
Total	1591	71	1106	78
Average	199	9 in. approx. low	138	10 in. approx low
Per cent	69		48	

load, a thing we should not have learned if we had drawn the 30-in. circle before shooting. These are important matters, and will have to await my next article in this series. In the meantime, I may usefully repeat the nominal percentage patterns associated with the various borings. They are, full choke—70 per cent; three-quarters choke—65 per cent; half choke—60 per cent; quarter choke—55 per cent; improved cylinder—50 per cent; true cylinder—40 per cent.

19 August 1967

the right way to test a gun (II)

In my previous article in this series I described the proper way of testing a gun for pattern. I now want to deal with the further interpretation of the pattern, and what to do if anything wrong is revealed.

Since my comments will be based on my earlier article, I had better run over its main points. Do not worry about the performance of your gun or cartridges unless your shooting is consistently bad under easy conditions, and then only after other possible causes have been explored. If the gun falls fairly under suspicion, it should be tested at 40 measured yards by firing *at least* six cartridges from each barrel at a metal plate or sheet of paper fully 4 ft. square. The gun should be carefully aimed like a rifle at an aiming mark in the middle of the target, and the centre of the pattern subsequently estimated by eye, *ignoring the aiming mark.* A 30-in. diameter circle should then be drawn about the centre so estimated, and the number of pellets within the circle duly counted and noted down. The position of the pattern centre in relation to the aiming mark should also be noted—whether it is high or low, or to the right or left, and if so, how much. The results of the six or more shots should then be averaged, including the deviation of the pattern centre from the point of aim.

I stressed the importance of not drawing the 30-in. circle before shooting, and the reason will now be clear. By the alternative procedure described, any failure on the part of the gun to throw its pattern truly to the point of aim is revealed, and the average amount of the deviation ascertained. This provides something definite to work on if remedial measures are indicated.

Choice of cartridge

Before going on to consider the interpretation of the patterns, it would be well to make the point that guns, by themselves, cannot make patterns: only gun-cartridge combinations can do that. So, if it is primarily the gun we want to test, we must be sure to test it with a strictly normal cartridge for the class of weapon concerned—unless, indeed, it has been specifically regulated for something different. Failing that, if the gun is an ordinary 12-bore game gun, with an improved cylinder right barrel and a half to full choke left, it would be well to test it with the Eley Grand Prix, loaded with $1\frac{1}{16}$ oz. of No. 6 shot, as being about the most reliably normal cartridge for such a gun. If, on the other hand, the gun is regularly used with some different sort of ammunition, such as the Eley Maximum, it would be well to test it with that cartridge, for in that case it would be the performance of that particular combination that needed investigation. But it should be borne in mind that no blame attaches to a gun unless it performs unsatisfactorily with normal ammunition.

Interpretation of patterns

The three essential things we want to learn from pattern tests are (1) the density of the pattern, as determined by the average pellet count; (2) the mean point of impact of the charge centre, as last discussed; and (3) the quality of the pattern, which I will now deal with.

Pattern quality is chiefly determined by two things—the uniformity of spread of the pellets over the circle, and the freedom from 'holes' or vacant patches. These two things should not be confused. By uniformity of spread, I merely mean that if we divided the pattern circle into three or four concentric zones of equal area, a uniformly spread pattern would give about the same number of pellets in each zone. But there might still be vacant patches.

In normal patterns, uniformity of spread depends chiefly on the degree of choke. If there is no choke, or very little, the pattern will be very uniform—we may expect to find as many pellets in the outer half of the circle as in the inner. If, on the other hand, the barrel is fully choked, the inner half of the circle is likely to contain about 60 per cent of the total pellets, and the outer half to be proportionately starved. (Note that a 21-in. circle contains about half the area of a 30-in.)

Uniformity is a *merit*. Dense-centred patterns look deadly, but they do not fill the bag so well as the others. It is a defect of choke boring that it normally reduces uniformity.

As for vacant patches, it is a great mistake to condemn a gun or cartridge because the patterns exhibit these defects. Admittedly, they *are* defects, for the ideal pattern would certainly have none of them; but we have never found out how to make guns that throw ideal patterns, and what we have to do is to try to form some idea of what degree of patchiness is normal. We shall then be in a position to judge how our particular patterns measure up to that standard.

Judging patchiness

When I am working on patterns, I usually take a 5-in. 'hole' as my standard of reference, and I have a little loop of spring-steel wire of this diameter attached to a handle by which I can quickly find out how many such holes the pattern contains. There is a surprisingly close and reliable relationship between the number of pellets in the 30-in. circle and the number of vacant patches of a given size it is likely to have, provided the pattern is of average merit. We can express this relationship as follows.

Number of pellets in 30-in. circle	*Normal expectation of 5-in. patches*
100	9
150	5–6
200	3
250	1–2
300	0–1

So, with an improved cylinder pattern of about 150, we could normally expect to find five or six holes the size of a small tea saucer!

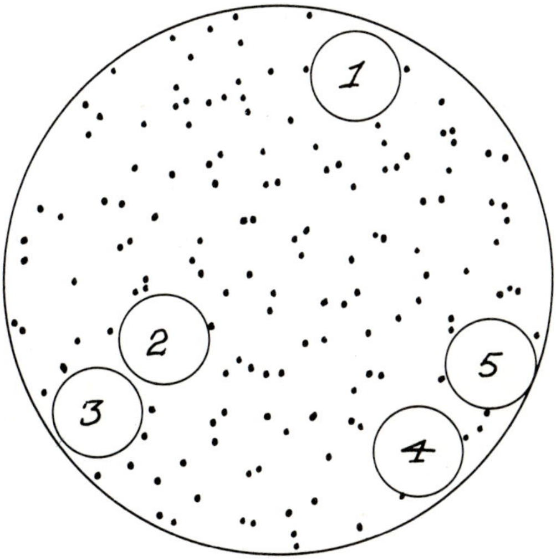

25. A typical good improved cylinder pattern at 40 yds. The load was $1\frac{1}{16}$ oz. of No. 6 shot (287 pellets). There are 146 pellets in the 30-in. circle, with five vacant 5-in. patches.

Never mind: *these are the patterns with which most game is shot.* Fewer patches would, of course, be meritorious: more, the reverse. The accompanying illustration shows a typically good 40-yd. pattern made by an improved cylinder barrel firing $1\frac{1}{16}$ oz. of No. 6 shot, comprising 287 pellets. There are 146 in the circle; they are well distributed; and there are five vacant 5-in. patches.

Before going on to remedies, I had better recapitulate the nominal density of various patterns. They are: Full choke—70 per cent; three-quarters choke—65 per cent; half choke— 60 per cent; quarter choke —55 per cent; improved cylinder—50 per cent. Always remember that uniformity of spread and freedom from vacant patches are far more important than precise density.

Remedies

There is no lack of remedies for defective performance as revealed by pattern tests. Poor density, bad distribution and undue patchiness can usually be put right by a skilful barrel regulator, and any of the well-known repairers will undertake this work. The cost is usually moderate.

Shooting low can be remedied by straightening the stock or adding height to the comb. Shooting high can be rectified by increasing the bend, though it is usually a good thing to have a gun which throws its charges well up to the mark. But stock alterations should only be undertaken on expert advice.

Finally, the reward for all the trouble of getting a gun absolutely right is *confidence* in it—the shooter's finest asset.

24 October 1967

velocity—how measured

Some observations of mine on the velocity of shot once provoked a comment and a query. The comment was, 'You referred to a velocity of 1,070 ft. a second as if it were quite good; but I remember reading about some cartridges that gave a velocity of 1,350.' The query was, 'How do they measure the velocity of shot? Don't they do it by the velocity of light?' Whereat I resolved to devote an article to velocity and how it is measured.

Let me say straight away that the comment I have just quoted betrays a confusion for which the professional ballisticians are to blame. They commonly use the word 'velocity' to describe two different things—the muzzle velocity and the regrettably so-called 'observed velocity'. The muzzle velocity is what the term implies: it is simply the velocity with which the shot leaves the muzzle of the gun. The observed velocity (in this country) is the average velocity of the shot charge over the first 20 yds. of its flight. So, the 1,070 f/s quoted was an observed velocity; the 1,350 f/s was undoubtedly a muzzle velocity. Moreover, they indicate no material disparity—they might almost have referred to the same shot charge.

In passing, I recognize good historical reasons why the observed velocity was so called. Originally, no means existed for observing the muzzle velocity. But they do now, and it would seem a great improvement if the average velocity was called simply that. The only snag is that one frequently requires to refer to the average velocity over some range other than 20 yds. So, as 'observed velocity' is thoroughly established, it would probably create more confusion than it dispelled to abolish it.

As for how velocity is measured, the short answer is that it is measured in the same way as the speed of a motor-car is measured—by timing it over a course. But owing to the high speed and invisibility of a shot charge, we obviously have to use a much higher-speed timing device than a stop-watch and we must also have some instantaneous means for conveying to it the 'start' and 'stop' signals.

The classical method

The classical method of measuring the observed velocity is by the Boulengé chronograph. In this, the timing device is an iron rod, which starts to fall vertically just as the shot emerges from the muzzle, and is nicked by a spring-loaded knife when the charge reaches the 20-yd. mark. As the rod always falls the same distance in a given time, the time taken for the charge to traverse the range can be determined by the position of the knife mark. Indeed, the observed velocity is read directly off a scale placed alongside the rod. The rod and the knife are each released electro-magnetically by the interruption of an electric circuit. The first (or rod) circuit is interrupted by the shot charge breaking a wire stretched across the muzzle of the gun, and the second (or knife) circuit by the impact of the shot on a special screen placed at the 20-yd. mark.

The measurement of the muzzle velocity is much facilitated by the fact that the emerging shot charge is borne, for the first few feet of its flight, on and in the expanding jet of high-velocity gas issuing from the gun. In consequence, it suffers practically no air resistance or loss of velocity over this part of its course. If, therefore, the average velocity is measured over a range of, say, not more than 10 ft., the result can be taken to be the actual muzzle velocity.

For measuring the very short time intervals involved, the preferred instrument nowadays is a form of electronic timer called a counter chronograph. In the particular model that many readers will have seen on the I.M.I. stand at Game Fairs, the timing element is a quartz crystal, which has the valuable property, when it is made to vibrate electrically, of doing so at a remarkably constant rate. The standard clock at Greenwich Observatory now depends on a quartz crystal for its timekeeping. The one in the kind of instrument used by I.M.I. probably vibrates at the standard rate of 100,000 times a second, and an ingenious arrangement actually counts and registers the number of vibrations undergone during the three-thousandths of a second or so taken by the shot to travel the first 5 ft. of its course.

Another electronic timer depends on the principle that if a graduated mug be held for an interval under a tap discharging water at a fixed and known rate, we can measure the interval by gauging the amount of water in the mug. But instead of using a constant stream of water and a graduated mug it uses a constant current of electricity and a standard condenser. The time interval is measured by measuring the amount of electricity that has flowed into the condenser. But

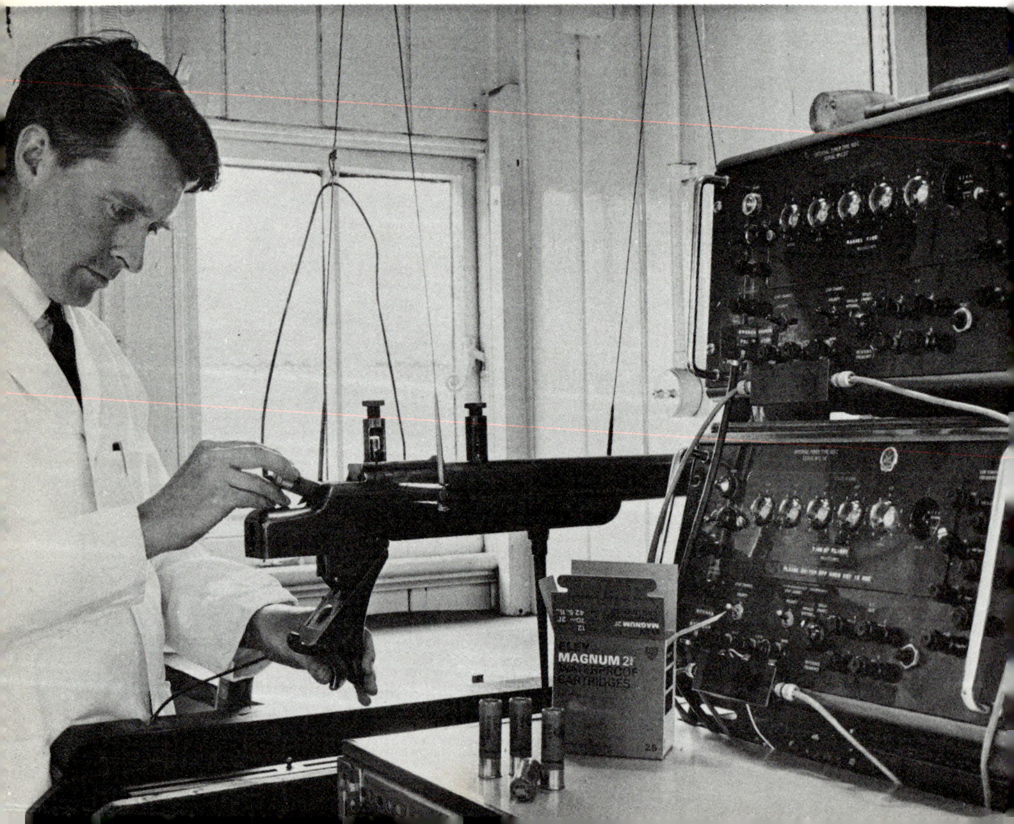

26. MEASURING THE VELOCITY OF SHOT

This modern counter chronograph at the I.M.I. factory gives a direct indication of the time up the barrel and the time of flight to the target.

I know of no chronograph applicable to ballistics that uses the velocity of light (*i.e.* 186,000 miles a second) as a measuring rod. That would be like using a stop-watch to measure the growth of a tree.

10 November 1961

pressure and velocity of home loads

There are three things the home-loader needs to know about his productions, namely, (1) pressure, on the score of safety; (2) velocity, on the score of penetration; and (3) pattern, on the score of effectiveness. All home-loaders can test their cartridges for pattern, but very few indeed have any idea of their pressures and velocities except so far as can be inferred from performance or from the submission of samples to one of the proof houses.

A few—a very few—dedicated home-loaders, and those chiefly in America, have pressure barrels and chronograph equipment. These are all very well for those who can justify the expenditure on the scope of their operations or the degree of interest involved, but for the majority they are, or should be, quite unnecessary.

There are two important principles in the testing of any material or equipment which are relevant here, and to what follows. They are (1) that tests should, as far as possible, be direct and not inferential—they should aim at providing a direct measure of the property or characteristic under examination, as found under practical working conditions; and (2) that the accuracy of the test should be related strictly to practical requirements—there is no point in weighing a sack of potatoes in milligrams.

So far as pressure is concerned, what the home-loader chiefly wants to know is whether his pressures are within safe limits. The majority, perhaps, would be satisfied with knowing just that one thing; and most of the remainder would be content with knowing whether they came into the useless, low, medium, high or excessive category.

As for velocity, this falls immediately under criticism as being only a guide to what the shooter really needs to know. The purpose of a shotgun is to kill small game—or to break clay targets. Common sense and experience have shown us that, to achieve this purpose, the pellets must have penetrative power; further, that the penetrative power of a given pellet is regulated by its velocity. But within practical limits we have no interest in velocity as such—it does not materially affect timing or lead. So, the direct test for killing power is shooting at game or targets. One stage removed, and more convenient in some respects, is testing for penetration, as our ancestors did, with their paper pads. Two stages removed, is testing for velocity.

Laminate crushers

In view of the fact that the home-loader needs only a feeble light to dispel much of the darkness in which he works, even the simplest means for affording him some guidance cannot be disdained.

I have accordingly thought that there might be some scope for a type of crusher designed for use in an ordinary gun, and have made some tentative experiments that are worth describing.

The crushers in question, as intended for roughly measuring the pressures developed by 12-bore ammunition, were $\frac{3}{4}$-in. discs of unidentified white metal foil, 3 mils ($\frac{3}{1000}$ in.) thick, and embossed by pressure against a knurled die to an overall thickness of 8 mils. They were thus thin enough to be shut up in an ordinary gun when placed centrally on top of the cartridge head. The overall thickness was measured before and after firing, and the difference taken as an indication of the pressure. Ordinarily, this difference would be referred to a table, which would give the corresponding pressure; but having no such table, I tested my crushers with cartridges known to be giving low, medium and full pressures respectively, with the following results.

	Reduction in thickness of crusher (mils)	*Approximate breech pressure (independently ascertained)*
1.	3	1·5 tons per sq. in.
2.	4	2·2 tons per sq. in.
3.	5	3·0 tons per sq. in.

Measurements were taken at three points around, but avoiding, the cap-chamber impression. They were then averaged and rounded off. Clearly, the material was insufficiently resistant, as there was total flattening at 3 tons, and no reserve for indicating excessive pressures.

Copper foil, embossed deeper and to a finer pattern, would probably serve. Guns with adequate headspace clearance are common or easily available.

Application

As for the general practicability of the method, it is at least worthy of consideration by any enterprising firm wishing to cultivate the home-loading business. There must be a considerable trade potential among those who would like to try loading their own cartridges, but are deterred by the present need for working so much in the dark with a risky medium.

I cannot imagine that there would be much difficulty in designing and producing a satisfactory crusher on the lines suggested, though it is indispensably necessary that means should be provided for avoiding the fiddling nuisance of shutting the crushers in the gun without displacing them from their central position on the cartridge heads. They could be gummed, and stuck on like postage stamps, though the gum would have to be soaked off before measuring.

To use these crushers to best advantage, a micrometer would, of course, be required, though the home-loader who made a habit of checking his pressures in this way would soon find himself forming the necessary conclusions by mere visual inspection. There is a conspicuous change of appearance according to the pressure developed, and if suitable photographic illustrations accompanied the instructions and the table, many would consider a micrometer unnecessary.

Scientifically, these crushers are defective because of the small amount of compression available for measurement, but this is partly compensated by the strong visual indication they provide.

Velocity

The measurement of the velocity of shot is a troublesome and expensive business. It was for this reason that I once made suggestions for putting on to a more scientific basis

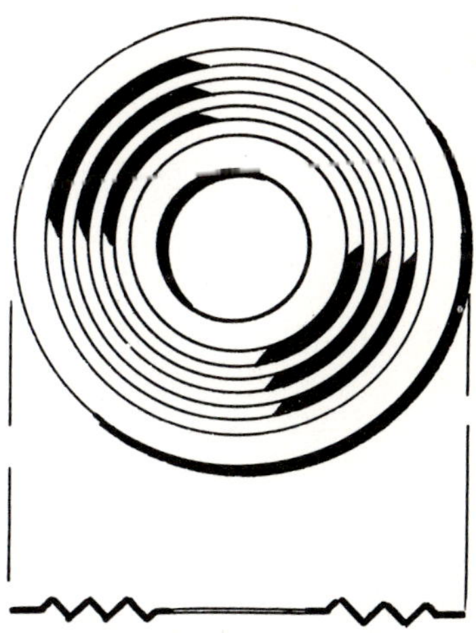

27. Laminate crusher
The ridging has been exaggerated for clarity.

the old trick of judging velocity by the degree of flattening of pellets against the pattern plate. The idea was to have a small piece of thick, polished steel plate in a pellet trap, at which one would shoot well-standardized cartridges, such as the Eley Grand Prix, from various distances. Pellets would be collected at each stage, and the average degree of flattening, as measured by micrometer, would be plotted on a curve against the striking velocities derived from the manufacturer's ballistic tables. By referring the average flattening of pellets from home-loaded cartridges to this standard curve, it would have been possible to read off directly the corresponding velocity, uniform hardness of shot being assumed throughout.

Unfortunately, this perfectly sound idea was spoiled by the perversity of I.M.I., who, I found, use shot of different hardnesses for their own cartridges.

In these circumstances, one's mind turns to the direct measurement of penetration, in which the shooter is really more interested than he is in velocity, as being more closely related to killing power. There would appear to be scope here for a revival of the special paper pads already mentioned, and known as Pettitt's pads. These were pads of standardized paper, about quarto size, or larger. When properly used, the sheets were separated and placed in a simple rack, and were usually shot at at a distance of 40 yds.

Payne-Gallwey gives a straightforward guide as to what constitutes satisfactory penetration. He says that a 12-bore gun with a standard game load of No. 6 shot should penetrate 24–25 sheets at the stated distance. As it can be contrived to use the same sheets several times, this would not appear to be an unduly troublesome or expensive method of proving the penetration of home-loaded cartridges. But Pettitt's standardized pads are no longer available, and so it would be necessary to standardize the paper or card used against factory cartridges, as in the case of my pellet-flattening proposals. I return to this subject in my next article.

1 April 1967

penetration tests for the home-loader

When I wrote about measuring the pressure and velocity of the home-loaded cartridge, I said that there was scope for reviving penetration testing as a substitute for testing for velocity. It is, in fact, more than a substitute, because it is getting nearer to what we really need to know about a gun. *Things are best tested by putting them through a measured exercise of the particular function in which we are interested.* Within ordinary limits, we are not interested in velocity as such: the variations normally met with have no effect on practical shooting, except so far as they affect penetration and killing power, which is what we really want to know. So, if we take some thoroughly well standardized factory cartridges, and test our home-loads alongside them, we can rest assured that, if they have the same penetrative power, they will have the same killing power, provided they give as good patterns.

Penetration tests have been criticized for lack of accuracy; but the variables encountered in penetration testing are obviously small when compared with the variables encountered by the same pellets when doing their job in the field. Further, these variables can be much reduced with care, so that the method is fundamentally sound.

A simple test

The usual way of carrying out a shotgun penetration test is to set up a rack of cards and shoot one or more shots at it, at a convenient range. The number of cards penetrated bv the pellets is taken as a measure of their penetrative power.

That needs elaborating. If, say, twelve pellets strike the first card, they will not all end up at the same place. Some of them will be very slightly larger than the others, or will be deformed less in the gun, and will have better penetrative power in consequence. So, we take the penetration as being the number of cards traversed by at least a certain proportion of the pellets—say, half. That would require, in the case under consideration, that we should start from the back and look for the first card containing not less than six holes. The number of that card, counting from the front, would thus be the index of penetration in that particular case. The fact that some of the pellets had passed clean out of the rack would not matter, provided it were less than half the total number striking the first card.

If the cards were of standard penetrability, as were allegedly those of the old Pettitt's pads, this single test would be enough. One would

28. Rack of cards for measuring the penetration of shot. This, rather than velocity, is what the sportsm[a]n really needs to know.

know (or be told) that, at a given range, a normal cartridge, loaded with shot of a stated size, should have a penetration index of so-and-so, as above defined. But as there is no such thing now available as cardboard of standard penetrability—and I doubt if there ever was—tests must be made comparatively. The standard cartridge is fired, and its penetration noted; then the home-load. *Shot sizes must, of course, be the same.* This will tell the average home-loader all he wants to know; but it may be noted that the ratio of the penetration values is theoretically the same as the ratio of the striking energies. Further, the square root of this ratio will be the same as the ratio of the striking velocities; and from this, if we were so disposed, we could work out the muzzle velocity or the observed velocity of the home-load in terms of the standard. But I would not encourage this line of enquiry: apart from the fact that it is working the method rather too hard, it is getting away from the practical conclusion aimed at.

Equipment and procedure

To carry out penetration tests, we need cards. The material known in the stationery trade as '10 sheet thick card' is suitable for testing normal loads. It is about ·025 in. or 25 mils thick. My supplier stocks it in sheets 30 in. by 22 in., and my last lot cost 10s. 9d. a dozen. Each sheet cuts into twelve pieces roughly 7½ in. square; and two sheets, yielding twenty-four cards, make a suitable rackful for testing.

The rack can be a very simple affair. Mine is a flat board, 18 in. long and wide enough to take the cards, which are supported, like pieces of toast in a rack, in saw-cuts made in two wooden stretchers, one on each side of the board mentioned. It is desirable that there should be a good finger breadth between the cards; that the slots should be clearly numbered from the front; that the supports should hold the cards at the edges only; and that the bottom of the rack should be solid and painted white, so that the pellets that have penetrated to each stage can be seen and counted where they have fallen.

Cartridges for testing, as well as the cards, should be conditioned in an ordinary dry indoor situation. Very dry or very damp weather should be avoided for the test, as affecting the penetrability of the card, and establishing false norms.

The rack should be set up at 40 yds., preferably in front of a target of some sort, which will enable the shooter to verify that he has aimed truly, and not merely put a few fringe pellets on his cards.

It is desirable that the first card should be struck by not less than ten pellets, and the cartridges should, therefore, be fired from the choke barrel. If there are fewer than ten hits, a second cartridge can be fired at the same lot of cards. A note should then be made of the number of pellets striking the first card.

Having shot off the standard cartridge(s) in this way, the process can be repeated for the cartridge under test. In each case, the last card showing not less than half the number of holes in the first card should be noted as being the penetration index of the cartridge concerned. Beware, incidentally, of counting deep dents as holes.

If, instead of working on the holes in the cards, we work on the number of pellets that have fallen at each stage, we can shuffle the cards and use them more than once without introducing any material error; but this needs something better than my simple rack, from which I lose a certain number of pellets. Some of the non-penetrators near the margins of the cards evidently rebound out from them.

Example

By way of a practical example, here is the result of a penetration test I carried out this morning on which I write. A certain cartridge was observed to leave much unburnt residue in the barrel, and from this and other indications was believed to have rather low ballistics. It was decided to check it against an Eley 'Impax', as being a corresponding load.

The Impax cartridge made twenty-one strikes on the first card, and the last card pierced by at least half this number was No. 15.

The unnamed cartridge made twenty-two strikes on the first card, and the last one pierced by at least half this number was No. 12.

The penetration of the unnamed cartridge was thus only twelve-fifteenths of that of the Impax cartridge, or 80 per cent, thus confirming my original suspicion. And if we do what I said we should not do, but which I cannot resist doing, and take the square root of this ratio as a measure of the relative striking velocities, we quickly arrive at the result that, if the Impax cartridge duly had its nominal velocity of 1,070 ft./sec., the corresponding velocity of the unnamed cartridge would have been about 950 ft./sec.—a perfectly reasonable result, and one duly borne out by subsequent test.

Here, then, is a simple, but nowadays much neglected, test, by which any home-loader can guide his operations.

8 April 1967

Section 10

PATTERNS AND PERFORMANCE

'From a practical viewpoint the patchiness of any given load at 40 yards is the most important attribute of your gun, and is all you need to know to estimate . . . the performance which the gun will give on game. It is not the number of pellets in a pattern, but the evenness with which they are spaced that counts.'

(Oberfell and Thompson—*The Mysteries of Shotgun Patterns*)

the hard-shooting gun

We seldom hear the expression 'a hard-shooting gun' nowadays, though our immediate ancestors were constantly using it. Why, I wonder, is that? Is it because we have become more precise in our ideas, and have discarded the vague notions conveyed by the phrase in favour of more exact conceptions of velocity and pattern? If so, it might well be yet another instance of some broad reality being lost in the search for scientific precision.

It is by no means easy to say exactly what our forefathers meant when they described a gun as being a 'hard-shooting' one. I do not think they meant merely a gun that was capable of killing game at long ranges, though no doubt that was sometimes part of the idea. My belief is that, to a given man, a hard-shooting gun was nothing more or less than a gun which filled his game bag better than another. I am reinforced in this belief by a story I have just read in J. O'Connor's book on shooting, about an elderly American character who had an old damascus-barrelled hammer gun with which he shot greatly to his satisfaction and which he swore was the 'hardest-shooting gun in Arizona'. But when at last he became persuaded that his old weapon was in a dangerous condition, and was induced to exchange it for a modern pump-gun, he found to his disgust that his new acquisition was not hard-shooting at all, but quite the reverse. It feathered and wounded a lot of birds without killing them.

The facts that emerged were that, over the years, the old hammer gun had lost any choke it ever possessed, while the new pump threw beautiful full-choke patterns. In short, there was nothing whatever the matter with the new gun except that it was totally the wrong gun for the man concerned and for his particular kind of sport. Presumably he was taking his birds at around 25 yds., at which his old cylinder gun threw a killing 36-in. pattern, wide enough to cover his considerable aiming errors. Not so the pump, which threw only a 20-in. pattern at that range, so that the old gunner was hitting most of his birds with the thin fringe of it, and not with the dense centre.

I suppose no man has ever done more to lead the present generation away from the conception of a hard-shooting gun and towards more exact methods of appraisal than Burrard, who, in Volume III of *The Modern Shotgun*, neatly summed up his attitude in the words, 'I prefer the unanswerable logic of the pattern plate to the reputed prowess of individuals.' How reasonable that sounds!—until one remembers that the function of a sporting gun is not to make patterns on a plate, but to make the best of its user's opportunities for filling his game bag. The game bag indeed is the only source of unanswerable logic in this matter.

So, although I would by no means advocate turning our backs on modern methods of appraising gun performance and reinstating our forefathers' vague concept of a hard-shooting gun, yet the latter, if I have interpreted it correctly, embodies a broader and more realistic view of the real merit of a gun—a view that includes three factors that must always be considered together if the best results are to be obtained in the field: the gun, the man behind it, and the kind of sport involved.

But there is an important corollary to all this. If anyone seeks to achieve the happy, original state of the old Arizona character by discarding his full-choke and adopting an open-bored gun, as being better suited to his kind of marksmanship and his kind of sport, he must beware of unsuitable cartridges, and especially high-velocity loads. Open-bored guns, particularly if old and bored to the upper dimensional limits of their proof category, need moderate- or standard-velocity loads and good wadding. Then indeed they are capable of establishing themselves as real 'hard-shooting', game-getting guns.

21 July 1961

buying design or performance

There is a principle, well known to engineering consultants, that plant and equipment can be bought either to a specified design or to a specified performance. If to the former, the purchaser must accept responsibility for the performance; but if to the latter, the supplier must be allowed the necessary latitude in design. The consultants must never try to specify both, as they did on one occasion in my experience, when the manufacturers were held not responsible for a disastrous failure on the grounds that the consultants had insisted on a design feature to which they (the manufacturers) had registered their disapproval.

This principle illuminates a point in connection with shotgun performance to which my attention has been drawn by the complaint of a reader. Having bought a Continental shotgun as a fully choked weapon, he subsequently discovered that the constriction of the bore was less than the 40 thousandths of an inch he had expected, and was inclined to complain that he had been deceived. He had not tested the gun to find out whether or not it gave full-choke patterns, whereby several ambiguities came to light.

The first lies in the various ways in which the performance of a gun is defined. When we stipulate that a gun shall be 'fully choked', are we specifying performance or design? If the former, then we presumably require one that will put 70 per cent of its charge into a 30-in. circle at a distance of 40 yds. But if by a fully choked gun we mean one having a muzzle constriction of 40 thousandths of an inch, then we are specifying design, and are not entitled to grumble if a gun so bored puts more or less than 70 per cent of its charge in the standard circle.

But unless he is contemplating firing some kind of solid projectile, I suggest that no shotgun user has the slightest interest in the degree of constriction in the muzzle of his gun. Different barrel borers have different ways of arriving at the same result, and provided the required pattern is duly attained the gunmaker should be regarded as free to bore the gun his own way. With modern cartridges he will probably use less choke than formerly; so to avoid any misunderstanding it is desirable, when having a gun made, simply to specify the performance required from each barrel in terms of the approximate percentage pattern. When buying one off the shelf, a critical user would be wise to have an understanding with the retailer as to what he means by the boring attributed to the weapon.

But even if we are prepared to disregard the bore dimensions of a gun as being a design feature, and to concentrate on performance as being the proper thing for the user to specify, there remains a strong ambiguity in merely stating the percentage pattern required unless at the same time we specify a particular load or cartridge. This is because a given gun will throw patterns that vary widely with different loads—a 25 per cent difference in pattern count is easily possible with different regular brands of cartridges. This is particularly the case with the more open borings. So if I am having a gun built or the boring altered to my order, I usually say that I want it to give a pattern of *about* so-much per cent at 40 yds. when firing a specified load of powder, shot and wadding; or alternatively a specified standard cartridge, if I know just what goes into it, and like what I know. I add that I am much more concerned about regular pellet distribution than I am about the precise pellet count.

20 April 1962

guaranteed performance

A Worcestershire friend has come to me with some trouble concerning his new Italian over-and-under. The case has several features of common interest, particularly to buyers of Continental guns, and is worth describing.

It appears that the gun was sold to him by the retailer as being a half choke and full choke. This should be noted, because it would appear to constitute a warranty on the part of the retailer, apart from any guarantee by the manufacturer.

When the reader tested the gun at the plate, however, he found that it gave only 50 per cent patterns with the bottom barrel and 57 per cent with the top, instead of the 60 and 70 per cent he had expected.

In the general case, the first point that would arise is, what does the description 'half choke' or 'full choke' mean? This is by no means a pedantic question, because the expressions have no commonly accepted meaning. Most men, perhaps, regard any description of the degree of choke carried by a gun as implying a standard of performance—specifically the capacity to throw a certain percentage of the charge in a 30-in. circle at 40 yds. But many men, including some of the most experienced, regard the degree of choke as implying a specific constriction at the muzzle, say, 35 to 40 thousandths of an inch for a full choke, and would not be satisfied with anything less.

Design or performance?

I have previously drawn attention here to a principle thoroughly well recognized by consulting engineers and others—that plant and equipment can be bought either to a specified design or to a specified performance. Broadly speaking, if a consultant specifies design, he must accept responsibility for performance; but if he specifies performance, he must allow the manufacturer or contractor all necessary latitude in design.

But when, in the case of a gun, a man specifies or requires a particular muzzle constriction, which is a design feature, there is a clearly implied performance specification behind it. He would not, for example, specify a full-choke constriction unless he meant to have full-choke patterns. I should say, therefore, that if a gun is sold as being a half choke or a full choke, or whatever it may be, without any qualification, it is implied that it is capable of the corresponding performance. If the gun proves to be incapable of that performance, I should not regard the retailer's ability to point to any degree of muzzle constriction whatsoever as letting him out of his implied warranty.

Continental choke markings

Coming back to Continental guns in general, the countries subscribing to the International Proof Convention have decided on a common marking to indicate the degree of choke of all shotgun barrels proved in their official proof house. The marking is by means of stars, *as determined by the muzzle constriction at the time of proof*, as follows:

	Tenths of a millimetre	
*	9–10	(full choke)
**	7–8	(improved modified)
***	4–5–6	(modified)
****	2–3	(improved cylinder)
CL		(true cylinder)

Since these markings are made by the proof authority, and are defined strictly by reference to bore measurement, they cannot in themselves be regarded as conveying any guarantee of performance. For that, one would still have to depend on whether the vendor offered the gun as being of a particular degree of choke, with all its implications as to percentage patterns. It would be up to the vendor himself to decide whether the markings on the barrel justified him in selling the gun with the performance-warranty implied by the corresponding description.

In the case of my acquaintance's gun, the famous manufacturer concerned, realizing, no doubt, the limited implications of the proof authority's markings, added a formal guarantee of his own that the ballistical characteristics of the weapon corresponded to the one-star and three-star markings impressed. This guarantee no doubt fortified the vendor in offering the gun as being a half choke and full choke, and reasonably so.

Gun and cartridge

But what does such a formal guarantee convey? So far, we have been considering the gun in a vacuum, whereas a gun by itself is incapable of any performance, except possibly as a club. Before my correspondent could establish a reasonable complaint concerning his gun, he would have to consider what are the implications of the maker's guarantee—and the vendor's implied warranty—in terms of loads or cartridges.

Bearing in mind, as I have said before, that a given gun is capable of throwing substantially different patterns with different brands of *good* cartridges, I think it must be accepted as a general principle that, when a maker guarantees the performance of a gun, he has the right to specify the load or cartridge necessary for the fulfilment of that guarantee, always provided that this does not involve the use of any non-standard components, or abnormal charges or methods of loading, unless expressly stipulated.

In the case of a ready-made English game gun, offered for sale on the home market, I should say that a description such as 'half choke' would imply that the gun requires a standard British game cartridge, like the Eley 'Grand Prix', in order to give half-choke performance; and that the maker would be justified in rejecting any suggestion that the gun should be capable of delivering half-choke patterns with a cartridge of substantially different characteristics.

But my acquaintance's gun is not English: it is Italian, and the fact has a bearing on the point at issue. First, it is bored tighter—·725 in., instead of our usual modern figure of ·729—and it by no means follows that a standard British cartridge, designed to give the best results in guns bored at anything from ·729 to, say, ·739, would deliver the densest patterns of which such a gun is capable. If the gun was bored with a standard cartridge in mind, it was almost certainly a standard Italian cartridge, which in turn might not show to best advantage in an English gun, or even a Continental one expressly designed for the British market.

There is a further point, significant in case of argument, that any Italian guarantee of shotgun performance will presumably relate, not to the British standard 30-in. circle at 40 yds., but to the Continental standard 76-cm. circle at 35 m. This is equivalent to a 30-in. circle at about 38 yds., and the difference could well mean that a gun which duly delivered a 70 per cent pattern by the Continental standard would deliver only 65 per cent by the British.

How tested?

Valid criticisms of shotgun performance can only be made on the basis of tests properly carried out. My friend says that he first bought a copy of my book *Shotguns and Cartridges*, and then followed my instructions 'to the letter'. But evidently not quite; for he fired only four cartridges per barrel, which is really not enough to get a fair average. I recommended six, from a previously fired barrel, as a minimum. Again, I suspect that, contrary to my instructions, he may have drawn the 30-in. circles on his paper-covered pattern board *before* he fired each round, as I believe many men do when testing their guns for pattern. Richard Arnold, I notice in *The Shooter's Handbook*, actually describes this procedure as part of the normal routine; but it is wrong, and would depress the results. The reason is that, however accurately the gun may be pointed, the mean point of impact of successive charge centres will not fall on the same place, but will make a group, perhaps the size of a dinner plate. The correct procedure, therefore, as used throughout the gun trade, is to shoot first, then to select the apparent centre of the pattern by eye, and finally to draw the 30-in. circle about the centre so estimated. I estimate that pre-drawn circles could readily make 5 per cent difference in the average pellet count, according to the type of boring.

The practical issue

I believe the foregoing gives a fair idea of the considerations chiefly arising in the interpretation of any guarantee of shotgun performance. I should add that I write on this subject, with its strong legal flavour, merely as an engineer, and I recognize that a long experience of specifications, contracts, guarantees and related disputes does not entitle me to speak with authority on any question of law. But the matter, as presented by my correspondent, is really nowhere near a lawyer's purview. It is a matter for the checking of testing procedure, and for trying a variety of other cartridges; also for remembering that shotgun performance figures are statistical rather than specific, and that pattern quality is far more important than marginal differences in pellet count.

8 July 1965

how to judge your patterns (I)

As readers of this book will now be well aware, shotgun patterns are judged in the first instance by the percentage of the total charge thrown into a 30-in. circle at 40 yds. The gun is fired at a whitewashed plate or paper target, preferably about 6 ft. sq. and not less than 4, set up at a distance of 40 yds. from the spot over which the shooter stands—not, as is sometimes thought, from the muzzle of his gun. The centre of the resulting pattern is then judged by eye, disregarding any aiming mark previously made on the target, and a 30-in. circle drawn about the centre thus estimated. The pattern is then usually contemplated for a moment, and judged as being good, medium or poor, according to the uniformity of spread of the pellet marks, and their freedom from undue central concentration, vacant patches and signs of 'balling', or the sticking together of small clusters of pellets, which is rightly regarded as a bad and dangerous defect. Finally, the number of pellets within or cutting the circle is counted and noted down; and when this has been repeated for not less than a half-dozen rounds, shot from a previously fired barrel, the average pellet-count can be worked out and the percentage calculated. Nothing less than this will enable a fair opinion to be formed of the effectiveness of a particular batch of cartridges in a particular gun. It is the procedure usually followed in the gun trade and by conscientious amateurs, who recognize that few things in the way of shooting can be more misleading or more hurtful to confidence than 'testing' a gun by firing a single round at a sheet of newspaper, stuck up at a distance that has not been carefully measured.

A defective method

But it will be clear that, however conscientiously this procedure is followed, it has some conspicuous shortcomings; the only quantitative information it yields is the actual pellet-count. The vital quality of uniformity is left to arbitrary assessment, and could obviously be judged differently by different individuals—or even by the same individual, according to mood, or how much time he had on his hands.

Recognizing this, many other methods have been proposed for the assessment of patterns. They chiefly rely on the same principle—that of dividing the area of the 30-in. circle into a number of fields, and counting the number of pellets included in each. Sometimes the fields are concentric zones or bands, and systematic inferences are made according to the number or proportion of pellets in each; and sometimes they are sectors of the main circle, divided again by concentric lines. A typical method, currently favoured on the Continent, consists of drawing an inner circle of half-radius, and dividing this by radial lines into four equal parts. The remaining outer zone is similarly divided by radial lines into twelve parts. This gives a total of sixteen fields, all of roughly the same area, and results are given by stating the number of pellets in each.

German thoroughness

A more elaborate method was that used by the *Deutsche Versuchanstalt für Handfeuerwaffen* (German Testing Institute for Small-arms) in the pre-war days. They used the familiar Continental 75-cm. ($29\frac{1}{2}$-in.) circle, divided into no less than 100 fields, comprising five concentric zones divided by twenty radial lines. A sportsman I know has one of their certificates relating to a gun he had tested in the 1920s, and and can describe in a fascinating way the formal, elaborate and painstaking tests carried out, including velocity and penetration, the 'nice little book' in which the results were recorded, and the meticulously handwritten certificate, resembling, I gather, an illuminated address, duly issued on completion of the trial. I wish I had space to repeat his description of the wonderful facilities possessed by the Institute, its many rifle ranges, its varied clay-pigeon layouts, its laboratories, clubrooms and restaurant—all open to the public at Wannsee, near Berlin—and maintained by the German gun trade and associated organizations. But this would lead me away from my point, which is to emphasize the fundamental deficiencies of this multiple-field method of assessing patterns.

More needed

If an ordinary 12-bore charge of game shot were fired into a 30-in. circle, making a pattern of, say, 150; and if the area included in the circle were divided up into 100 equal fields, there would obviously be an average of $1\frac{1}{2}$ pellets to each field. Owing to normal imperfections in the pattern, the number striking any particular field might range from nothing to, perhaps, five or six; and it is characteristic of these small numbers that they are just as quickly conveyed to the eye and mind by strokes, or dots, or fingers held in the air, as they are by arithmetical digits. Indeed, dots (or pellet marks) convey more: they indicate position as well as quantity. So, the numbered multi-field diagrams, such as one sees reproduced in Continental gun and cartridge advertisements, are at best an imperfect record of actual patterns, and the data for some system of evaluation.

What is clearly needed for the sound assessment of patterns is the recognition of those qualities which determine practical effectiveness in the shooting field—the real game-getting qualities—and the setting up of corresponding standards, in terms of which these qualities in actual patterns can be numerically expressed. To be practical, the method must be capable of quick and easy application, otherwise it would be only of academic interest.

There is no doubt as to what constitutes the game-getting qualities in patterns. They are (1) an appropriate degree of overall concentration, having regard for the kind of sport in view, (2) freedom from undue central concentration, and (3) freedom from vacant patches. Point (1) is, of course, covered by the familiar conception of percentage density, and is the only quality ordinarily admitting of quantitative expression. Point (2) usually goes by default in assessing patterns, and what is really a defect is occasionally pointed out as a merit. Point (3) corresponds to the quality more often expressed as uniformity of spread. Its importance is sufficiently recognized, but, again, it lacks quantitative interpretation.

The Oberfell and Thompson method

I have already referred here to various aspects of the work of the American investigators Oberfell and Thompson, which is not so well known in this country as it deserves to be. In their book, *The Mysteries of Shotgun Patterns*, they describe a method of assessment which covers all the requirements I have indicated, and is easy to apply. It is based, first and foremost, on an analytical approach, through the medium of the mathematics of probability, or the laws of chance. In case this should alarm any practical reader, I hasten to say that their theoretical work was fully supported by actual testing, and that their conclusions, which I have checked pretty thoroughly on many patterns taken by myself and others, are usually so accurate as to be slightly uncanny.

First, a word on the basis of their method. If a charge of theoretically perfect shot was fired, undeformed, from a similarly perfect true cylinder barrel in absolutely still air, it might be thought that it would, of necessity, reach the target in the same compact mass as that in which it left the barrel. But, in fact, the powerful resistance of the air would cause both lateral and longitudinal dispersion of the pellets. At first, it would tear off the outer ones from the protected inner mass, into which it would then go riving and sundering until they were all travelling more-or-less independently. And they would not, except by inconceivably remote chance, arrive at the target in perfect 'pepper-pot' formation, nor, except by an equally remote chance, would they all arrive together. In fact, the general character of the formation in which they *would* arrive, expressed in terms of the degree of central concentration, and the number of vacant patches of a given size, is capable of being mathematically calculated. This establishes a standard of normality in terms of which actual patterns can be assessed.

As for the detailed method, I leave that until my next article. I will only say now, as a random example of the kind of thing that may be expected, that the typical, good, improved-cylinder pattern shown on page 50 of my book *Shotguns and Cartridges*, on being checked by the Oberfell and Thompson method, shows *exactly* the number and size of vacant patches predicted.

2 September 1965.

how to judge your patterns (II)

In the first part of this article, I wrote of the inadequacy of the ordinary method of assessing shotgun patterns, in which the only hard or quantitative information noted is the number of pellets striking within a 30-in. circle at 40 yds., the vital qualities of uniformity of spread and freedom from vacant patches being left to the arbitrary and qualitative assessment of the tester, according to his preconceptions and experience. I referred in passing to the methods favoured on the Continent of dividing the area in the standard circle into a number of fields and noting the number of pellets in each, but I pointed out that this in itself does not constitute an assessment of the pattern but only a record of it, and maybe a poor record at that.

I concluded that a sound method of assessing patterns required the quick and easy evaluation, on a quantitative basis, of those qualities that determine their game-getting (or target-smashing) effectiveness in the field, namely, an appropriate degree of overall concentration, according to the kind of sport concerned; freedom from undue central concentration and freedom from vacant patches. I went on to mention the method described by the American investigators Oberfell and Thompson, in their book *The Mysteries of Shotgun Patterns*, as conforming to the stated requirements, and undertook to describe it, which I will now try to do, having satisfied myself over the past year or two of the soundness of the authors' ideas.

Theory and method

Oberfell and Thompson start off with what all the checks I have been able to apply confirm is a sound theory—namely, that the distribution of pellets in a shotgun pattern is *basically* regulated by chance, and is amenable to mathematical prediction according to the theory of probability. This gives them certain standards to which I find that good, normal patterns conform with an uncanny degree of precision. Further, the practical researches by which they confirm and elaborate their theory build up into a consistent body of information which entitles their conclusions to respect, even when they are occasionally at variance with one's long-standing preconceptions.

So much for the preamble: now for the method. The gun is shot in the ordinary way at a plate or paper target 40 yds. from the shooter's position, and a 30-in. circle drawn about the pattern centre, as estimated by eye. The 30-in. area is then divided approximately in half by a concentric circle, 20 in. in diameter, and the number of pellet marks counted, first those in the 20-in. circle, and then the remainder in the outer zone, giving, by addition, the total.

The number of vacant patches in the pattern within the 30-in. circle is then ascertained. For this purpose, the authors have selected a 5-in. circular patch as being most suitable, having regard for the size of the vulnerable area of most game birds, and the diameter of clay targets. (A 5-in. transparent disc, fitted with a cork handle, is convenient for checking the number of pellet-free patches.)

Evaluating the pattern

With the above information, and a knowledge of the total pellets in the charge, the pattern can be assessed.

First, the overall *percentage density* is worked out in the ordinary way. (The authors call this—regrettably, in my opinion—the 'pattern efficiency', thereby implying that a dense pattern is more efficient than an open one, which, of course, for many kinds of sport, is not the case.)

Next, the *distribution factor* is ascertained. This is simply a measure of the degree of central concentration, and is the relationship between the number of pellets in the 30-in. circle and that in the 20-in.

Last comes the *patchiness factor*, which is determined by the number of complete, 5-in. diameter, vacant patches in the pattern.

The authors then give two tables by which the merit rating for the distribution factor and for the patchiness factor can be determined, and simple rules for combining them to give an overall assessment of the quality of the pattern. This part of the book is rather overwrought in the authors' anxiety to be understood by 'persons of the meanest intelligence', and can best be summarized by the two graphs following, which I have adapted from those given in their text. I do so

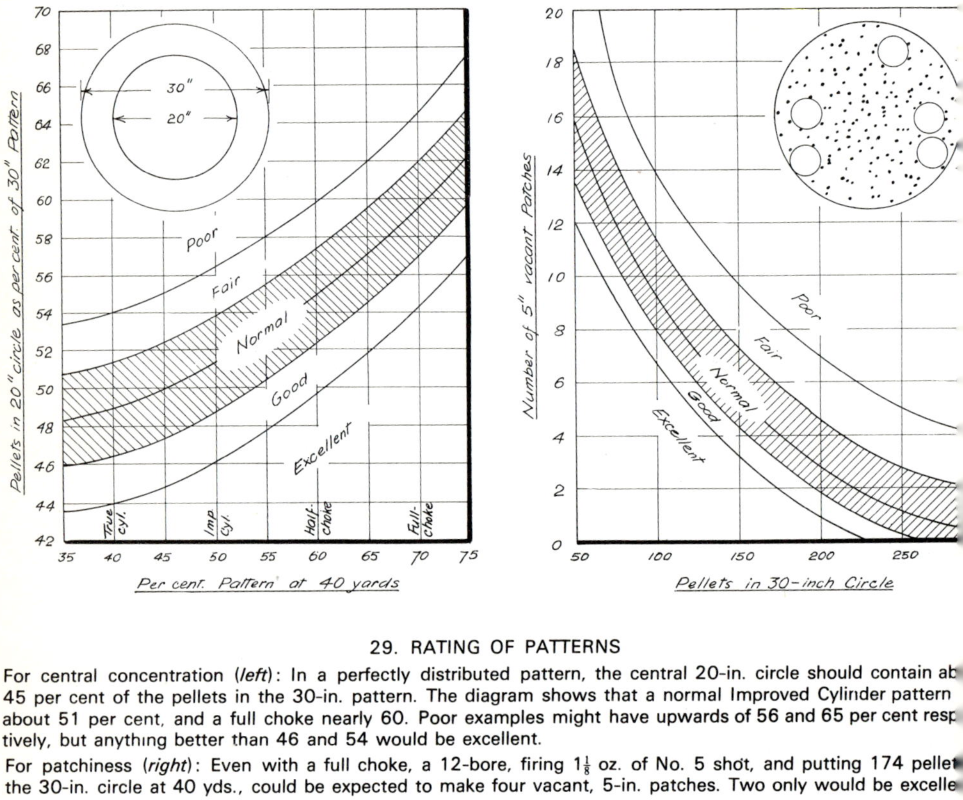

29. RATING OF PATTERNS

For central concentration (*left*): In a perfectly distributed pattern, the central 20-in. circle should contain ab 45 per cent of the pellets in the 30-in. pattern. The diagram shows that a normal Improved Cylinder pattern about 51 per cent, and a full choke nearly 60. Poor examples might have upwards of 56 and 65 per cent resp tively, but anything better than 46 and 54 would be excellent.

For patchiness (*right*): Even with a full choke, a 12-bore, firing $1\frac{1}{8}$ oz. of No. 5 shot, and putting 174 pelle the 30-in. circle at 40 yds., could be expected to make four vacant, 5-in. patches. Two only would be excelle

with due acknowledgement. Those who wish to follow the method in detail should get the book, which is published by the Oklahoma State University Press. I thoroughly recommend it, despite the fact that pidgin-English chapter headings like 'Know your Know-how' and 'Know more Know-how' make my pedantic prickles stand right up. After all, the book *does* bear the imprimatur of a university.

For the rest, it contains many ripe conclusions derived from the authors' research, experiments and field tests, as well as an extensive bibliography and numerous tables, and I can best devote the remainder of this article to bringing out some of its more oustanding points.

Nothing perfect

The perfect pattern is a will-o'-the-wisp: some degree of patchiness (based on the authors' 5-in. standard patch) is to be expected in all cases, unless there are at least about 280 pellets in the 30-in. circle—corresponding, say, to a full-choke or 70 per cent pattern made by $1\frac{3}{16}$ oz. of No. 7 shot. This can be seen from the right-hand curve opposite, where the shaded zone covering normal results first strikes the zero line at about that figure. A pattern of 144 pellets, as nominally made by the improved cylinder right barrel of a 12-bore game gun, firing $1\frac{1}{16}$ oz. of No. 6 shot, could ordinarily be expected to show six such patches (reading from the central curve of the normal zone), which is, in fact, the number to be found in the typical pattern of this sort shown on page 50 of *Shotguns and Cartridges*. This degree of imperfection in the normal pattern is something to be emphasized, because I have known men to condemn a gun or cartridge outright on less evidence. Those who have guns capable of substantially better performance with the cartridges available are lucky, or have been particularly well served.

Incidentally, the normal relationship between number of pellets and number of vacant 5-in. patches, as indicated by the curve, is so far reliable that, when dealing with the average run of patterns, it is possible to estimate closely the total number of pellets in the 30-in. circle by merely counting the number of patches, and reading off the total pellets from the curve. I have amused myself by doing this in many cases, and have been struck by the curiously high standard of accuracy shown by the results.

The authors make the admirable point that, from a practical point of view, the patchiness value of a pattern at 40 yds. is the most important test of a gun–cartridge combination. 'It is all you need know . . . to estimate with a reasonable degree of accuracy all of the gun's patterning characteristics, and the performance the gun will give on game for all practical shooting distances. *It is not the number of pellets in a pattern, but the evenness with which they are spaced that counts.*'

Chokes and cylinders

A related point is brought out by the left-hand curve, which shows the markedly increased degree of central concentration to be found in the higher-density patterns thrown by heavily choked guns. When to this we add the fact that the outer zone of such patterns exhibits a markedly higher patchiness, especially when using large shot, the dependence of the users of such guns on a high standard of marksmanship for the realization of the advantage they theoretically possess is emphasized.

On the other hand, the authors' researches support the rehabilitation undergone by the true cylinder barrel in recent years. If for no better reason than the higher proportion of undeformed pellets it discharges, one feels that the *quality* of the true cylinder pattern should be higher than that of the choke. The authors confirm this. They find that, *for a given number of pellet strikes*, the merit-rating of the true cylinder pattern is highest. Thus, a true cylinder makes as dense a pattern at 30 yds. as a half-choke at 40; but it will be a better-quality pattern, other things being equal, with fewer patches and less central concentration, and in practical effectiveness will have less than its seeming or nominal disadvantage in respect of range. No wonder some men swore by those old B.S.A.s, with their true-cylinder right barrels.

9 September 1965

the element of chance

Even if a shotgun threw perfect 'pepper-pot' patterns—that is to say, patterns in which the pellets were invariably spaced with perfect, geometrical regularity—a target of given size would not always receive the same number, even though it were fairly caught every time within the pattern circle. Obviously not: if the target were small enough, or the pattern coarse enough, it might fit into one of the regular gaps. On the other hand, it might receive one or two hits. It is only if the theoretically perfect pattern were extremely fine in relation to the size of the target that one would approach the condition of hitting it with certainty, and with the same number of pellets each time, accurate shooting being assumed throughout.

When it is considered how far actual patterns fall short of perfection, it is clear that the scope for variation in the number of hits scored on the target is greatly enlarged. A perfect gun might put, say, 150 pellets into the 30-in. circle (707 sq. in.) every time at 40 yds.; and a given bird might regularly present a silhouette of 20 sq. in. to the gun. In these circumstances we might say that the bird would receive 150 pellets divided by 707 and multiplied by 20, or rather more than 4. This is the basis on which Burrard calculated effective ranges—by relating pattern density to the areas presented by the vulnerable regions of various kinds of game, and regarding the effective range as the greatest distance at which the pattern would be dense enough to score the minimum number of hits necessary to produce a fatal result, as determined by experience. I.M.I. adopted the same basis for the effective range tables published in *The Shooter's Year Book.* So did I for the comprehensive range charts given in *Shotguns and Cartridges.*

Modest expectations

But this method of assessing the range of a gun depends very much on averages, and if we are to accept it, we must not pitch our expectations of consistent performance too high. If we are satisfied with nothing less than 100 per cent returns from accurately aimed shots, we must be prepared to confine ourselves to shooting within much shorter distances than those commonly accepted as being within effective range. If, on the other hand, we wish to take full advantage of effective range, as commonly understood, we must tolerate something less than 100 per cent kills for equally accurate shooting.

In what I have previously written on this subject, I have not attempted to get to grips with this question of what to expect from accurate shooting at full range. Yet it is not too difficult to form some idea. If, in given circumstances, a target receives on the average a certain number of hits, it is possible to calculate by the laws of chance within what limits the number of hits from individual shots is likely to fall. Further, if we have quite made up our minds as to how many hits are needed to make a certain kill, we can then work out in what proportion of shots the number of hits is likely to fall below this

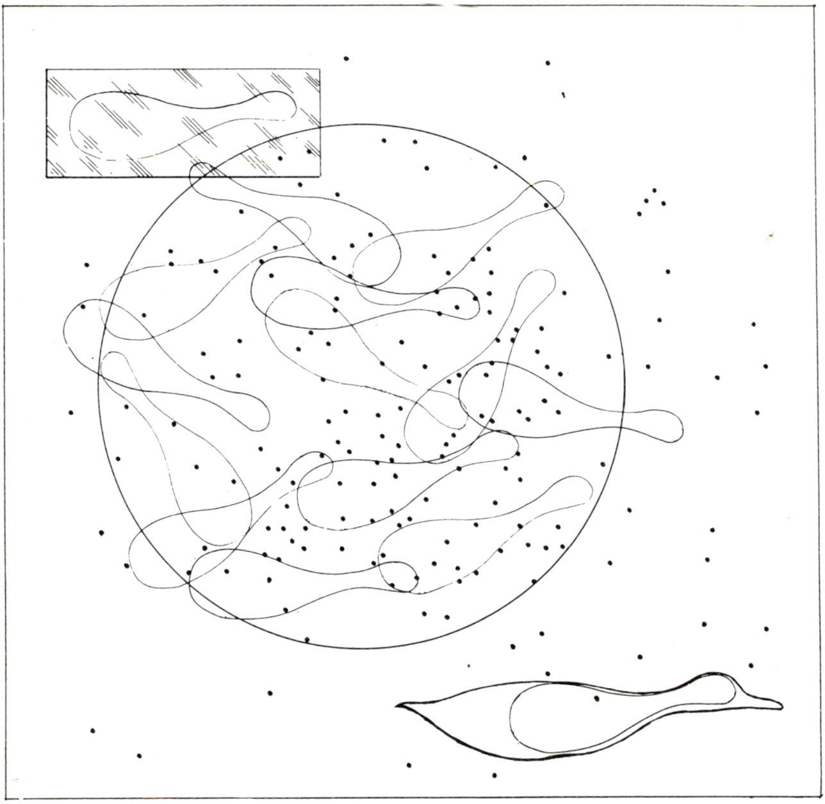

30. A MATTER OF CHANCE

Experiment to indicate the variations to be expected in the number of pellets striking the vulnerable parts of a mallard at 40 yds. This is an actual full-choke pattern made by $1\frac{1}{2}$-oz. No. 4 (American) shot in a 30-in. circle.

figure. This, then, will give us a guide to the sort of results we are entitled to expect from accurate shooting at the range concerned.

An experiment

Calculations on these lines can be neatly checked by practical experiment, and as the experimental method is likely to be of more interest to readers, I will give a practical example. One takes an actual pattern, which is thoroughly representative of the performance of the gun-cartridge combination under test, and applies to it, by a suitable random method, a transparent cut-out representing the vulnerable area of the bird or other game concerned. This is repeated a large number of times—say, at least 100—and each time the number of pellet marks covered by the cut-out is noted and recorded. If these results are tabulated and analysed they will usually be found to conform to theoretical predictions.

The most convenient way I have found for performing this experiment is to reproduce the chosen pattern by photography to about the size of a dinner plate, and to place it flat down on a table. A small transparent celluloid slip, carrying the outline of the bird's vulnerable area, reduced, of course, to the same scale, is then dropped on the pattern from a height sufficient to ensure a random fall. As we are supposed to be examining the probable results obtained by accurate shooting, a circle is drawn enclosing the bulk of the pattern, and any 'shots' falling wholly outside it are regarded as misses, and ignored.

. . . and an example

I have chosen for my example a pattern made by a fully choked, $2\frac{3}{4}$-in. American 12-bore firing a magnum cartridge loaded with $1\frac{1}{2}$ oz. of American No. 4 shot, corresponding to English No. 3. The pattern, which is reproduced on the opposite page, was made at 40 yds, and includes 136 pellets, or 67 per cent of the charge in the 30-in. circle. This circle has been taken as the boundary circle for the present test, as the remainder of the charge was widely scattered, and was no doubt largely made up of low-energy 'fliers'—that is, badly deformed pellets trailing along wildly at the rear of the shot-string, and of well below average killing power.

Also shown in the illustration are a mallard, drawn to scale, and the area within the bird's outline regarded as being the vulnerable region of its anatomy.

The result of 100 successful 'shots', made in the manner described may be tabulated as follows.

All cases received 1 or more pellets
94 cases (94 per cent) received 2 or more
81 cases (81 per cent) received 3 or more
72 cases (72 per cent) received 4 or more
58 cases (58 per cent) received 5 or more

The average number of hits was 6. According to my calculation, there was an even chance of individual hits falling between 4 and 8, and a 100 to 1 chance of all of them falling between 0 and 12. Both predictions were correct: 55 per cent fell between 4 and 8, and all fell between 0 and 12, this latter figure being the highest recorded.

Interpretation

What are we to make of all this? If we take it, as the best American authorities seem to do, that it takes a minimum of five pellets to make sure of a clean kill with mallard, it seems that, even at this modest range of 40 yds., a full choke and a magnum load of $1\frac{1}{2}$ oz., aimed truly, could only rely on 58 per cent of clean kills. If, on the other hand, we take it, as we have widely done in this country, that four hits will account for any mallard, the percentage goes up to 72.

But we must recognize that there can never be any hard and fast rule as to how many pellets are necessary for a clean kill. Much must always depend on where they strike. So, even if our experiment gives a fair picture of what is likely to happen in practice, in terms of hits, the actual bag produced by 100 accurately aimed shots would be better than 58 or 72. It would include a number of birds which, though struck by fewer than the minimum number of pellets considered necessary for a *certain* clean kill, were killed none the less. And it would include others not killed at all, but nevertheless fairly fetched down and duly brought to bag.

But whatever the figure might be whipped up to in this way, one thing stands out very clearly. This was an actual pattern, and a good average one at that; and it was made at the modest range of 40 yds. If, therefore, our experiment was a valid one, as it appears to have been, the outlook for consistent performance at extended ranges, even with magnum loads, is not very bright.

In the meantime, it is only fair to note that although the Americans are so largely responsible for the magnum cult, their principal gun and cartridge manufacturers, in their more sober pronouncements, have no delusions. 'A 40-yd. shot is a long shot,' the Ithaca company say; 'a 50-yd. shot is a very long shot; and a 60-yd. shot is a *whale* of a long shot.'

22 July 1967

the all-important wad

The whole subject of shotgun performance is haunted by wads—those insignificant-looking little lumps of felt, or some modern substitute, inserted between powder and shot in the cartridge. No gun, however costly—however carefully made and regulated—can give of its best unless it is loaded with efficient wadding, and the performance of *any* gun can be reduced to an abysmally low level by failure on the part of this vital component to do its proper job.

The prime purpose of the wad is, of course, to act as an obturator—that is to say, a seal—between the powder gases and the shot. If the seal is not effective throughout the whole of the brief interval occupied by the shot in its course up the barrel, things will start going wrong. From the viewpoint of the powder, any escape of gas will lower the pressure and the temperature, and therefore the efficiency of combustion, so that some part of the charge may escape unburnt. Velocity, and therefore penetration and killing power, will accordingly suffer. From the viewpoint of the shot, any escape of white-hot gases intermingling with the pellets may fuse numbers of them together, so that they travel as a single projectile of greater energy and ranging-power than those that remain correctly in a state of isolation. This is 'balling'. It is highly objectionable, and can be dangerous. Even if the aggregations comprise only a few pellets, there is an obvious loss of pattern quality, while the larger aggregations, sometimes comprising a considerable part of the charge, can travel great distances and inflict serious injury on anyone in the way. Burrard recalls a case, originally reported in the *British Medical Journal*, of a man whose jaw was thus broken at a distance of 133 yds. The wound contained an agglomeration of pellets weighing a third of an ounce. I have seen worse examples at the pattern plate, and have received several accounts of birds more or less blown to pieces at full range. There are other aspects of balling which I cannot consider now. For the moment, I will merely add that, apart from the possibility of their causing balling, powder gases escaping into the shot charge can be highly destructive of pattern quality.

Other functions and effects

But the wad does more than act as a seal: it also transmits the thrust of the powder gases to the shot charge, and in so doing acts as a cushion. In this capacity it modifies the initial acceleration of the shot, and therefore the force tending to crush, deform and possibly cold-weld the pellets, particularly those at the rear of the charge. And according to whether the cushion is a soft or a hard one, it modifies the volume available for the initial expansion of the powder gases, and thus affects the pressure, temperature and efficiency of combustion. Significant differences in velocity—say, as much as 10 per cent—can thus be produced even by what may appear to be unimportant changes in wadding material.

Again, according to the hardness or softness of the wad, and the variation of these qualities throughout its mass, factors emerge which influence the pattern. If this last point sounds vague, it is because we are getting into matters which elude precise definition or measurement, and which can only be evaluated by practical experiment. In this category come, for example, wads of special shape, such as hard wads with a frontal cavity, which have been claimed as giving extra dense patterns, particularly with small shot.

An important incidental function of the wad is to sweep out of the bore all residue remaining from the previous shot, and, if possible, to remove any leading.

Properties and types

But nothing avails a wad unless it efficiently performs its prime duty of sealing off the powder gases. This is a task that may be made more difficult by charges developing relatively high pressures, by guns with long chamber cones, by those of maximum bore dimensions within their proof category, and by small-bores as opposed to those of larger calibre, since in their case the wad is called on to undergo a proportionately larger expansion in order to make an efficient seal.

For all these reasons, it is clear that wads should have a good reserve of obturating capacity, particularly if the cartridges may be called on to function in a variety of guns, as is the case with those loaded by the big manufacturers.

Obturating capacity depends fundamentally on the extent to which the wadding material is capable of translating the longitudinal thrust of the powder gases into a lateral thrust against the barrel wall. The material must thus have plasticity, and what engineers would describe as a high value of the Poisson's ratio, which for present purposes can be taken simply as the amount of swelling produced by a given squeeze. It is no exaggeration to say that the world has been combed for wadding material, and it is unfortunate that one of the very best—high-quality wool felt—is so expensive that the big manufacturers do not use it. I do not even know where it can be had nowadays. Brown felt can be good, but is not so consistent. The so-called vegetable felts have some good points, but lack the obturating power of wool. Cork is a bad obturator—curiously so, for it accepts a large measure of compression with hardly any change in its lateral dimensions.

Partly for economic reasons, and partly in the hope of combining desirable features, many composite wads have been tried. The popular French 'Iris' wad is a good example—a piston of cork with a piston ring of felt. Westley Richards use a somewhat similar composite wad in their well-known 'Game Load' cartridges*.

But the most striking development in wads in recent years is undoubtedly the American plastic wad, now usually associated with some form of shot protector.

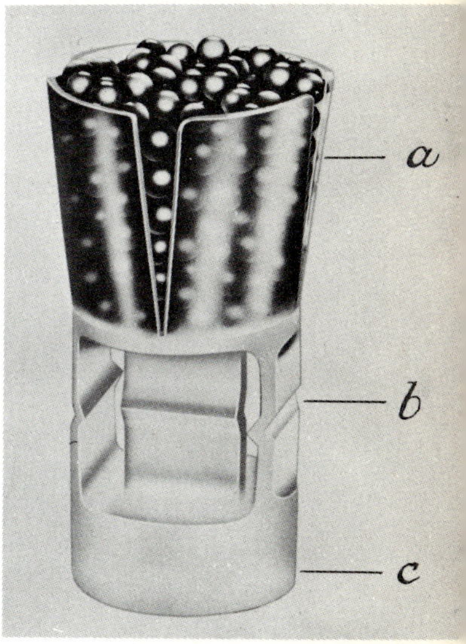

31. THE WAD OF THE FUTURE?
A typical American plastic wad incorporating: *a.* a split protective shot cup which folds back on the emergence of the shot charge from the muzzle; *b.* a collapsible portion to cushion the initial rapid rise of gas pressure; and *c.* a cup-washer skirt to seal the powder gases.

The plastic wad

In these wads, which I believe are made of polyethylene, obturation depends on a short rearward skirt which acts like the cup-washer on a bicycle pump. To get this thing right, so that it reliably seals the bore on the one hand, and does not do so sufficiently tightly to cause juddering and rivelling on the other, must have been quite an achievement. The necessary degree of cushioning in these wads, in the absence of any useful elasticity on the part of the material, is obtained by interposing a collapsible portion between powder and shot. The shot cup, developed from the original Winchester Mark V shot collar, is usually now part of the wad. It protects the shot from contact with the bore, and from balling by the intrusion of powder gases. Impressive claims

* Manufacture now discontinued

are made for these new-old developments. Still more impressive is the scale on which they have been applied in recent years, and the success they appear to have enjoyed. We may be sure that the eminent manufacturers have had their troubles, and can only hope that they have been entirely overcome. If so, the plastic wad with the integral shot cup may well be the type of the future.

First things first

In this brief review, I have unavoidably been more concerned with principles than with practice. Home-loaders may have scanned these lines in vain for the answers to their own wadding problems. Still, I hope I have made it clear that it is almost impossible to exaggerate the practical importance of the wadding component in the shot charge. One is tempted to say that it comes first. At least, if it fails everything fails. Some home-loaders who write to me take the cartridge case first; then they consider what load of powder and shot they wish to use, and the amount of case required for the turnover or crimp. What is left over is considered the appropriate space for the wadding. If good results follow from this approach, it is sheer good luck, and undeserved good luck at that.

In this matter, our muzzle-loading forebears had an advantage over us. They had to exercise deliberate choice in the matter of wadding, and on the whole were more knowledgeable about it than we are. The subject is worth all the attention we are likely to give it.

2 March 1967

charge elevation an advantage

For a modest household, we eat a lot of game, mostly of my providing; and this year I have been disconcerted by murmurings from the domestic authorities to the effect that I am putting more lead into my birds than usual, and not, perhaps, giving them enough law. This strikes me as odd, because I am certainly not taking them at any closer range than hitherto, yet there seems to be some substance in the complaint.

What, if anything, can have happened? I am still using the Eley Impax cartridge, with its modest ounce of No. 6 shot, which I find fully adequate for all ordinary game shooting, and a rough check yields no evidence that the new plastic issue makes any closer patterns than the paper variety. My gun, it is true, is a new one, but I have checked it carefully for pattern, and it does not come under suspicion. The right barrel is supposed to be an improved cylinder, and it does in fact throw good improved cylinder patterns, like my old favourite. The left barrel is, admittedly, more closely choked, but I have made very little use of it, and the difference is insignificant to the present problem.

There is one thing: my new gun shoots high—about 7 in. at 40 yds.—whereas the old favourite shot true to the point of aim. Could this be it? It is worth considering.

Doctrine

In my early days, I was always assured by my elders and betters that birds missed are invariably missed below and behind. It was explained that, even when they appeared to be flying level, they were in fact usually rising, and that it was necessary to blot them well out to make sure of hitting them.

I have long since outgrown any subservience to this doctrine. Deliberate observation on many occasions spent with the beaters showed me that on flat ground, partridges and grouse and other non-soaring birds frequently go away pin-pointed against the background, so that a moderate amount of aiming over would be sufficient to ensure a miss. Further, many birds which are still climbing strongly in relation to the ground are declining in the shooter's view when they become shootable, and need to be shot under rather than over.

If, when I was a young chap, I had a spell of missing, I remember that I was induced by my early training to believe that I was shooting under my birds, and that I tried to improve matters by blotting them out ever more strongly. I am sure that that did not always work, and that I must have done a good deal of missing over until I recovered my form.

Practice

But these questions of overall performance cannot be settled by reference to individual types of shots. The point at issue and of interest is whether, taking one shot with another, I tend to shoot low, and whether this is true of most other shooters. If so—if, that is to say, we all tend to take our birds with the upper part, or even the upper fringe, of the pattern—we should obviously benefit by using a gun which tended to throw its patterns high. More birds would thus be hit with the central pellets, which are not only less scattered but also have more individual energy. True, such a gun would increase the missing of descending birds, or birds which, though still ascending, are declining in the shooter's field of vision; but these are a minority in ordinary mixed shooting, and would thus not affect the general proposition.

What evidence is there of a general tendency to shoot low rather than high? There is certainly a universal agent at work in favour of such a tendency, in the shape of the force of gravitation. Most of us, irrespective of age and stamina, become conscious of it at the end of a long day, when it would be a refreshing boon to shed something from the weight of our guns, and particularly from the muzzle end. This, of course, is one of the best arguments for the short-barrelled weapon, which not only relieves the shooter of weight, but also tends to throw its charges somewhat higher. 'Better charge elevation', I remember, was one of Churchill's battle cries, when he was campaigning to establish his 25-in. barrelled guns in public favour.

Missed under

Any shooting-school coach who can see his pupil's shot charge in the air would, I am sure, testify to the far greater proportion of sporting-type targets that are missed under rather than over. We ourselves, particularly in the case of the closer shots, can often verify that our less workmanlike efforts are the result of shooting too low—seldom indeed are birds tailored, except below and behind. Again, two experienced trap-shooters were quoted to me the other day as concurring in the opinion that, when they were tired, they shot better with the upper barrels of their over-and-unders than they did with the lower. Note that this is the barrel of the superposed weapon which tends to shoot high, sometimes by a very considerable margin.

Gunmaker's duty

I used to say, and I have no doubt that I have said here, that it is the gunmaker's duty to make his guns shoot true to the point of aim; that it is the gun-fitter's duty to ensure that the line of aim comes easily and naturally to the shooter's master eye; and that it is the shooter's duty to learn to point his gun in the right place. I was hard on the gunmaker in this matter, and used to insist that he was perfectly free to play his part in several ways. He could alter the overall slope of the rib. He could, more subtly, modify the vibrational whip of the barrels by changing their external contour. He could even resort to less conventional methods, of which perhaps more later.

I was scarcely less hard on the gun-fitter, who, I considered, should not be expected to compensate for idiosyncratic pointing errors on the part of his client. This, I admit, was a rigid doctrine, but it seemed justified by fact that if the gun did not shoot true, and if the gun-fitter compensated for this, and possibly also for his client's habitual pointing errors, as revealed at the time, the poor shooter would be without any firm basis to work back to if ever he had a bad spell of missing. He would not know where his gun shot, or where his eye was supposed to be, in relation to the line of aim provided by the rib, and could only flounder back to his original form.

A merit

But rigid opinions tend to relax with time, and perhaps it is just as well that they do. If, owing to the ever-present force of gravity and to the frailty and susceptibility to fatigue of the human frame, it is the universal tendency of shooters to shoot low rather than high, it would count as a merit, and not as innaccuracy, if guns threw their charges somewhat above the point of aim, say to the extent of 6 in. or thereabouts at 40 yds. I put this point occasionally in reply to readers' letters, and I believe most gunmakers would agree. In any case, the immediate evidence points to the conclusion that, with a somewhat high-shooting gun, and with everything else unchanged, I am putting rather more pellets in my game. This can only mean that I am shooting more accurately—that I am benefiting from this built-in compensation for an innate low-shooting tendency. True, I may miss over on more occasions, but if I do better on the whole, as I seem to be doing with this new gun so far, I shall have cause for satisfaction.

16 December 1967

cast-off and point of impact

In a previous article ('Choke—a Neglected Aspect') I made the point that unless the user of a full choke could rely on taking his birds or clay targets with the dense, central part of his patterns, he might as well be shooting with a cylinder gun. And in arguing this I was not referring to the wild fringe that accompanies even the best of patterns, but to the outer zone of the familiar 30-in. circle at 40 yds. The margin available for the accommodation of error is indeed small: a mere 10 in. at 40 yds. may be sufficient to bring the target into a part of the pattern where the average density by no means corresponds to the 70 per cent nominally associated with full-choke patterns. It may only be 50 per cent, or even less, which could be equalled or bettered by improved cylinder boring. Conversely, if the shooter with a heavily choked gun is skilful enough to centre his charge on the target, it receives more pellets than the overall pattern density would imply.

But however skilful the shooter, he cannot benefit in this way unless his gun always centres its charge at the point of aim. Two sources of error arise here. In the first place, no gun consistently centres its charge on the same spot in relation to the line of sight from round to round. In other words, the mean point of impact of individual shots (M.P.I.) wanders around erratically, and makes a 'group', just as the bullets from a rifle do. And in the second place, the gun may not group truly at the point of aim.

There is a particular source of error arising in this latter connection which I would like to deal with here. It arises from cast—the lateral bending of gunstocks practised by gunmakers to bring the breech of the gun easily in line with the aiming eye: cast-off when the stock is bent to the right, and cast-on when it is bent to the left.

Non-alignments

It is generally recognized that when a gun is fired and before the charge has left the muzzle, the barrel undergoes vertical movements whereby the line of departure of the shot is not coincident with the centre line of the bore, as positioned immediately before the pulling of the trigger. It is also recognized that these vertical movements are partly due to the jump of the gun as a whole, and partly to the whip or vibration of the barrels. For the moment, I want to forget the whip and concentrate on the jump.

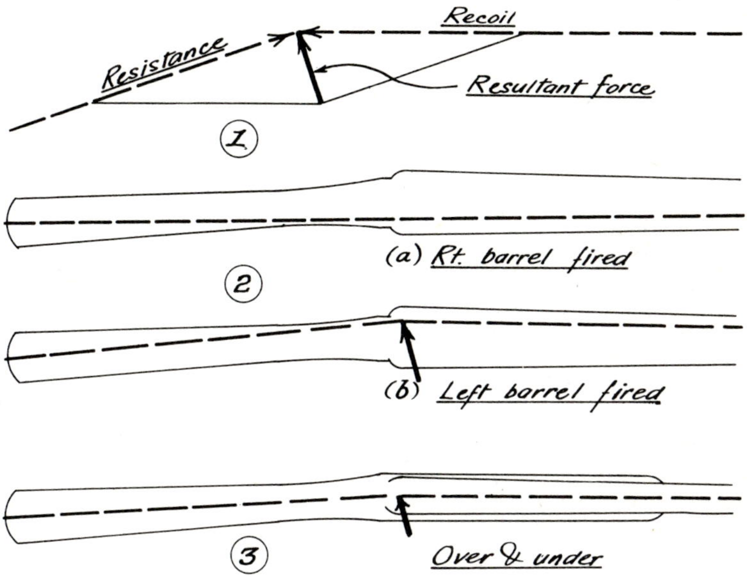

32. CAST-OFF AND POINT OF IMPACT

1. Recoil and resistance out of line produce a resultant force.
2. A cast-off side-by-side does not give rise to a resultant when (*a*) the right barrel is fired, but does so (*b*) when the left is fired.
3. A cast-off O/U gives rise to equal resultants with both barrels.

The downward bending of a gun, as necessary to adapt it to being fired from the shoulder, means that the thrust of the recoil, and the reaction to it offered by the shooter's shoulder, do not take place along the same line. The situation is as represented by my diagram figure 1; and elementary mechanics teaches us that in these circumstances there is a resultant force developed as represented by the heavy arrow. If we regard figure 1 as representing a side view of an ordinary gun, the resultant force will operate to cause an upward jump of the barrels on firing; *but if we regard it as representing a cast-off gun viewed from above, the resultant force will throw the barrels to the left.* This is the basic fact to which I want to draw attention; but in practice it undergoes significant modifications, not only by barrel vibrations, but according to whether the gun is a side-by-side or an over-and-under, and whether the right barrel or the left is fired. Other considerations involved are whether the gun is firing a heavy charge in proportion to its weight or a light one, and also the degree of choke.

Side-by-side

My second diagram, figure 2, represents a side-by-side gun with normal cast-off, viewed from above. Owing to the convergence of the tubes, the axis of the right barrel is in line with the butt, as shown at (*a*). In consequence, there will be no lateral resultant force, and the barrel may be expected to shoot truly for direction. The axis of the left barrel, however, makes a considerable angle with the direction of the recoil-resisting force, as indicated at (*b*), and in this case the gun will be thrown to the left, and will shoot to the left—not much, perhaps, but maybe enough to signify. Owing to the lateral stiffness of the barrels, their vibrations will be substantially confined to the vertical plane, and will not affect these conclusions.

This left-shooting tendency on the part of the left barrels of ordinary side-by-side game guns is most noticeable (*a*) when they carry much choke; (*b*) when shooting a full load, such as the Eley Maximum; and (*c*) at intermediate rather than at full ranges. Light, short-barrelled guns firing lively game cartridges also exhibit it conspicuously. It may even make some small contribution to what I believe is a statistical fact—that more left-crossing birds come to grief than do right-crossing ones.

Over-and-unders

My third diagram, figure 3, represents a similarly cast-off over-and-under. Here, both barrels make the same angle with the line of action of the recoil-resisting force, and both will experience the same thrust to the left. But whether they will actually shoot to the left depends on the incidence of barrel vibrations, which in this case will operate in the horizontal plane. If, at the moment when the charge is leaving the muzzle, the barrel is vibrating to the right, it may neutralize, or even reverse, the effect of the leftward thrust on the gun set up by the cast-off. Further, the incidence of these horizontal vibrations will vary according to whether the gun is firing a light trainer load, a regular $1\frac{1}{8}$-oz trap load, or an Olympic trench load of $1\frac{1}{4}$-oz.

But the upshot may well be that most O/Us carrying appreciable cast-off shoot to the left. As a practical example, I may recall the case of a reader who came to me a year or so ago with the complaint that his Merkel shot conspicuously to the left—if my memory serves, enough to prejudice his performance. The gun was cast-off; and so I recommended him to fit a temporary offset butt-plate to neutralize the cast. He did so, and immediately cured his gun's error.

Points to note

There are several lessons in all this. If you find that the left barrel of your cast-off side-by-side gun shoots to the left, or both barrels of a corresponding O/U, do not blame the gun or the gunmaker—blame the fundamental laws of mechanics. *If you are a serious trapshooter, you may be wise to adopt a straight stock, and to make any necessary adjustment of fit on the comb height.* If you are a game shooter, or a rough shooter, or any kind of choke-addict, you would do well to recognize the facts described as yet another possible impediment to the realization of the full, theoretical advantages of choke boring.

29 April 1967

Note: Evidence coming to light after this article was written suggests that if a gun with a cast-off stock is sufficiently stiff in the grip or 'hand', it will throw to the left, as indicated; but that otherwise the stock may undergo a degree of crumpling under the thrust of the recoil, and thus cancel the effect described, or even reverse it.

spreading shot for skeet

It has from time to time been suggested to me that there is a considerable potential demand in this country for a dispersing or spreader cartridge which would enable trapshooters and others to use their heavily choked guns for skeet or game shooting. The Americans have their 'brush' cartridges and their scatter loads, the Continentals have their *cartouches dispersantes*, but here so far as I am aware, nobody markets anything to correspond. I have indeed heard that there are some of the F.N. wide-shooting cartridges about, loaded with square, or, rather, cubic shot—the so-called *plomb carré*—but at the moment of writing I have not been able to get any confirmation, and it seems that if anyone wants cartridges of this kind he had better be prepared to load his own.

I was accordingly pleased to have an invitation from Mr. M. J. Raymont to see some of these cartridges being tested at his well-known Lower Lake shooting grounds at Upton Cross near Liskeard in Cornwall, which I duly accepted. The results were interesting and encouraging, and seem to be well worth reporting.

Cartridges

Three kinds of 12-bore cartridges were used—Eley Special Trap-shooting, and two others described as standard trap loads but incorporating alternative dispersion devices. The Eley cartridges were fired only to provide a standard of comparison. They were loaded with $1\frac{1}{8}$ oz. of No. 7 shot. Of the two kinds of dispersion cartridges (I do not like the word 'scatter' in this context—it implies a disorderly process rather than the regulated enlargement of spread aimed at), one incorporated a modification of the old Greener plan. The shot charge was divided into four equal parts by three transverse polythene discs, about 15 mils thick. Otherwise the cartridges, which were crimp-closed, were quite normal. The other cartridges used the device favoured by the Americans. The shot charge—also $1\frac{1}{8}$ oz. of No. 7—was again divided into four equal parts, but this time by a cruciform longitudinal spreader, made of thin cardboard which looked as if it had originally formed part of a cartridge carton, and about 30 mils thick. These spreaders are made by cutting two small oblongs of cardboard, the same length and width as the shot column, and fitting them together at right-angles by means of two slits, each running halfway up the mid-line.

The spreaders, as recovered from the ground after firing, looked a good deal thicker than I myself would have thought of using, and I believe there may be a significant point here which I will come to.

Decisive results

All shots were fired at 20 yds., out of consideration for skeet shooting, and, except as indicated later, from the fully choked barrel of an A2 Browning over-and-under. Subject, as always, to the possibility that a different gun or shot size might have given a somewhat different verdict, the results were decisively in favour of the American-type concentrator, as opposed to the Greener. Both gave fairly consistent results, so that only five rounds were fired in each series. But the quality of the patterns thrown by the former was notably superior to that of the latter.

The accompanying pattern diagrams were copied from projected photographs of typical patterns obtained. Diagram *A* was made by ordinary Eley Special Trapshooting cartridge. Diagram *B* was made with the American-type spreader; and diagram *C* was made by another ordinary Eley S.T. cartridge, but fired in this case from the skeet barrel of a Brno over-and-under. The caption gives further data.

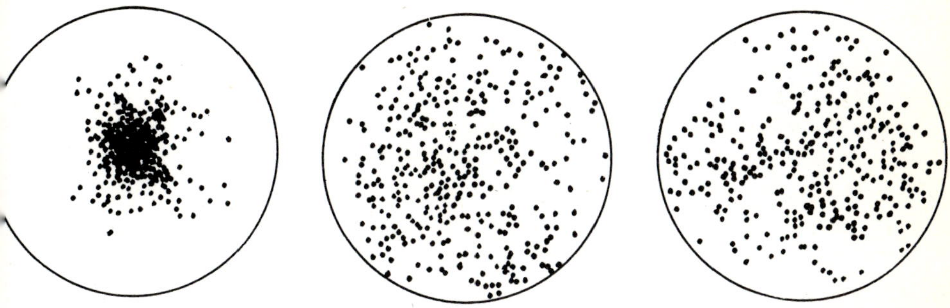

A B C

3. Patterns made in a 30-in. circle at 20 yds. by $1\frac{1}{8}$ oz. of No. 7 shot in each case. *A*. Full-choke barrel, normal cartridge. *B*. Full-choke barrel, spreader cartridge. *C*. Skeet barrel, normal cartridge.

Because of its limited scope, the test could obviously not be regarded as a rigorous examination of the comparative merits of the different spreaders tried; but I think it provides a fair indication that a fully choked gun firing a normal trap load incorporating an American-type spreader, as described, is capable of giving patterns comparable with those of a standard cartridge in a true cylinder or skeet barrel. One-gun owners of heavily choked weapons who are also home-loaders, and who would like to improve their chances at skeet or game, have clearly something worth exploring here.

Speculation

How do these spreaders work? So far as the Greener type is concerned, I would guess that the multiple top-wads, mixing with the shot charge at all angles, and communicating lateral components of the heavy air pressures to which they are subjected to the little groups of pellets they obstruct, cause piecemeal dispersions in unpredictable directions—which is exactly what the resulting patterns look like.

The American-type spreaders seem to work in a different way. I noticed that, after firing, they are heavily indented over the whole of their surface by the pellets of the charge. This is evidently because a charge of shot in a gun behaves to a certain extent like a liquid, converting the forward thrust of the powder gases into a lateral pressure against the bore of the gun, or against any other longitudinal partition, such as these spreaders provide. If the spreader is capable of yielding to this lateral pressure (to which the choke, incidentally, contributes), it will yield; and if it is capable of rebounding, it will rebound.

I believe therefore that when a shot charge associated with such a spreader emerges from the muzzle, the spreader to some extent recovers or rebounds from the heavy compression to which it has previously been subjected, and in so doing effects a regular lateral dispersion of the pellets. If this is a true theory, the degree of dispersion would be amenable to some degree of control by varying the thickness and elasticity of the material used for the spreaders. Further, the spreader would not have to be cruciform: it could be a central core of some elastic material, such as the ebonite rod used, I believe, in the Baschieri & Pellagri dispersion cartridge. Here is an opportunity for some interesting experiments.

26 May 1966

shotgun vagaries

Although most of my correspondents refer to their guns as being of the neuter gender, the rest, without exception, write of them as being feminine. American shooters go further, and freely call their favourite fowling pieces after an eponymous heroine of the name of Betsy. There is matter here for speculation.

Is it that men get fond of their guns, and assign to them the sex that is the natural recipient of men's affections? Or could it be that the shotgun is tacitly recognized as possessing some feminine attributes? A cynic might say that we have something there—capriciousness, unpredictability and a tendency to be swayed by considerations making no appeal to reason, for example. Without endorsing anything that a cynic might impute to our better halves, there is no doubt that something resembling these qualities attaches strongly to the shotgun.

I have here, for example, a normal English game gun. It is a 12-bore with 28-in. barrels and weighs 6 lb. 6 oz. It is bored improved cylinder in the right barrel and half choke in the left. If we look up the tables in *The Shooter's Year Book*, we find some information that should define its performance. The right barrel should put 50 per cent of its charge in a 30-in. circle at 40 yds., and the left 60 per cent. The charge should have a spread of 51 in. and 45 in. respectively at the same distance, and the corresponding effective ranges against partridges should be 42 yds. and 47 yds. True, the gun is a high-quality one, and was required to give a specified performance with a certain charge, so that in all probability it will indeed give that performance *with that charge*—or it will do so provided the charge has been correctly loaded into a normal case, and is associated with the right kind of cap, and good-quality wadding of the proper kind. And provided, too, that the shot is a fair sample, and that the crimp or turnover has been made so as to develop the right resistance.

A matter of statistics

But it must always be understood that, even if all the foregoing provisos are duly fulfilled, the performance of the gun is not to be taken as specific for each shot. Rather it is no more than a statistical evaluation of a series of shots—say, not less than six, and preferably ten. Individual shots within the series may be 5 or 10 per cent up or down from the average, on any point of performance. That is why it is impossible to test a gun by firing a single shot at a newspaper.

And if all the provisos are *not* fulfilled—if the wadding only, for example, is inadequate or defective—then performance may start going badly off the rails. Pattern percentages may fall well below the nominal standard, and pattern quality much farther. Again, an unsuitable cap, which does not give a flame of the volume and temperature necessary to ignite the powder as thoroughly and as quickly as it should be ignited, will lower the ballistics and reduce the effective range. On the other hand, a closure that is too tight, and especially one that has been recklessly sealed with varnish, may raise the pressure to an excessive degree, and scatter the pattern to the winds.

It is not easy to give representative figures to illustrate the effects of abnormalities in loading a proper charge, but I can recall pressures as low as 1·9 tons and as high as nearly 5 tons from allegedly correct quantities of powder and shot in a 12-bore gun. (The right figure should have been about $2\frac{3}{4}$ tons.) And in the course of experiments with wadding, I have had almost everything possible from a given gun, ranging from patterns of correct density and unexceptionable quality, to those which were so patchy as to make hitting a matter of chance—not to mention 'balled' patterns, in which a large part of the charge, fused into contact by hot gases escaping past the wadding, travelled like a solid ball.

Nor is there any guarantee of velocity with a correct charge. For example, in some of my early and misconceived experiments with cork wadding, cartridges otherwise correctly loaded gave muzzle velocities well below the minimum standard necessary for effective use against game.

New possibilities

And when we depart from the charge with which a gun has been regulated, or with which it has been proved in the field to shoot satisfactorily, we enter into a whole new realm of vagaries. Even a moderate change in shot size can produce a significant change in the percentage patterns thrown. For example, a full-choke barrel which gave a 70 per cent pattern at 40 yds. with No. 4 shot should not be expected to give more than about 65 with No. 7. I say *expected*, but then some guns behave unexpectedly in this matter, and display a marked preference for shot of a certain size, with which their performance does not follow the normal trend.

Again, changes in charge weight, though within the normal range for a gun of given bore and chamber length, may produce disproportionate changes in performance. Variations of this sort are usually most conspicuous with guns of liberal bore dimensions within their proof category, and with only a slight degree of choke. A variation of twenty points in the pattern percentage thrown by such barrels by no means exceeds what may be expected with different normal loads —say, as between $1\frac{1}{8}$ oz. of shot in a high-velocity cartridge and 1 oz. in a low-recoil brand. And these are variations in *average* performance with the cartridges in question, and not the differences between top and bottom individual results.

Further, although, as I say, variations of this sort are usually most conspicuous with barrels loosely bored and only slightly choked, they are by no means confined to such barrels. Still, it remains generally true that the more tightly bored and more fully choked barrels tend to exert a firmer and a more consistent control over the performance of the shot charge.

Shooting low

It is not only *how* a gun shoots, but *where* it shoots that may be appreciably affected by changes in the loading within normal limits. If, with the load for which it was designed, a gun shoots true to the point of aim, it may be expected to shoot progressively lower as the load, and more particularly the powder charge, is increased. General Journée, perhaps the greatest authority on shotgun performance who has ever lived, describes some revealing experiments on this subject in his classic, *Tir des Fusils de Chasse.* He took a selection of double guns, and fired them for mean point of impact in relation to point of aim at 10 m., and with progressively increasing powder charges. Theoretically, one would expect the M.P.I. (in a gun without cast) to move outwards and downwards from the appropriate barrel-axis as the charge was increased, and with some curious and unexplained divagations this is substantially what happened. Journée concluded that, beyond a certain charge, all guns shoot lower as the charge is stepped up. ('*Tous les fusils de chasse . . . portent, a partir d'une certain charge, d'autant plus bas que le charge est plus forte.*') With maximum charges, there is always the possibility that the dense centre of choke patterns will pass below the point of aim—a point especially worthy of the attention of shooters who measure their prospects of success in terms of charge weight.

Normality still normal

In all this, I have been chiefly concerned with those vagaries in shotgun performance that can be laid at the door of the cartridge. But the gun, and particularly the boring of the barrels, is capable of making some curious contributions which I have no space to go into now. One example must suffice—the improvement in pattern density and quality observed by Oberfell and Thompson when they deliberately roughened choke tubes, which cuts dead across all expectations.

But there are two things I must emphasize in conclusion—first, that any good gun may be expected to perform at least satisfactorily with any good-quality commercial ammunition designed for it; and secondly, that all shooters should nevertheless test their guns for pattern with any cartridge they intend to use regularly.

19 January 1967

the all-round gun—a will-o'-the-wisp

The tendency of men to seek the realization of their ideals, and to be undeterred by delays, difficulties and disappointments, must assuredly be counted one of the finer manifestations of the human spirit. Recognizing that, I always consider sympathetically the many requests I receive for advice on the choice of an all-round gun.

These requests usually start off in moderate terms. Typically, the writer wants a gun for general mixed shooting in this country. He specifies his usual game—pheasants, pigeon, woodcock and other varieties amenable to the same treatment. He adds that most of it is walked-up. But before I have time to reflect that this looks like an easy case, he adds that he wants to be well equipped to deal with duck 'and the occasional goose'; and for good measure he is quite likely to add that he is interested in clay pigeon shooting in the close season. I suppose that the people who run matrimonial bureaux receive essentially similar requests from those seeking a wife who will be as beautiful as Helen, as wise as Aspasia, as chaste as Diana and as seductive as Phryne—as well as having, as a matter of course, a constitution of iron and the strength of a donkey. The comparison is not far-fetched: such women, I am sure, are comparatively common, whereas guns to the implied specification are simply non-existent.

I have often testified here, in one way or another, to the versatility of the ordinary double-barrelled, double-triggered 12-bore gun, as overwhelmingly favoured in this country: to its instant choice of close or open boring; to the lightness, balance and fast-handling quality that are capable of being built into it; to its supremacy in the matter of sustained fire-power; and to the way in which, without venturing into abnormalities, it can be adapted to specialized duties by choice of weight, boring and chambering. But in this last consideration lies the clue to the impossibility of specifying in detail the all-round gun.

The gun of (nearly) all work

The point can best be brought out by considering a normal English game gun as provided for general mixed shooting in this country, and checking its suitability for all the occasions contemplated by my typical correspondent. The normal gun is fairly represented by a side-by-side hammerless ejector, bored improved cylinder in the right barrel and half to three-quarters choke in the left. It has $2\frac{1}{2}$-in. chambers and 28-in barrels, and it weighs, say, 6 lb. 6 oz. to 6 lb. 8 oz.

Such a gun would be suitable for firing anything from the 1-oz. Impax cartridges to the $1\frac{3}{16}$-oz. Maximum, though the latter would be best confined to strongly built specimens of not less than $6\frac{1}{2}$ lb. in weight. In any event, the gun would be suitable for firing the old standard 12-bore load of $1\frac{1}{8}$ oz., and would thus be in every way suitable and efficient for the whole range of game met with in the course of shooting of the kind under consideration, as well as sporting clays. That, of course, is why it is so popular. Loaded with No. 8 shot, it would cope well with snipe; with No. 6 it would be ideal for pigeon and all medium game; and with No. 5, 4 or 3, it would do well with the larger game and wildfowl, subject, as always, to its being held straight and confined to its proper limits as to range.

In passing, its suitability can always be further enhanced if full use is made of the flexibility provided by its two degrees of choke and its double trigger. I believe that only a minority of shooters do this: the general tendency is to fire the right barrel first in all circumstances. This is excusable with shots that have to be taken very quickly—indeed, it is done by unthinking reflex action. Besides, more often than not, it is the right thing to do, because such shots are usually taken at close to moderate range. But the shooter who has formed the habit of getting off his choke first when it offers the better chance will put more game in the bag than one who neglects this advantage.

The gun with special duties

Much can be done to adapt our normal game gun to special duties by merely altering the boring, and without going in for longer chambers and greater weight. If the emphasis is on driven game, it may be advantageous to have both barrels open-bored. In that case, the gun would also become suitable for skeet. If, on the other hand, wildfowl figure largely on the programme, choke in both barrels is indicated, except, perhaps, for decoy work at moderate range, or duck-shooting by 'tapping-in' to inland pools and streams with good bank cover, when most shots may be taken at close to moderate distances, according to circumstances.

But, of course, any such adaptive modification of our standard game gun is a move in the direction of specialization, and a move away from the all-round gun. So, to an even greater extent, is any increase in the chamber length and weight designed to permit the use of heavier charges. The shooter who seeks *any* extreme in his weapon, whether it be maximum range for flight shooting, maximum spread for skeet, minimum weight for the avoidance of fatigue or minimum recoil for the avoidance of gun-headache, must be prepared to make sacrifices of the all-round gun concept, in one direction or another. This applies with particular force to the trapshooter. The highly specialized nature of his sport really does seem to require a specialized weapon, differently stocked, differently furnished and usually of a different type—that is to say, an over-and-under. The fact that exceptionally gifted individuals, such as Percy Stanbury and the late Herb Parsons, seem to find no difficulty or disadvantage in using a side-by-side double for trapshooting would certainly not justify my encouraging an uninformed enquirer in thinking that this sport can be pursued with any all-round gun.

Evading the compromise

But if the inherent properties of the conventional gun prescribe the terms of the compromise implicit in the idea of all-round utility, it is clear that other types of weapon, with other properties, might offer the desired compromise on better terms. Given sufficient flexibility, they might even enable all compromise to be evaded. The suggestion provokes an enquiry well beyond the scope of this article, in which I can only give an indication as to where it might lead.

A gun, chambered for the heaviest-loaded cartridge required, made of lightweight materials, but avoiding the heavy recoil otherwise implied by the use of a suitable, energy-absorbing moving-breech system and/or a muzzle brake, and fitted with a variable choke on its single barrel, might seem to be ideal. Such weapons, of course, exist, but they are not ideal: it is even doubtful if they offer all-roundedness on better terms than does the conventional gun. In fact, they bring with them a whole new family of disabilities, most of which I have mentioned here from time to time, and which have prevented them from attaining any dominant position in the gun markets of the world. Perhaps a better kind than any we have seen may yet appear. If so, it should be welcomed, and I would like to preserve an open mind. But in the meantime, the all-round gun, strictly so regarded, must be classed with the will-o'-the-wisp and the rainbow's end.

11 March 1965

Section 11

IN THE FIELD

'A sportsman ought to be, and usually is, a man who takes a delight in using a gun and *his brains.'*

(The Badminton Library—*Shooting*)

basic wing-shooting

I fully expected that some observations I once attributed to Messrs. Jennings & Groves, when I reported on their new 'Singlepoint' sight,* would attract comment and questions. These were their observations on the application of their sight to shotguns, . . . in the course of which they said, 'No lead is required, because, in keeping the spot on the target, a perfectly timed swing is ensured right through to the pressing of the trigger. In fact, it has been found that experienced shots, in their first few rounds with Singlepoint, are inclined to shoot ahead of their target because, due to force of habit, they swing the spot ahead. Once this fact is grasped, 100 per cent kills usually ensue.' I recognized at the time that the prospect of attaining 100 per cent kills to cartridges might have some attractions for the average shooter, and so I added a cautionary note. I said, 'I am not to be taken as endorsing this, and the makers themselves are insistent that these observations are only tentative, and that they have much yet to learn about the subtleties of binocular vision in this particular application.' Mr. Groves, with whom I discussed the matter at the time, was emphatic on this point. Still, they had experimented, and these were their findings, and they could do no other than report what they had found.

The interesting thing about their observations is that they appear to re-establish the old cart-wheel theory of shooting moving targets, now, I should have said, thoroughly discredited, and I think it might be useful, particularly to beginners, to run over the various ways in which moving targets can in fact be hit with a gun.

The cart-wheel theory

Having mentioned the cart-wheel theory, perhaps I had better get that out of the way first. It has been attributed to an American wildfowler, presumably a very good shot, who explained his success by

* *Note:* This is a sight, applicable to shotguns, in which a spot of light is projected rearwards into the shooter's right eye, and is superimposed by him on the target as viewed with the left.

saying that he always imagined himself as being situated at the hub of a revolving cart-wheel, the duck being in a position on the rim in line with one of the spokes. All he did to make sure of his duck was to keep his gun moving as if it were part of the spoke concerned, whereupon the shot charge would inevitably and necessarily follow the line of the spoke and duly connect with the target.

I have no doubt that this is what the good American sportsman *thought* he did; but I equally have no doubt that if he actually did it, he would have come home with an empty bag. A few years ago, in fact, I carried out an experiment in which I reproduced the conditions faithfully in miniature. I used a gramophone turntable as my cart-wheel, and fixed a little 'gun' at its centre, capable of projecting a steel ball accurately along the line of an imaginary spoke to a small target situated at the rim. When the turntable was stationary, the ball hit the target every time; but when it was made to rotate, the ball went far behind the mark—all as required by elementary kinematics.

Human complications

There is indeed no difficulty in laying down the law on just how a gun must be pointed and swung to hit a target moving more or less across the line of sight. No experimenting is necessary: the principles concerned are too simple and too well understood for that. But when we introduce the human factor—when we try to reconcile what a shooter tries to do with what he does, and what he does with what he thinks he does—we find that things are no longer simple. Kinematics cannot help us here, except, perhaps, to puncture some illusions.

Undoubtedly the best way to get an insight into these matters is to consider the required movements of the gun first, before examining the complications introduced by the shooter.

There are four basic ways in which a gun may be made to hit a crossing, or partially crossing, target. They are as follows, and are illustrated in my correspondingly numbered sketches on the opposite page.

1. Here the gun is swung so that its muzzle has the same actual speed as the target, whereby it will score a hit if fired when pointed straight at the mark.

2. This is the 'interception' method. The gun is fired when it is stationary and pointed ahead of the target by an amount sufficient to ensure that the shot charge will intercept it in its flight.

3. In this, the 'lead-and-swing' method, the gun is swung to cover

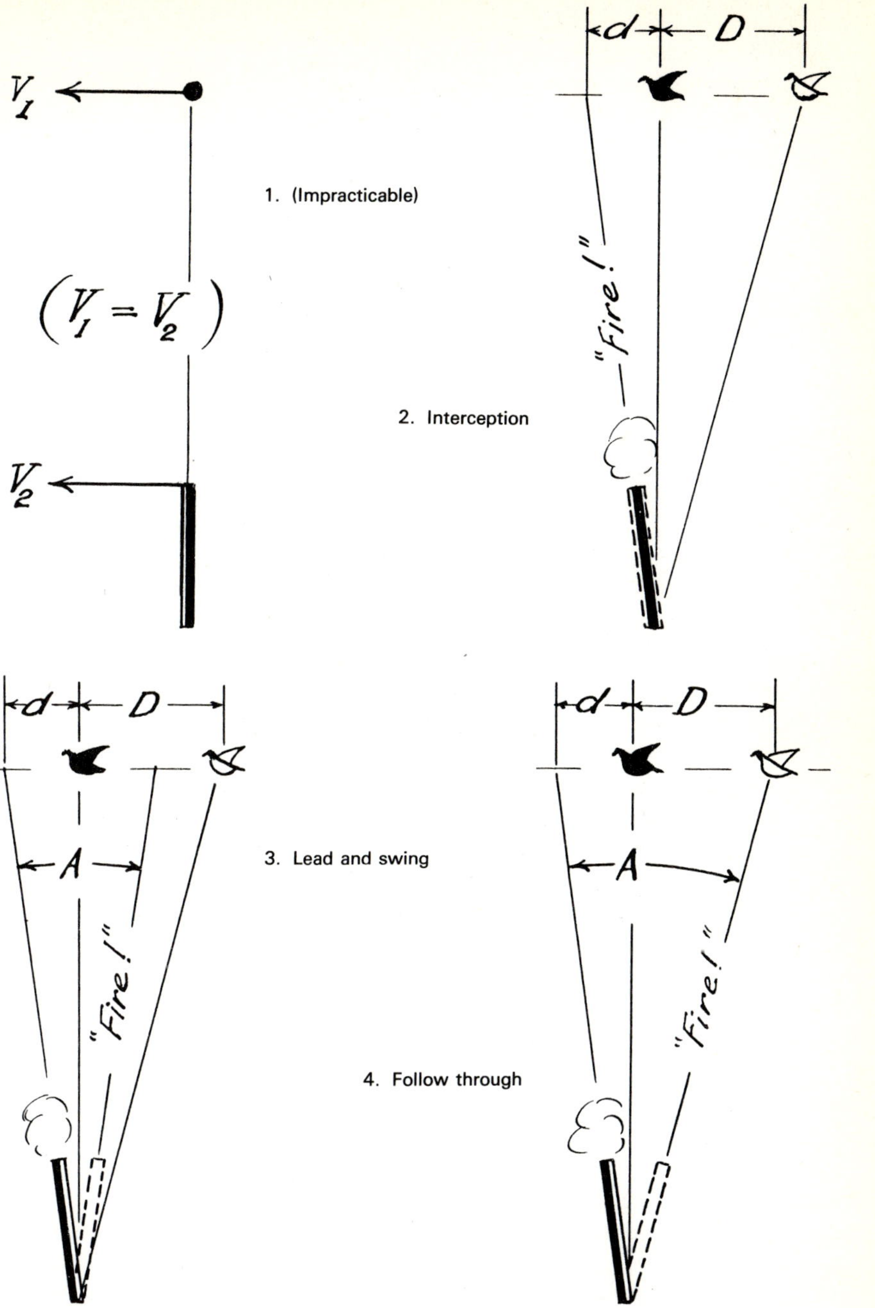

34. BASIC WING SHOOTING

nce travelled by bird during ter's reaction time . . . D

Distance travelled by bird during flight of shot . . . *d*

Angle traversed by gun during shooter's reaction time . . . *A*

and gun at instant of decision oot . . . — *'Fire'*

Bird and gun at instant of discharge

a point a fixed distance ahead of the target, and is fired without any interruption of the swing. (This corresponds to the cart-wheel case, except that the gun is not laid along the spoke pointing towards the target, but along one of the spokes ahead of it.)

4. This is the 'follow-through' method. The gun is swung to overtake the target from behind and to carry on past it, when it is fired at the appropriate distance ahead, as in 1. But this method cannot be fully understood without reference to the shooter, as will be seen.

The shooter's part

Method 1 is not practicable, since, for a full crossing bird, it would be necessary to swing the muzzle at 30 or 40 or even more miles an hour, which simply could not be done.

The interception method (2) gets used for quick snap-shots. Its great defect is that it is at the mercy of any changes in the shooter's reaction time, due to food and drink or fatigue, etc. From the time his brain says 'Fire' to the time he actually pulls the trigger may be only a quarter of a second when he is rested and alert. After lunch, say, it could well be a third of a second. If he still used the same lead, he would miss a 30 m.p.h. crossing bird by over $3\frac{1}{2}$ ft. behind.

The lead-and-swing method (3) gets over this difficulty. It is not only independent of changes in the shooter's reaction time but also of variations in the ignition time of his weapon. It must have been the regular technique of the old flintlock shooters, who otherwise could never have had their wonderful successes. Even today, it is the standard practice of many shooters—perhaps most of them—but is recognized as inferior to the follow-through method for fast work, particularly at driven game. It tends, indeed, to a slower style, and is, of course, absolutely dependent on the maintenance of the swing.

The great merit of the follow-through method (4) is that it enables the shooter to think that he is shooting straight at his bird. He does indeed give the mental order to fire at that instant, but his reaction time, plus the ignition time of his gun, ensures that an interval, perhaps about a quarter of a second, will elapse before the shot leaves the muzzle, by which time the gun will have raced ahead to give the appropriate lead.

The method would appear at first sight to be doubly vulnerable: first, by variations in the shooter's reaction time, and, secondly, by variations in the speed at which he swings his gun past the target; but there is a compensatory principle at work here which does not seem to be generally understood, but which reduces the net effect of these variations. Thus, if, because of fatigue or the like, the shooter slows down his rate of swing, his reaction time is also likely to have increased. So, if he still says to himself 'Fire' as his gun points at the target, his gun, though moving more slowly, will have more time to race ahead before it goes off. The upshot is that this is probably the best and most consistently successful technique to those who practise it.

Some conclusions

Coming back to the 'Singlepoint' sight, since this cannot in any way affect the kinematics of shotgun shooting, it can only affect the subjective aspect, and I believe that it merely makes shooters using the follow-through method more conscious of the fact, as I said at the time. As for the American cart-wheel shooter, I have long been convinced that he also used this method, and received the same impression of shooting straight at his birds.

There are two points that I should mention in conclusion. First, that it is possible to combine some of the methods described. For example, with very tall birds, I think there is a tendency to adopt a lead-and-swing technique, reinforced by a follow-through urge at the last moment. Secondly, on the kinematics side, there are some factors of a second order of importance which I have ignored for simplicity.

30 March 1968

the master eye

Whenever I come across a writer on shooting going through the time-honoured ritual of explaining the master-eye doctrine, I shift uneasily in my seat and feel my didactic prickles rising. The latest occasion was in a new American publication. There the writer, aided by a photograph of a nice, clean American male instructing a charming feminine neophyte, explained how, by pointing at an object with both eyes open, and then closing them successively without moving the finger, it can be demonstrated that one eye—the 'master'—alone determines the direction of pointing, and must be afforded facility for doing the same with a gun. There the young couple, who would understandably have more interesting things to discuss, were dismissed as having fulfilled the whole purpose of their demonstration.

I noticed that in the photograph the young woman was pointing with her right hand and arm; and it may be comfortably taken that, like most people, she was right-eyed. In that event, if she decided to pursue her man by taking up his hobbies, and was fitted out with a normal gun, all would have been well within the present context. But if not—if, for example, she turned out to be right-handed and left-eyed, or right-handed and equal eyed, *which the test described might have failed to reveal*—she would have had trouble with her shooting until her case was truly diagnosed. If only for a minority, therefore, this business of master eye is worth pursuing a little further.

Basis of mastery

Mastery on the part of one eye may well have a physical basis. There are several links in the visual chain: the optical lens which projects an image on to the retina, the retina which converts the light image into nerve impulses, the nerves connecting the retina to the brain, and the visual centre of the brain itself; and it is clear that there can be some condition or derangement affecting one or more of these links which reduces the efficiency of the eye concerned, and leaves the other in a state of dominance—at least, for so long as the condition or derangement persists.

But even if there is no such specific basis for mastery, mastery usually exists. Why, I can only speculate; but I believe that it is a consequence or a homologue of right- or left-handedness. When our anthropoid ancestors adopted an erect posture and thus freed their fore-limbs from all locomotive duties, so that they became the direct and active agents of the brain, a bias in favour of one hand or the other acquired a survival value. Ambidexterity might be all very well, and even advantageous, for peaceful and deliberate activities; but in sudden emergencies it might well involve split-second hesitations that could be fatal. So, I take it, our brains developed a bias, but one not derived from any structural modification. My medical friends, indeed, assure me that autopsy reveals no traces of any such modification. Yet, even without it, the bias can be very strong, and one would expect it to be reflected in other functions controlled by the same brain. One would expect, for example, a right-handed man to be to some extent right-footed or right-legged as well as right-eyed. If he were left-eyed, one would look for some defect in his right, if only a degree of astigmatism, say, not present in the other.

Theory

But, strong though it may be in relation to its primary purpose, the brain-bias that determines right- or left-handedness has strict limitations. It does not weaken the other hand or impair its capacity for skilled activity, except as determined by use and habit. The boxer, the games player, the typist, the violinist or pianist—all or any of these making regular use of their left hands find them in no way inferior to their right, even though they may be strongly right-handed in the ordinary sense. Still less, therefore, would one expect the left eye of a right-handed, right-eyed person to be incapacitated from taking charge of a particular operation, subject to training and to its having no specific defect.

So, I believe that anyone possessing two good eyes, free from any inequality of which they are ordinarily conscious, should not be deterred from using a normal gun from the appropriate shoulder merely because his master eye *appears*, from the simple test first described, to be on the other side. In the first place, the test may be delusory: it may be unduly influenced by which arm does the pointing. And even if it is not delusory, the other eye can usually—and sometimes very easily—be trained to take over, being much aided in this by the presentation of a gun barrel beneath it, which acts as a signal or command to it to do so.

Practice

The foregoing is not merely theory: I have proved it in practice and by repeated experiments over the years. Typical results were obtained with the help of two schoolgirl nieces staying with me while this article was being written. Rosemary and Catherine are 17 and 15 years old respectively. They are both bright girls, but are innocent of any knowledge of guns or shooting, and thus had the great merit of not knowing what was expected of them. Both are normally right-handed. Doing the usual pointing test, using the right arm, revealed that R. was decidedly right-eyed and C. left-eyed. Repeating with the left arm showed R. to be still right-eyed, though rather less decidedly so, while C., of course, remained left-eyed.

The experiments were then repeated, with the addition of a 2-in.

strip of blackened plywood, with a $\frac{1}{2}$-in. hole at one end, and used as a peep-sight. With the peep-sight at her left eye and pointing with her left arm, R. changed from right-eyed to left-eyed—repeatedly and consistently. Conversely, when pointing with her right arm and with the peep-sight at her right eye, C. changed from left-eyed to right-eyed. Both girls, of course, had both eyes open and unobstructed all the while, except for checking the direction of pointing.

These experiments fairly indicate the way in which the non-master eye is capable of responding to a signal to take charge. A gun-breech and gun barrel can well provide such a signal.

Of course, it may be objected that these subjects were both young and adaptable girls, whereas a mature man might find it almost impossible to accomplish any corresponding switch. But the several correspondents who have written to me about their master-eye problems may reasonably expect to be able to train either of two good and apparently equal eyes to take charge, subject to snapping and aiming practice with the other eye slightly dimmed. Half shutting it may do, though it is possible that a pair of tinted glasses with one lens removed might do better.

7 July 1966

'pointability' in guns

A curious recurring phenomenon in my correspondence is presented by those readers who tell me that, although they shoot happily with both eyes open when using an ordinary side-by-side gun, they feel an urge to close the non-aiming eye when using an over-and-under. They may even find that they have to do so if they are to maintain their standard of performance.

This, added to several other observations that I have in mind, suggests to me that it might be well to take a critical look at accepted doctrine on the subject of the 'pointability' of guns, which, it can readily be shown, is inconsistent with experience.

But first we must be clear on what we mean by pointability. This is not a dictionary word, and so I can only offer my own definition. I should say therefore that pointability in a shotgun is that quality which enables the shooter to direct it *visually* as required in relation to the target.

As for the accepted doctrine, it appears to comprise three main articles, namely:

1. Long guns are more pointable than short.
2. A gun with a single or narrow 'sighting plane' is more pointable than one with a double or broad sighting plane. (This is usually taken to mean that a single-barrelled gun or an over-and-under is more pointable than a side-by-side double.)
3. Pointability may be improved by sighting devices, such as raised and/or file-cut ribs and foresights, as well as by certain adventitious features, notably conspicuous hammers or standing breeches so fashioned as to serve as backsights, or even muzzle attachments.

Long barrels versus short

I have little to say on the first point of the doctrine under review, except that I believe the superior pointability of long barrels is exaggerated by their advocates. In the act of shooting, the eye is ill situated to judge the length of the barrel; indeed, I doubt if a man putting a strange gun to his shoulder with his eyes closed, and then opening them, could form any reliable idea of the barrel length. But what the eye is well situated to judge is *angular* movement and *angular* lead as necessary for shooting, and these are the same for long barrels as for short. I have recently been doing some shooting, for the first time, with 25-in. barrels, and I cannot say that I find them in any degree less pointable than 30-in.

Inconsistencies

But it is the second article of the familiar doctrine, as stated, that is chiefly open to criticism. There is indeed a broad mass of historical fact and practical experience that cannot be reconciled with the alleged superior pointability of the single-barrelled or O/U gun. Thus the O/U, the obvious and original form of double gun, was evolved when sitting targets were the only kind attempted. When improvements in ignition made wing-shooting feasible the side-by-side double totally superseded the older weapon—this, be it noted, during the muzzle-loading era, when it was as easy to make guns one way as the other. It is inconceivable that a weapon of inferior pointability should have been deliberately adopted for a more difficult kind of sport, unless it had some marked advantage in another direction, sufficient to cause its particular weakness to be overlooked. But in that event it would have been quickly found out, and the earlier form would have been revived, if only as a rival form possessing an important advantage. As we know, nothing of the sort happened, and the side-by-side double long remained, and still remains, the favoured weapon of the large majority of British and Continental game shooters, including many of the leading pigeon shooters of the Mediterranean countries. The known preferences of these latter, engaging, as they do, in what may well be the most exacting of all kinds of competitive shooting, on which there is the heaviest betting, are alone sufficient to challenge conventional pointability doctrine.

What the eye sees

The facts of experience and the fallacies of unthinkingly repeated views on pointability may be expressed in the following simple propositions, which anyone can easily verify for himself by practical experiment.

1. *A single barrel (or the upper barrel of an O/U) is, by itself, nearly or completely unpointable under normal open-sky conditions.* When a clean, blued barrel is viewed as in Fig. 35 opposite, a zone of sky, as marked AA, is reflected back to the eye from the surface of the barrel with very little loss of intensity. If the sky BB surrounding the forward end of the barrel is of the same shade as that at AA, the barrel will be substantially invisible to an eye focused on a distant target, and the only pointable thing will be the foresight. (Try this with an ordinary gun turned over sideways.)

2. *A rib on a single barrel (or O/U) is useless as an aid to pointability except so far as its surface is non-reflecting.* If a rib has a reflecting surface like that of the barrel, it will simply acquire a corresponding degree of invisibility under the conditions assumed. It is not enough that the surface should be matted or knurled: some such finishes have little more than a token value. But a really deeply file-cut rib makes an eminently pointable dark strip or line.

3. *On the other hand, a rib on a double barrel, even if it has a fully reflecting surface, can be strongly pointable by virtue of the deep shadows cast on either side of it.* The higher the rib, the stronger the shadows.

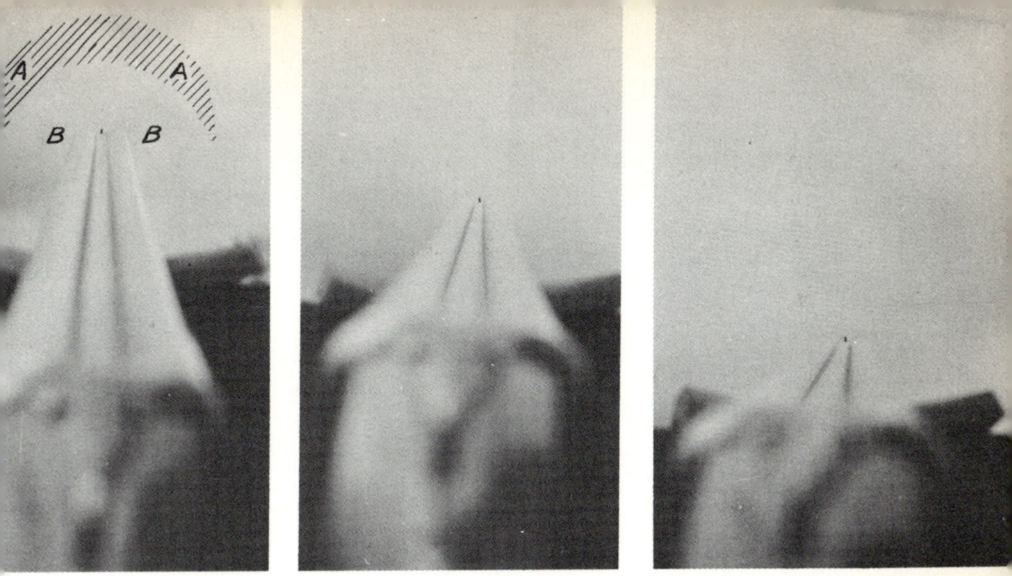

35. POINTABILITY IN GUNS

ree stages in preparing to shoot. *Left* Individual barrels, even at this stage, are rendered nearly invisible by ylight reflected from zone A-A. *Centre* The rib itself is no more visible than the barrels. *Right* At the oment before firing, the barrels are invisible, and pointability depends entirely on the strong shadows outlining the rib and on the foresight.

ote: The gun was a normal gun with well-blued barrels and a plain hollow rib. The sky was overcast. The camera was focused on the foresight.

Hence the success of the old Manton elevated rib: it made the double gun more pointable than it had ever been before. The high, narrow Churchill rib is exceptionally pointable for the same reason. To achieve something of the side-by-side gun's pointability in an O/U, the Browning people have reproduced the essential features of its appearance in their 'Broadway' model by using a very broad rib with two deep, longitudinal grooves in it—a graceful compliment to a rival type of weapon!

Sighting devices

I have no criticism to offer of the third article of the common doctrine, as set out above. But these aids should not be overworked. If they are, they may attract *conscious* attention to the gun, and thus defeat their purpose, which should be to raise its subconscious visual impact to the optimum level, but not beyond. What that level is depends partly on lighting conditions.

* * *

I think it will be clear to anyone who makes a few experiments on the lines indicated that there is no evidence of any superior pointability on the part of single barrels or O/Us. Failing a really effective non-reflecting rib, or other surface, there is less, as my correspondents first mentioned appear to have found out. The popularity of the O/U among trapshooters must be sought elsewhere—probably in its second barrel's high-shooting tendency, not to mention certain non-ballistical factors outside the scope of this article.

14 July 1966

mind, eye and gun

Recently, John Marchington wrote truly of the importance of the right mental state in shooting—of the need to set worries and distractions aside, and to concentrate on the task in hand. He might have added something about the kind and degree of concentration necessary for the best results, for that is hardly less important. There is a principle here which my little springer bitch, Shelagh, brings home to me very nicely at times.

When I am sitting under a hedgerow, eating my pocket lunch, I occasionally throw her bits of crust, which she catches with nonchalant ease. She is, indeed, a bonny catcher, and provided I give her a reasonably good throw she never misses. I notice, incidentally, that in maintaining this high level of performance, she does not squint along her muzzle in order to point her nose at the right place in relation to the flying fragment, nor, I am sure, is she in the slightest degree concerned whether her said muzzle affords her a broad or a narrow sighting plane. Her whole attention is obviously concentrated on the piece of crust: what follows is left to the subconscious working of her co-ordinative machinery. For all practical purposes, as I say, it never fails.

Another story

But when I mentioned crusts, I did so deliberately, for it is not necessarily the same with other offerings. For example, even among dogs, Shelagh is notable for a very sweet tooth, and if I round off my lunch with a bit of butterscotch or the like, her attitude undergoes a marked change. As I unwrap the toothsome morsel, the pupils of her eyes dilate, and she visibly stiffens as she concentrates her whole being on the possibility of its coming her way. And if I indulgently throw it to her—this thing that she so much desires—she makes a fierce bite at it, and as often as not misses it clean! There, indeed, I see her master, fairly reflected! If ever I am more than ordinarily anxious not to miss a particular bird—if my concentration is too tense; if it lacks the redeeming measure of detachment or relaxation—then I am almost certain to do what I am so anxious not to do. It would seem that what is really needed is not concentration, but something more diffuse—say, preparedness, but a relaxed preparedness.

And yet another

There is, of course, an essential difference between a dog catching things thrown and a man shooting at moving targets. The dog operates entirely with her own physical facilities, all under the direct control of her brain, whereas the man has to use an intermediary in the shape of a gun. And it is odd that, even now, we do not all know or cannot all agree, exactly what part can best be assigned to the gun in this combined operation called shooting, in which eyes, brain, nerves and muscles count for at least as much as the gun itself.

It is possible, for example, for the connection between gun and shooter to be entirely muscular and tactile—dependent, that is to say, solely on the muscular sense of position aided by the sense of touch. Respectable shooting can undoubtedly be done in this way, for example, by shooting from the hip at rabbits bolting in covert. There was even the American instructor who could shoot skeet blindfold, merely by listening to the sound of the trap release, and letting off his gun in the familiar direction after the familiar interval.

There must be many—driven game shooters in particular—who would say that they shoot in essentially the same way, except that they substitute a sight of the bird for the sound of the trap and prior knowledge of the target's path. In other words, they would say that they are in no way dependent on, or conscious of, any sight of the gun in the act of shooting.

Fitting unnecessary?

Yet these are the very shooters who go to most pains to ensure that their guns really fit them, so that, when they are thrown up, the rib is accurately aligned with the eye. If these shooters were really independent of any sight of their barrels, much of the business of fitting, as commonly understood, would be unnecessary. All that would be needed would be to fit the gun for an easy presentation posture and for the comfortable absorption of recoil. The shooter, having then found out by trial at the plate or otherwise just where his gun shot *in relation to his muscular and tactile sensations,* could go right ahead. Apart, perhaps, from having adopted a more comfortable posture, he would be on all-fours with the hip-shooter.

But that, I am sure, would never do. It would certainly not do for me, even though I count myself among those who are independent of any sight of the gun—at least, when I am shooting well and quickly. I can only conclude that *we all, to some extent, rely on the visual alignment of our guns—the aimers or 'pokers' consciously, the trap shooters semi-consciously, and the fast workers at driven game subconsciously.*

But if we admit this, the question properly arises as to whether the subconscious view of the gun can in any way be exploited to aid accurate shooting? This is where the rib merchants come in. Perhaps they are right—at least for themselves—in the importance they attach to this widely disregarded feature of the double gun. And then, what about the foresight? Are we right in allowing the best gunmakers to vie with one another in reducing this vestigial object to the vanishing point? Perhaps some of us might do better with a thing like the American 'Raybar' sight, which glows like the carbuncle in my old-fashioned tie-pin, and is almost as large.

A long-lost view

I raise this matter, not by way of idle speculation, but because of a disconcerting experience I had the other day. I was doing a bit of swinging and snapping practice in my study, and I happened to be wearing a pair of long since superseded reading glasses. As my eyes are now, these glasses give me a needle-sharp vision of things about 4 ft. away; and on the occasion mentioned they presented me with a view of the muzzle and foresight of my gun which I realized I had not had for years. I could not help thinking that such a sharp picture, even if only subconsciously seen, might be a much more valuable aid to gun alignment than is the relatively muzzy picture I see in the ordinary way.

There are indeed times when none of us see much of our guns, consciously or otherwise. When shooting in the open, reflected skylight often makes the barrels become nearly, or even completely, invisible. Under these conditions, the foresight and the groove on either side of the rib are the only things to be seen. Without them—and in some guns they amount to very little—the shooter would be reduced to the hip-shooter's method of pointing by unaided instinct.

It could well be advantageous in such circumstances to increase the subconscious visual impact of the gun—perhaps by merely adding a more conspicuous foresight, which would be a very easy thing to try. But it would be necessary to avoid making the gun *too* conspicuous, for this might draw conscious attention to it, and thus encourage an aiming or poking tendency, with its inevitable loss of speed and accuracy. This may explain the inconclusive nature of the experiment of making the top rib of a gun stand out by running a length of sticky white tape along it. The carbuncular Raybar could also fall down on the same account.

5 May 1966

shooting ailments

Guns, like some horses, can do damage at both ends. Apart from their effect on the object of pursuit, they can inflict anything from discomfort to severe pain on their users—to such an extent, indeed, as to rule out shooting as a rational amusement. What is more, a given gun-cartridge combination which one man may find comfortable to use may be objectionable to another, apart from any obvious explanation based on the fit of the gun, or on the fitness, physique or robustness of constitution of the shooter.

Gun headache is, of course, the chief of these shooting ailments. It is also the most baffling, as evidenced by the absence of any generally accepted diagnosis, notwithstanding the number of eminent medicos who have also been shooting men, and have been moved to express opinions on the subject. Burrard quotes the late Dr. C. J. Heath, a past President of the Wildfowlers' Association, as being of the opinion that gun headache is nothing more than mild concussion produced by repeated recoil. Major Hugh Pollard is of the same opinion: gun headache, he says, is simply a total of minor concussions. Churchill, because of his great experience as a coach, is worth quoting at length. In the latest edition of his book, *Game Shooting*, he says, 'Once, when a great variety of powders were available, some would claim that they were headache-free from using one brand, and others swore by another; but there was no agreement on the universal panacea for gun-headache. There couldn't be, because the powder in the cartridge is not the cause of it. Recoil, the note of vibration of the explosion, are all called in to account for the trouble; but, actually, gun headache is simply the consequence of a fault of style. It means that the shooter is taking the recoil shock with a loosely held head. Set the head down into the shoulders, though without raising the shoulders; stiffen the neck muscles, and gun headache will vanish.'

Not so easy

All these opinions are probably valid so far as they go. Churchill's experience, in particular, may have justified him in believing that he had found the main cause and the appropriate cure. But his own experience, as revealed in the observations I have quoted, should have shown him that he was not in possession of the whole story. 'Some would claim,' he says, 'that they were headache-free from using one brand (of powder).' Surely, if reputable witnesses, having no possible axe to grind, say that in certain circumstances they are free from headache, their evidence should be accepted; and if it is inconsistent with some preconceived theory, the theory should be modified to accommodate it.

Similarly, the cumulative minor concussion theory is inadequate to cover certain types of case. We not only have those last quoted, in which a mere change from, say, a slow-burning to a fast-burning powder effects a cure, as it sometimes does, without in any way affecting the number and severity of the concussions (unless indeed it were to make them *more* severe), but we also have those curious cases in which the headache appears to arise from what is heard, rather than what is felt in the way of recoil. For example, one of my correspondents complained of getting a headache by merely firing a single shot from a Browning two-shot automatic. I myself find the metallic ring given out by these guns in certain circumstances curiously painful, even when standing 2 or 3 yds. away, and I can well imagine how much more painful they might be to a sensitive ear right alongside the receiver, from which the noise—apparently a sharp, metallic impact—seems to come. Blast, too, particularly from muzzle brakes, can be decidedly distressing. So, even accepting it as a fact that the mechanical jolt of the recoil is the main predisposing cause, we cannot rule out a number of other causes.

Liver and migraine

So far I have not mentioned that marvellous biochemical factory, the liver, which is stated to have at least 500 known functions, to which additions are constantly being made. It seems most unlikely that the liver can be directly provoked by shooting into causing its owner a headache; but I am certain that, by some malfunctioning or special activity, induced maybe by over-indulgence in food or drink, or by an east wind or sudden drop in temperature, it is capable of giving rise to a *tendency* to gun headache. Let those who cultivate hangovers testify! They might stiffen their neck muscles to a state of total rigidity and yet find it agonizing to bring an empty gun smartly into their shoulders, let alone fire it.

Migraine sufferers, too, seem particularly prone; but I suspect that they are only a special case within the liver bracket, for my own experience suggests that the liver plays a leading part in this distressing complaint. It also suggests that the migraine subject, above all others, is likely to be sensitive to the kind of powder he uses—whether it is fast-burning or otherwise. The principle here is the one to which I have referred more than once when dealing with recoil. It is the principle that things capable of causing sensation, or it may be pain, can fail to register fully on the nervous system if only they are fleeting enough. So the migraine man, having done everything else he can to avoid trouble—having checked the firmness of his hold and of his neck muscles, and eschewed heavy or high velocity loads—would be well advised to try a cartridge loaded with the fastest-burning powder he can get, which, in the Eley range, is Neobel No. 1. The Impax cartridge, loaded with a flat ounce of shot and with this powder, is, I believe, the best readily available answer to gun headache.

Eley headache powder

For example, I am not a migraine sufferer, but I get a touch of it occasionally, as I did one morning last week, when I went out to see if I could find a woodcock. (I am writing in January.) I was rather dreading letting my gun off when a 'cock offered me a chance of a lightning snap-shot, which I successfully took before I had a chance to think or hesitate. I was pleased with the shot and with my spaniel's quick find and efficient retrieve; and it was only when I had put the bird in the bag that I realized that the shot, far from giving my head the painful twinge I had expected, had, quite clearly in retrospect, momentarily *suspended* the pain. This was an Impax cartridge in a 6 lb. 3 oz. gun, and a most efficient combination against game; but how efficient it might have proved as a headache cure if I had gone on to fire 100 such rounds, I am not, of course, in a position to say.

Minor ailments

I have devoted most of my available space to gun headache because of its distressing and frequently elusive nature. But if they are more easily diagnosed and cured, some of the other shooting ailments can be both painful and troublesome.

Bruising, for example. Some of my young readers come to me with bruised shoulder trouble due simply to their stuffing their $2\frac{3}{4}$-in. chambered 12-bores with loads out of all reasonable proportion to the gun's weight. To keep recoil within reasonable limits, a fixed-breech gun needs 6 lb. of weight for every ounce of shot.

Bruising of cheekbone or arm is a different matter, and is usually due either to a badly fitting stock or to incorrect mounting or hold, or possibly to a combination of these causes. It can only be diagnosed by observation of the victim in action . . . though an experienced man could, in many cases, identify a particular stock as likely to give trouble with a man or boy of known physique.

Bruising of the second finger usually suggests a stock that is too short, though it can be exaggerated by a badly shaped trigger guard or by a loose hold. The well-known Southampton gunsmith and coach, Mr. G. T. Cox, has suggested that to cure loose hold or prematurely relaxed hold, the shooter should mentally count, *bang*, one, two, three, before relaxing his grip. The more familiar remedy is a little rubber cushion of the kind sold for the purpose.

Some users of long-recoil automatics also seem to suffer from excessive or objectionable recoil—even from a $7\frac{1}{2}$-lb. gun firing an ounce of shot! In this case, which came to my notice only the other day, I suspect that the main trouble was excessive lubrication of the magazine tube.

But, broadly, if only one can steer clear of gun headache, the other troubles are amenable to expert diagnosis and cure.

3 March 1966

Section 12

RANGE

'I am sure that many a man forms an unduly low opinion of his ability, and much reduces his average of kills to cartridges, not because he deliberately fires at birds that are out of range, but because he simply cannot judge when they are.'

36. Vertical range is commonly over-estimated. Pheasants coming over this *Wellingtonia Gigantea* would often be considered out of shot; but the tree is no more than 114 ft. (38 yds.) high. The figure arrowed is that of a tallish woman.

estimating range

Range is a matter of vital concern to the user of the shotgun—not so much because of its relatively low muzzle velocity, but rather because of the extremely rapid falling-off in the effectiveness of the charge of shot, partly by loss of velocity and partly by the scattering and stringing of the pellets. From one point of view, this rapid loss of effectiveness is a merit: without it, shooting as a social amusement would hardly be feasible in a densely populated country. As it is, no matter how many shots are fired from a particular location, or in what direction, nobody beyond a couple of hundred yards, say, can possibly get hurt.

But as between the shooter and his quarry, this characteristic imposes severe limitations. A particular gun and charge of powder and shot that may be effective at 40 yds. may well be highly inefficient at 50 and totally useless at 60; for even if the individual pellets retain sufficient velocity, and therefore energy and penetrating power, at this last range, they are likely to have lost the coherence necessary for a killing pattern.

In these circumstances, one would expect that shotgun users as a body would have developed a highly realistic attitude towards the matter of range, as determining the kind of gun, the weight of charge and the degree of choke necessary for the effective pursuit of a given kind of game in given circumstances. One would also expect them to regard an ability to judge distances instantly and accurately as a prime qualification for using a gun; but in fact these things are undoubtedly not so.

Doctrinaire notions

It is impossible to read many shooting books without coming up against a body of doctrinaire opinions on the subject of the ranges involved in shooting. The most familiar of these is that wildfowling involves long shots—much longer than game shooting. From this springs the idea that success in wildfowling depends on a heavy, long-cased, fully choked gun, firing maximum charges of large shot. The truth is that although wildfowling in certain circumstances requires the longest possible reach, and the delivery of the heaviest possible blow, there is a great deal of duck-shooting, at least, which can be most efficiently, conveniently and comfortably enjoyed with an ordinary game gun. One distinguished duck-shooter I have in mind, who probably shot more duck in a season than the average coastal gunner shoots in a lifetime, used an ordinary game gun and No. 7 shot. His success came from a realistic assessment of the conditions of his particular kind of sport.

Another rigid opinion, to which I am surprised that Burrard lent himself, is that whereas driven birds are usually taken at short range, in rough shooting 'the long shot is the rule'. Although much depends on individual circumstances, a long and varied experience of rough shooting has convinced me that this long-shot tradition is utterly false; that the rough shooter who arms himself in conformity with it is at a disadvantage; and that, in any case, it is a bad tradition to inculcate in the beginner to whom these remarks are chiefly addressed, as encouraging him in the idea that he is expected to take long shots when rough shooting. Taking one kind of sport with another, the rough shooter who is a good tactician, who beats his ground the right way, and above all, who *keeps quiet*, will have his full share of close shots.

As for judging distances, and particularly heights, I believe the average standard is low. I am sure that many a man forms an unduly low opinion of his ability, and much reduces his average of kills to cartridges, not because he deliberately fires at birds that are out of range, but because he simply cannot judge when they are. And if the standard for distances is low, that for heights is lower. On the one hand, pheasants are described as 'archangels' when they are perhaps only 30 yds. up or less. This does no harm; but on the other hand, flighting duck are fired at at the most impossible ranges, sometimes quite innocently.

The beginner can build up his distance-judging ability in two ways. He should find out by measurement what is the length of his average pace. He should then, on his walks, frequently estimate, and then proceed to check, the distance of various objects that lie in his path. This is amusing as well as good practice.

Heights are more difficult. A well-grown hedgerow elm of fair height may be 25 yds.; the village church spire may be 30; a local factory chimney or 'folly' may be 35. These things can usually be checked and advantageously studied. Again, the width of the muzzle-end of the barrels of a 12-bore gun at 40 in. from the eye covers about 30 in. (say, the wing-span of a mallard) at 20 yds. With this knowledge, and a little rule-of-three figuring, some useful range-finding can be done.

15 March 1963

effective range

A correspondent's recent question about the 'maximum killing range' of his gun, which I had to translate into maximum *effective* range before I could begin to deal with it, has made me wonder whether it is possible to lay down any maximum killing range for a shotgun. I doubt it. It would first be necessary to define the term. The maximum killing range of a gun, one might begin, is the maximum range at which—what?—could be killed—and by what? Is it the greatest range at which the smallest and most delicate bird ever likely to be pursued with the gun in question could be killed by the largest ball that would fit the bore? Hardly, for that would run us into hundreds of yards. Or is it the greatest distance at which the same bird, or some other bird, could be killed by the largest size of shot (whatever that may be) normally used in its pursuit? That sounds more reasonable, but it nevertheless lands us plump into the region of freak shots. Single pellets, penetrating by easy routes into the vital regions of birds or animals, can sometimes produce spectacular results, beyond all reasonable expectation. If only a man fires a sufficiently large number of cartridges at excessive ranges, he will in time bring off enough freak shots of this kind to start a saga in which the leading role may be assigned to himself, his gun, or even his brand of cartridges. No part, be it noted, will be assigned to those birds which, though fairly centred in what remained of the pattern, were only wounded.

In the days when gunmakers published far more testimonials than they do now, one saw much of this kind of thing in the tribute of enthusiastic users, recounting their fabulous shots. Yet, when discounted for that human weakness which tends to make us all extol our more cherished personal possessions (and, by implication, the judgement, etc., with which we acquired them), such accounts afford little evidence of the real capacity of a gun, which can only be defined in terms of the *maximum effective range*, or the range within which it is reasonably certain that a given bird will be killed if fairly caught by the pattern made by a given load. The table of effective ranges given in the I.M.I. *Shooter's Year Book*, though it makes less exciting reading than testimonials of the kind to which I have referred, should be accepted as a code of practice by all who seek to kill their game cleanly and avoid wounding.

2 February 1962

calculating effective range

Since I wrote the preceding article I have had several requests for information on other aspects of the same subject. So I think it would help many readers and interest more if I set out the method I used for calculating the range of a gun. Readers can then work out for themselves the range of other guns and other loads.

Just a word of recapitulation on the method. It is that originally worked out by Burrard in *The Modern Shotgun*. Its basis is that the *effective* range of a shotgun (which is always less, and may be much less, than the range at which kills may occasionally be made by lucky pellets striking vulnerable spots) is the greatest range at which the gun can be expected to put a killing number of pellets into a given bird when it is fairly caught in the pattern circle. Obviously, the range will vary with the degree of choke, the weight, size and velocity of the shot and the kind of bird.

How many pellets?

As for what constitutes a killing number of pellets, that is taken from much practical experience to be two small shot for small birds such as snipe; three medium shot for birds such as pigeon or pheasants; and four large shot for geese. For the rest, the method depends on measuring the sizes of the vulnerable regions of various birds, and relating these, as targets, to the known patterns thrown by various guns, loads and borings. There is no theory involved: the method merely brings together two sets of practical measurements, and is endorsed by experience.

Now for the actual working. Proceeding on the lines described, we get the following minimum patterns as being necessary to ensure consistent, clean kills.*

Game	*Shot size*	*Min. pattern*
Snipe	8	270
Woodcock	7	150
Squirrel	7	180
Partridge	6	130
Grouse	6	130
Pheasant	6	120
Pigeon	6	130
Rabbit	5	120
Teal	5	110
Duck	4	80
Hare	4	100
Goose	3	70

* I have rounded up and otherwise slightly amended the minimum patterns above to agree with the figures I subsequently published in *Shotguns and Cartridges*. Also, I give below (*a*) the minimum pellet energies that require to be associated with these patterns for effective use against game; and (*b*) a table of pellet energies at various ranges.

(*a*) Minimum pellet energies (Burrard):

Large birds (e.g. geese)	1·5 ft.-lb.
Medium birds (e.g. grouse)	0·85 ft.-lb.
Small birds (e.g. snipe)	0·5 ft.-lb. (but see page 223 and the footnote on page 216).

(*b*) Striking energy in ft.-lb. for individual pellets fired at observed velocity of 1,070 ft. per second:

Size of shot	*Range in yards* 30	35	40	45	50	55	60
3	4·48	3·92	3·43	2·99	2·59	2·23	1·94
4	3·54	3·08	2·66	2·30	1·97	1·68	1·42
5	2·60	2·23	1·90	1·61	1·36	1·14	0·93
6	2·03	1·71	1·44	1·20	1·01	0·82	0·67
7	1·52	1·27	1·06	0·86	0·70	0·57	0·45

All the shooter has to do to find out the effective range of his gun and cartridge is to decide what is the range at which they are capable of making the appropriate minimum pattern. One more table will enable him to do it. It is a table giving the percentage patterns thrown by various borings at all ranges. It is true enough for all gauges except the very small ones (28 and ·410) which would need to be plated to find out to which lines their barrels belonged.

Percentage patterns for all ranges

Range (yds.)	*30*	*35*	*40*	*45*	*50*	*55*	*60*
Imp. cyl.	72	60	50	41	33	27	22
Half choke	83	71	60	50	41	33	27
Full choke	100	84	70	59	49	40	32

The calculations in a typical case can best be shown by an example. Thus:

Question: What is the longest range at which I ought to shoot at mallard with the half-choke barrel of my $2\frac{1}{2}$-in. 16-bore, firing No. 4s in a standard cartridge?

Answer: The standard load for a $2\frac{1}{2}$-in. 16-bore is 15/16 oz.; and 15/16 oz. of No. 4 shot contains 159 pellets. From the first table, the minimum pattern required is 85, which is about 53 per cent of 159. From the second table, we see that a half-choke barrel will give this percentage at between 40 and 45 yds., and rather nearer the latter. So the practical answer would be about 40 yds.

Particulars of the number of pellets in game charges may be found in the I.M.I. *Shooter's Year Book,* from which I have calculated the first table and adapted the second.

But it must be remembered that calculations of this sort depend for their realism on guns and cartridges that give something like standard performances. If, having worked out an answer of this sort, you go out with some unknown, super-velocity fireworks, like those of which a correspondent recently wrote to me, which gave less than a true cylinder pattern from a half-choke barrel, I certainly cannot answer for any disappointment you may suffer.

9 February 1962

the balanced long-range load

I remember that when my professional wildfowling guide of the 1930s felt dissatisfied with his marksmanship, for which he set a pretty high standard, his remedy was an 'extra pinch' of powder. Black powder, of course, is especially tolerant of such arbitrary treatment, and if that extra pinch restored a temporary loss of confidence it was probably a good thing, even though its overall ballistical effect may have been bad. It is only too likely that it increased those things which did not need increasing, namely, muzzle velocity (and to a lesser extent striking velocity at full range), and diminished the very thing on which the long-range gunner, using large shot, chiefly depends for the best results, namely, density of pattern.

I recall that on one such occasion, when the extra pinch had failed to produce the desired effect, and my old friend was seeking what to blame, I said 'Leave it to me—*I'll* load you up some cartridges that won't let you down.' The cartridges I loaded for him (3-in. 12-bore) were based on opposite tactics to those he employed. I reduced the powder charge and stepped up the shot, at the same time reducing the size from his favourite BB to No. 3. I resorted to guile by marking the over-shot cards with the former size, knowing, as I did, that anything smaller would be viewed with distrust, not to mention contempt; and when I presented them to him I assured him that he would find them really hot stuff. In due course, I asked him how he had been getting on with them, whereupon he grinned with satisfaction and assured me that they were 'proper mustard'.

Experienced wildfowlers will recognize the circumstances in which my tactics were successful; but now that we have another shooting season on us, with a new entry of young wildfowlers, many of whom will be inclined to seek success in ballistical superlatives, it might well be profitable to examine the 'proper mustard' recipe more closely, if only for their sake.

Key to success

The key to successful long-range shooting is the balanced load. But before going on to discuss the balanced load, I had better say what I mean about successful long-range shooting. I mean shooting under such conditions that an accurate shot results in a reasonably certain kill—in other words, shooting within the effective range of the gun, which excludes all long-range flukes, such as can be brought off occasionally by firing excessively large shot at fowl at inordinate ranges.

It will be clear that in order to fulfil the conditions stated, pattern density and pellet energy must be co-ordinated. It is no good having a dense pattern and registering several hits on a bird unless the individual pellets have the striking energy necessary to penetrate to a vital organ. Equally, it is no good having pellets with abundant striking energy unless there are sufficient of them to ensure that the bird can only escape through holes in the pattern—or, what is worse, cannot escape wounded, perhaps by a single pellet striking it in a non-vital part.

It must be admitted straight away that we lack the knowledge necessary to lay down with precision the pattern density and pellet energy best suited for shooting wildfowl. Many years ago, Burrard made a gallant attempt to arrive at some practical values for minimum patterns, and his results, with some modifications, have been used by I.M.I. to arrive at the effective range table printed in *The Shooter's Year Book.* This assumes that large birds, such as geese, require at least four pellets for a clean kill, each having a striking energy of not less that 1·5 ft.-lb. This implies a minimum pattern of seventy in a 30-in. circle at the appropriate range. Duck would need a minimum pattern of eighty and should succumb to a lighter blow; but all the evidence coming my way suggests that we may have under-valued in the past both the minimum patterns and the striking energies required for these two birds. So, for present purposes, at least, I am going to take it that for long-range work both goose and duck shooters should aim at a minimum pattern of eighty, and a minimum pellet energy of 1·5 ft.-lb.

Balanced loads

The accompanying back-to-back diagrams give the key to well-balanced wildfowling loads conforming to these requirements. The right-hand diagram gives the range to which a fully choked gun may be expected to throw any given charge between 1 oz. and 2 oz. so as to make the required minimum pattern of eighty in a 30-in. circle. For example, if we take $1\frac{7}{16}$ oz. of No. 3, we see by following the dotted line up to the No. 3 curve and then across to the range scale, that this minimum pattern would be thrown to a distance of 55 yds. If we want to find what energy the individual pellets would have at this range, we continue across to the No. 3 curve on the left-hand diagram, and then down to the base line, as shown, where we find the energy would be just over 2 ft.-lb. This would make a well-balanced load, with an effective range of 55 yds. There would, of course, be a small margin of energy in hand, but there always should be when pattern is failing.

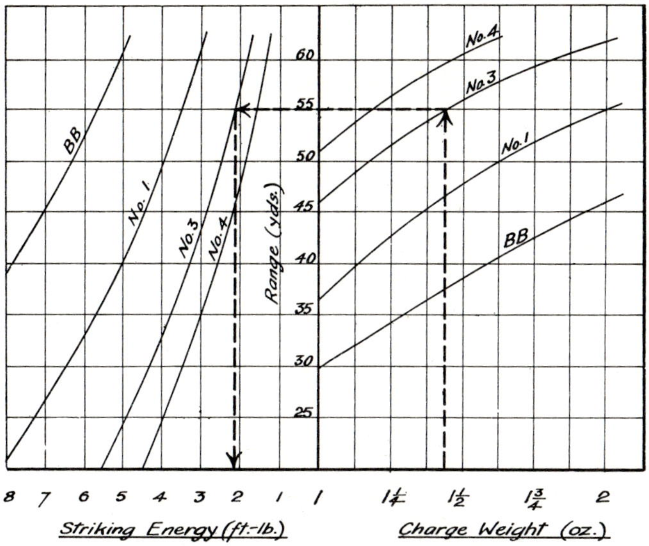

37. KEY TO BALANCED LONG-RANGE LOADS

The right-hand diagram shows the ranges to which a fully choked gun will throw various charges of Nos. 4, 3, 1 and BB to make a minimum pattern of 80 in a 30-in. circle. The left-hand diagram shows the striking energy of corresponding pellets at the given ranges and normal velocities.

For this reason, No. 4 would not quite meet the stated conditions: pattern might be adequate at 60 yds., but not pellet energy. Still, it would do very well on duck at more moderate ranges.

Equally, No. 1 would not make the best-balanced load for this charge. The minimum pattern would not go beyond 47 yds., at which range energy, at $4\frac{1}{3}$ ft.-lb. would exceed requirements.

As for BB, the lack of balance is outstanding with this particular charge weight. The minimum pattern is down to about 37 yds., at which distance the energy would be over 8 ft.-lb.—far in excess of requirements. It is a size for 4-bores and punt guns—or for dependance on long-range flukes.

All the same, there is no categorical answer to those who would exchange pattern density for pellet energy within moderate limits, other than the undeniable fact that, as pattern becomes thinner, so do the chances of hitting a vital spot. One can only do what I have done here and decide first what best meets the needs of practical experience, and then find the prescription that best conforms.

3 November 1966

Note: in the second edition of *The New Wildfowler* I have suggested the following minimum striking energies: duck, $1\frac{1}{2}$ ft.-lb; the smaller geese, 2 ft.-lb; Canada geese, 3 ft.-lb.

Section 13

SHOT AND SHOT SIZE

'Birds are not killed by guns, but by charges of shot, and then only by those pellets, travelling with adequate velocity, which the regularity and density of the pattern, combined with the skill of the shooter, are together capable of bringing to bear.'

(The author—*Shotguns and Cartridges*)

the right size of shot

From the Rhodesian Copper Belt comes an appeal to me to settle a modest alcoholic wager concerning the best size of shot. I am used to these arbitrations, but the present case is especially interesting because of the extreme opinion of one of the parties to the argument, who is stated to hold the view that the best size of shot to use in a 12-bore against geese is AAA at thirty-five pellets to the ounce, or SSG at fifteen.

Shot sizes are, of course, perennially arguable because of the strong compensatory principles at work, which, within limits, appear to make the matter one of personal choice. On the small side, and under normal conditions, the limits are fairly obvious, for experience quickly shows up the lack of penetrating power of unduly small shot. (Our forefathers' belief in its *superior* penetrating power could only have been based on pure conjecture.) The unsuitability of unduly large shot, however, is by no means so obvious, for at close ranges there may be not only superabundant pellet energy, but also a sufficiently close pattern to make reasonably sure of a kill. And even at the longer ranges the user of such shot may not be impressed by any obvious sign of its deficiencies, for the striking energy of individual pellets will still be high, and if only one or two of them happen to connect they may score a spectacular kill. A few such kills, particularly if a man is a poor shot, may fill him with vainglory and give him far too rosy an opinion of the merits of his load, which may indeed allow many birds to escape—scot-free or pricked or wounded—through the inadequacies of the pattern. Deliberate reliance on the long-range flukes which large shot can occasionally bring off is, of course, downright cruel, unsporting and unethical.

Experience the only guide

For the best results—for consistent kills by well-aimed shots within the effective range of the gun and load concerned—the choice of shot size is, in fact, limited by the need for keeping individual pellet energy and pattern in step. Neither is much good without a due measure of

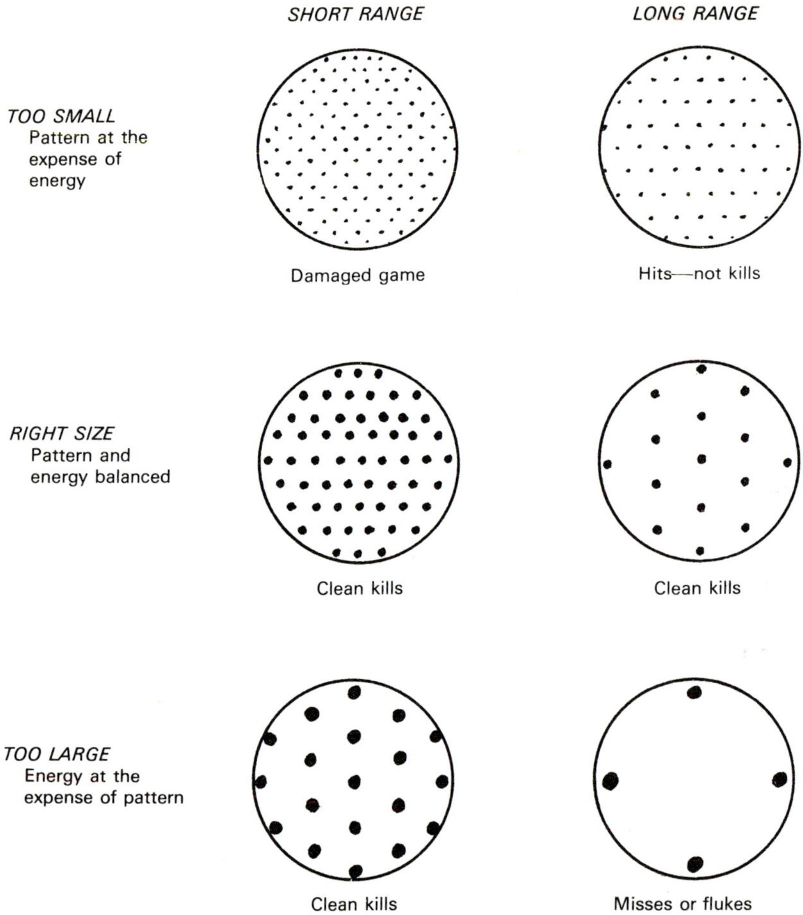

38. Diagrams illustrating the general effect of right and wrong shot sizes.

the other. Pattern without energy means hits but not kills. Energy without pattern means trusting to luck. Theoretically, given the weight of shot, the boring of the gun, the kind of game and the greatest range at which it is normally taken, it should be possible to say exactly what size of shot would be likely to deliver the heaviest blow to the bird in terms of total energy. But in the absence of factors expressing the practical imperfections of patterns, calculations made on these lines give a shot size which experience has shown to be too large. The only sure guide is, in fact, experience, of which there is fortunately a large store for the uncommitted shooter to work on.

The following table gives what I believe to be the verdict of generations of shooters.

Partridge	6	Rabbit	5 or 6	Mallard	4
Grouse	6	Hare	4	Teal	5
Pheasant	5 or 6	Woodcock	7	Geese	1 or 3
Pigeon	5 or 6	Snipe	8	Squirrel	7

The uncommitted man can safely adopt the sizes given and forget the subject so far as standard charges and normal conditions are concerned. Light loads and open boring tend to justify a smaller size and may require the acceptance of a shorter effective range. Heavy loads and close boring operate conversely; but I cannot find any justification for using AAA or SSG in 12-bore charges against geese. The latter would not even stack. I would recommend anyone with strong leanings towards abnormally large shot to test his gun for patterns at the *measured* distance at which he believes it to be fully effective, and to ask himself frankly how much he is depending on luck.

The diagram on the previous page is intended only as a visual aid to beginners in memorizing the chief pros and cons of large and small shot.

18 July 1963

shot sizes and patterns for geese

When I wrote an article on 'The Case for the Big Bores, and the Outlook', I felt sure I should attract criticism, or, at least, comment, from the ranks of the goose-shooters—a tribe of specialists, as I well knew, with strong individual views. In the circumstances, I counted myself lucky to have drawn nothing more embarrassing than the cool and constructive observations (not to mention the sound sporting sentiments) of a correspondent who signed himself 'Home-loader'.

In my article, I suggested (1) that geese required a minimum 30-in. pattern of seventy; (2) that a 4-bore, firing 3 oz. of No. 1

shot, might have an effective range of 75 yds.; and (3) that the corresponding figure for an 8-bore, firing 2 oz. of No. 3, might be 65 yds. The stated minimum pattern, I should add, was that considered necessary to ensure the four or five hits required to make reasonably certain of finding a vital spot.

'Home-loader' raises two main points. He suggests that the 1·50 ft.-lb. commonly quoted and used as the minimum pellet energy for geese may not be enough. He quotes practical experiments implying that pellets having no more energy than this are incapable of adequate penetration—at least, of the powerful breast muscles and sternum protecting the heart and lungs of these birds—and from this he concludes that a pellet energy of the order of 3·00 ft.-lb. may be necessary. This is a big jump and one that he correctly states would reduce the effective range of Nos. 1 and 3 shot.

Lack of evidence

This, of course, is much fought-over ground, on which no final victory has ever been won, or is ever likely to be, and, at the risk of disappointing those who enjoy a good verbal shindy, I had better say that, in this matter, I count myself a mere seeker after knowledge or, at best, an assessor of evidence. Theory is of little use here unless it runs hand-in-hand with practical experience. Acceptable evidence, as I have already said, is hard to come by. Most of that on offer is useless, as when an eminent gunmaker such as the late W. W. Greener writes that 'with No. 1 shot in one of our (8-gauge) choke-bore guns, we can warrant to kill ducks at 130 to 140 yds.'. His subsequent remarks make it clear that what he is thinking of is single-shot flukes, which is the category into which much other such evidence fits.

Even the most experienced and scientifically minded goose-shooter, who had consistently preserved notes of his sport, could say little more than that he had tried various specified loads and shot sizes, and that he had found some of them more effective than others. He could not reliably quote actual ranges, and he would never know to what extent his failure to kill individual birds outright was due to his fault or that of his pattern. And he would be most unlikely to have established any definite standards by which to judge the consistency of his results, or to have carried out systematic post-mortems on a sufficiently large number of birds, killed outright, and wounded but brought to bag, to bring out clearly the limits of effectiveness of his various charges and shot sizes. Yet, without something of that sort, we are working in the dark.

Exhaustive experiments

The only way to bring the subject into the daylight would be for someone to do for geese what F. C. Bellrose did for duck. Bellrose, working for the Illinois State Conservation Department, shot large numbers of mallard flighting just over the tops of trees of measured height. The birds brought down were X-rayed and classified according to the number and location of hits, etc., and various supporting experiments were carried out. The whole thing was done on an exhaustive scale, and enabled some hard inferences to be drawn. They were not altogether flattering to the power of the gun.

So far as I know, nothing in any way comparable has ever been done for geese, but Bellrose's results tend, by inference, to support 'Home-loader's' view that our popularly accepted ideas on the minimum pellet energy needed for the larger birds are too low. I myself have had this impression for a long time and I recall that, in *Shotguns and Cartridges*, I arbitrarily stepped up the figure for duck from the commonly quoted figure of 0·85 ft.-lb. to 1·00 ft.-lb. For the same reason, when assigning the effective ranges I did to 4-bores and 8-bores, I kept a good margin of striking energy in hand. At the 75 yds. I gave for the 4-bore, the remaining energy or striking energy of the No. 1 pellets assumed would have been not 1·50 ft.-lb. but very nearly 2·25 ft.-lb. At the 65 yds. I gave for the 8-bore, the corresponding figure for the No. 3 pellets would have been 1·75 ft.-lb.

The verdict of experience

Are these energies enough? I believe they are and I base that, not on any theory, but on the broad record of experience, as I interpret it. Even if 'Home-loader's' experiments had proved conclusively (which he does not claim) that it needs 3·00 ft.-lb. of pellet energy to penetrate the more impenetrable parts of the anserine anatomy, it does not follow that it would pay to work to that figure. The large shot thus needed, the fewer pellets in the charge, and the resulting more open pattern would mean foregoing the chance of scoring hits on more vulnerable spots. Besides, one must allow for the crippling and shock effects of pellets which, though they do not penetrate a vital organ, expend their destructive energy in knocking the bird's flying machinery out of action, whereby it may be brought immediately to bag.

If, on the other hand, one were to prescribe 'Home-loader's' tentatively suggested 3·00 ft.-lb. as a limiting figure, it would require some drastic revision of current ideas on the effectiveness of goose loads.

To bring out the point, I have worked out the remaining energies at extended ranges of the three most popular shot sizes for geese, namely, BB and Nos. 1 and 3. They come out as follows:

Striking energies of large pellets at various ranges (ft.-lb.)
(observed velocity 1,100 ft./sec.)

Range (yds.)	*50*	*60*	*70*	*80*	*100*
BB	6·80	5·45	4·34	3·47	2·20
No. 1	4·00	3·30	2·56	1·98	1·20
No. 3	2·77	2·10	1·59	1·20	0·69

As will be seen, this would rule out No. 3 altogether, beyond game-shooting range, no matter what the charge weight or calibre of the gun. I am sure that my Irish readers in particular, who, I believe, are much addicted to No. 3 for goose-shooting, would reject this limitation, as I would myself, despite my strong sympathy for 'Home-loader's' point of view.

Effective range

But even if we are prepared to settle for a much lower figure than 3·00 ft.-lb. for our minimum pellet energy, the problem of effective range remains open. It is a problem of charge-weight and gun-cartridge performance, and can only be expressed in terms of the range at which a particular combination will demonstrably make a killing pattern—one that will fairly reliably put four or five or more pellets into the bird every time, if held straight.

30 September 1965

shot sizes for clays

When I was a budding young engineer, under articles to a Westminster consultant and living in London, I used to seek relief occasionally by paying a visit to the old Worcester Park shooting ground, and having a hundred clays on the sporting layout under Arthur Hearn. There I have spent some happy hours walking-up single and double rises in rough cover, then proceeding to driven partridges or grouse and ending up with high pheasants from the 120-ft. tower.

One or two things stick in my mind about those occasions. I used to use a normal game gun and No. 7 shot; and it is significant, though not related to my present theme, that I seemed to score better on the walked-up double rises than on the singles. What is more to the point is that it seems in retrospect to have been a fairly common thing for me to say, 'That's funny: I thought I had that one,' and for Hearn to reply, 'It's all right: it was well inside your pattern.' Hearn, of course, could see the shot, and was thus able to assure me that what I sometimes thought were misses were really failures on the part of my gun and cartridges to make a sufficiently dense or regular pattern at the range concerned.

The elusive clay

The ordinary clay target is indeed an elusive object for the shotgun. Having a diameter of about $4\frac{1}{4}$ in., it presents an area of about 14 sq. in. when seen directly from underneath. In this, its most favourable aspect, it provides a mark little larger than the vulnerable region of a partridge, as measured by Burrard. But its more familiar aspect, as presented in particular to the trapshooter, is edgewise or only slightly tilted, when it affords a mark normally not much exceeding 4 sq. in., or, say, two-thirds that of a snipe. Further, although close shots are common in skeet, the trapshooter must be prepared to take these tiny targets at distances up to, or even exceeding, 50 yds. in handicap events. Small wonder that scores of 100 straight were practically unknown before crimp-closed cartridges became general.

So far as I can ascertain, no scientific study has ever been made of the vulnerability of the clay target, so that we do not know with any certainty just what is the best combination of pellets and striking energy to score a 'kill'. Indeed, any such study would be of doubtful practical value because of the many variables at work, including, as they do, variations in the composition of the target, changes in its brittleness according to temperature, and the endless permutations and combinations of rate of spin and number and incidence of shot.

Two sorts of luck

One thing we can be sure of is that trapshooting under handicap conditions stretches the available gun–cartridge combinations to the limit of their performance—beyond the limit, indeed, tolerable in game shooting, where the unwritten code bars shooting at birds at ranges exceeding those at which the combination of pattern and pellet energy is adequate to ensure a clean kill. It seems to me that the trapshooter, undeterred as he is by any such ethical considerations, can, does and sometimes must rely to *some* extent on luck. Thus, trap speed plus reaction time might be sufficient to defeat a man with small shot: he might be incapable of getting on to his target while his pellets retained sufficient energy to break them. But if he changed to a larger size, he could certainly break those he hit, even if he lost others through his more open pattern—hence, no doubt, the C.P.S.A. rule limiting shot size. Under similar conditions, a man of faster reaction time, but not so good a shot, might do better with smaller shot but a rather less tight boring, the one relying partly on what we might call the luck of the strike and the other on the luck of the spread.

Experience teaches

Subject to such variations in favour of individuals, experience should have decided, long since, on the best recipe for success in clay target shooting. But speaking as an enquiring onlooker and not as a regular practitioner in this particular sport, I find it hard to resist the conclusion that in this country we are inclined to favour shot that is a size too large. I find support for this conclusion in comparative statistics kindly supplied to me by I.M.I. and the Federal Cartridge Corporation of America, which I have interpreted to give the following table, using English shot sizes throughout.

It clearly implies different interpretations of practical experience on the part of British and American shooters. Can they both be right?

9 July 1964

Preferred shot sizes
($1\frac{1}{8}$-oz. loads)

	U.K.	*U.S.A.*
Trap	7	8 (ordinary shooting) 7 (handicap shooting)
Skeet	7 and 8	9 ('overwhelmingly preferred')

home-made shot

A Dundee reader, with a good Scottish sense of thrift, writes to me on a subject which evidently strikes some lively sparks of interest among home-loaders, judging from the correspondence I received when I last raised it. He says:

> 'Again I see that the price of cartridges has risen to around 18s. for a box of twenty-five. To the average shooter, this seems a staggering amount.
>
> 'I agree that almost everything is going up—except the price that poulterers pay for game. Woodpigeons are still making only 9d., shot rabbits 2s. 6d., hares 3s. and white hares 1s. 6d. And so it goes on until the average shooter asks himself, "Can I afford it? Why don't I start making my own shot?" I used to do so . . . clean lead can be had for 25s. for 28 lb.; yet 28 lb. of shot costs around £4.
>
> 'If anyone can inform me how to make good lead shot I should be most grateful. All my efforts so far have produced only pear-shaped shot.'

I was interested, therefore, to remind myself in detail of an Irish reader's method of making shot with only the most primitive facilities, about which I was told some time ago. This shot, according to his account, was quite free from tails, and, when rubbed up with a little black lead, was indistinguishable from the boughten article.

At the time, I made some experiments on my own account, and was fully satisfied that good, round shot could be made at home, and by simple means, by anyone prepared to take the trouble. It also became clear to me that the process had a fascination of its own, like many other handicrafts. There is scope for skill and care, and for the refinement of technique, with a goal of perfection always just out of reach. So, even without the economic urge, many home-loaders might be tempted to make their own shot once they had got the hang of the thing.

The short-drop system

The key to successful home-made shot is the short-drop system. Everybody knows that commercial shot is made by dropping molten lead from a height into water, and the mistake that most amateur shot-makers fall into is trying to do the same thing. It was the mistake I made as a boy, when I tried to drop shot from an upstairs window: the tear-shaped pellets I produced aptly symbolized my own disappointment.

The idea of the long-drop system is to give the tail of molten metal, inevitably formed when the drop separates from the mass in the perforated container, time to become absorbed in the body of the pellet before the latter hardens. This requires a free fall in air for a distance which is proportional, among other things, to the size of the pellet.

But in the short-drop system an entirely different principle is employed. Water, which, contrary to a common impression, plays no part in the formation of long-drop pellets, now has a vital role. The molten metal, as before, escapes from perforations in a container, but the container is only about one-eighth to three-eighths in. above the surface, according to the size of the pellets being run. The effect is that, as the molten drop of metal separates from the mass, and while it still has a full-length tail, its forward portion makes contact with the water, and is immediately cooled and checked. The tail, still molten, then collapses into the body of the pellet, by which it is completely absorbed and rounded off by surface tension.

If everything is correctly adjusted—the temperature of the mix and the height of the drop are the chief variables—there will be no signs of departure from the true round; but otherwise there may be a vestigial tail, like that of a guinea-pig, or even a negative tail—in other words, a minute dimple.

Apparatus

The apparatus used by my original Irish correspondent was simple in the extreme. It comprised merely an iron bar, $2\frac{1}{2}$ in. by $\frac{1}{2}$ in. and 9 in. long, in the middle of one side of which a 1-in. hole was sunk to within $\frac{1}{32}$ in. of the total depth. This thin floor was drilled with a number of small holes—about the size of a sewing needle for No. 8 shot.

In use, the bar was heated bright red-hot in a turf fire, and then placed over a container of water, about $\frac{1}{8}$ in. above the surface. Clean, greased sticks of lead, about $\frac{1}{2}$ in. square, were then melted down in the hole in the bar, the water level being maintained carefully constant. The resulting shot was 'perfectly spherical'.

In my own experiments, I used a steel plate with a shallow $1\frac{1}{4}$-in. iron ring brazed on it, enclosing the perforations, and heated from above by an ordinary plumber's blowlamp. I only pursued these experiments far enough to satisfy my curiosity concerning the general feasibility of the method before publishing anything about it. There is no doubt about the feasibility, and the fact that one can start getting encouraging—and fascinating—results at an early stage.

If I were setting out to make my own shot as a regular thing, I should contrive an iron pot, electrically heated if possible, otherwise by blowlamp, in which to melt my metal. I would have a screw-down valve in the bottom of the pot to release the molten lead in a regulated manner; and I would discharge it horizontally into a small, flat-bottomed sieve adjustably mounted over a generous water container, the level in which would be maintained by overflow as the shot displaced the liquid. If one intended running shot of different sizes, one would need other sieves with different-sized perforations.

In my experiments, the size of the pellets produced by a given sieve varied materially—probably as a result of temperature fluctuations. With a better set-up, such as I have described, I should expect less variation. Still, I have little doubt that the shot would need grading for size in suitable riddles. I would make these from large, flat tin cans. Also, to eliminate defective pellets, it is desirable to discharge them down a 15° inclined plane with a transverse gap at the bottom, adjusted for width so that only truly round specimens can jump it. Defective ones fall through, and can be collected for re-melting. All the necessary equipment can be made by an amateur, but I will refrain from giving further details, which anyone inclined to take up shot-making will readily work out to suit himself.

Metal

An admitted snag about home-made shot is the difficulty of arriving at the right lead alloy. Factory shot is made of lead, alloyed with about 1 per cent of antimony for game cartridges, 2 per cent for trap, and up to 4 per cent for Olympic trench. The antimony gives hardness. Arsenic is also added to increase the surface tension of the molten metal and thus to facilitate the manufacture of truly round pellets. The quantity needed is very small—about one-tenth that of antimony.

The professional way of adding the antimony and arsenic to the molten lead is to prepare bars of metal known as 'temper bar'. These are of fixed weight and contain a high and known proportion of the constituents to be added. To a given weight of pure molten lead it is then only necessary to add so many of these bars to arrive at the right alloy. But temper bar is not an article of trade, and so the amateur shot-maker will usually be reduced to using plain lead. Old battery plates have been suggested as a source of antimonial lead, but the proportion of antimony—probably less than 1 per cent—is swamped by about 9 per cent of tin. Ordinary printing type, on the other hand, contains up to 20 per cent of antimony, and probably no other alloy; so the local printer might be worth interviewing for old type-metal as a source of temper bar. Unfortunately, this seems to be one of those cases in which familiar trade sources of common materials are inaccessible to the amateur because of the small quantities he requires. Still, if I were setting out to make shot regularly, I would risk a brush-off from one of the lead-base alloy specialists, such as McKechnie Bros. Ltd., of Rotton Park Street, Birmingham 16.

1 June 1968

Section 14

RECOIL

'Guns, like some horses, can do damage at both ends.'

searchlight on recoil

All shooters of an enquiring turn of mind owe a debt to the late Sir Gerald Burrard for the light he threw on the shotgun. I myself acknowledge that debt with gratitude. Yet I am sure that if he were alive today, he would be the last to claim either the infallibility or the finality that some of his admirers attribute to his writings. In saying this, I am thinking particularly of the subject of recoil, of which his treatment, viewed in retrospect, was notably inadequate. Yet it is one on which his conclusions are still quoted as if they were holy writ. Indeed, a modern writer has done so with a degree of dogmatism that makes me think it would be worth while to take a broad look at the whole subject in the light of present knowledge.

It is impossible to discuss any subject intelligibly unless the parties talk the same language. On the subject of recoil, the ballisticians do not usually talk the language of the ordinary shooting man. By recoil, they mean either the momentum of the recoiling gun or its kinetic energy—usually the former. And since momentum is weight multiplied by velocity, they commonly express this momentum in terms of the velocity of recoil of a particular gun. They may even express it in terms of the horizontal distance travelled by a heavy pendulum, of known weight and proportions, into which the gun may be clamped for testing purposes.

The ordinary shooting man, when he speaks of recoil, means none of these things. In most cases, he could not even define momentum or kinetic energy, and it would not be of the slightest service to him in this context if he could. What in fact he means by recoil is what his gun *feels like* when he fires it. Perhaps he does not feel it at all, in the excitement of shooting. Or perhaps it gives him no more than a friendly and reassuring punch, pleasantly indicative of its energetic action on his behalf. Or it may kick like a mule, and bruise his shoulder or his face, or give him a headache. These are the ordinary man's criteria of recoil, and to him *they are the things that matter.* The ballistician's criteria of momentum and kinetic energy, etc., are of significance to the shooter only inasmuch as they determine his sensations. As a matter of fact, they *do* determine them, but only broadly; for a given *momentum* of recoil may produce different *sensations* of recoil in a given man under different conditions, to a degree that may be highly significant. It may represent the difference between comfort and discomfort, or between gun-headache and no gun-headache, or between enjoying shooting and giving it up.

Dynamic and sensible recoil

It is impossible to discuss recoil, therefore, unless we distinguish between (*a*) what I call dynamic recoil, which is recoil measured in terms of kinetic energy, or momentum, or gun-velocity, and (*b*) what I prefer to describe as sensible recoil, using the word 'sensible' in accordance with its primary meaning, which my dictionary gives as 'capable of being perceived through the senses'. I would define sensible recoil as 'the recoil felt by the shooter . . . the net effect of the dynamic recoil on his physical and nervous organisation', and the student, writer or ballistician must not fall into the error of thinking that this aspect of recoil is less significant than the other, merely because it is less easy to understand and less amenable to quantitative analysis or expression. In fact, we know more about the relation between dynamic and sensible recoil than we did in Burrard's day, and later in this article I venture to offer a suggestion for reconciling an outstanding conflict in the practical evidence on the subject.

But, first, it is necessary to be clear about the facts of dynamic recoil. The basic proposition here, derived from Newton's third law of motion, is that the rearward momentum of the recoiling gun must always exactly equal the forward momentum of the issuing charge; and the unnamed disciple of Burrard I have mentioned categorically denies that recoil is affected by anything else whatsoever. By way of general comment, I would say:

1. The proposition referred to is not, in fact, rigorously true of *any* actual gun. (Technical readers may be reminded, though others should skip this parenthesis, that, inasmuch as a gun barrel possesses inertia and is not perfectly elastic, *some* part of the energy of recoil will always be lost by being converted into heat through mechanical hysteresis. This is unlikely to be of any practical significance, but I mention it as a warning against working Newton too hard.)

2. The proposition is not even approximately true (*a*) of any gun with a muzzle brake, or (*b*) of one in which any part of the recoil energy is utilized for the operation of a self-loading mechanism, or is

absorbed internally in any other way. This last case includes that of the humble rubber recoil pad.

3. Even if the proposition were always true, it would remain possible for the final momentum of recoil to be attained in different ways—slowly or quickly, according to the kind of powder used. The point will be seen to be of immediate significance.

When we come to consider sensible recoil, we are confronted with a direct conflict of evidence. On the one hand, there is the long-standing and eminently reasonable belief that slow-burning powders, giving a low rate-of-rise of pressure, reduce sensible recoil. The suggestion here is of a cushioning effect, as otherwise provided by a rubber recoil pad, or, more effectively, by the American 'Hydro-Coil' device, which makes use of an hydraulic cylinder and a coiled spring. On the other hand, we have I.M.I.'s prolonged researches which I have described in *Shotguns and Cartridges*, in the course of which it was found that a team of shooters, firing many thousands of cartridges loaded to give the same velocity to the same shot charge, and therefore developing the same *dynamic* recoil, unanimously voted that the variety giving the least *sensible* recoil were those that, unknown to them, had been loaded with the fastest-burning powder.

This conclusion is equally reasonable, and accords with universal experience. We all know that, because of the time-lag between stimulus and sensation, hurtful things hurt much less—or even not at all—if they happen very quickly.

The evidence of the popular belief in the low recoil of the slow-burning powders can be discounted on the grounds that, in the past, most of such powders gave somewhat low ballistics. But there is no such escape from the apparent conflict of evidence between the I.M.I. researches and the Hydro-Coil—both are fully backed by instrumental evidence. So it would seem that sensible recoil can be reduced either (*a*) by increasing the rate of rise of pressure transmitted to the butt plate, or (*b*) by reducing it!

Paradox explained

My personal explanation of this paradox is that it does not exist: both sides of it are true within appropriate limits. As the rate of rise of pressure for a given dynamic recoil increases, sensible recoil increases with it, up to a point—the peak of sensitivity. But when that point is reached, sensation can hardly keep pace with stimulus. Beyond it, as the rate of rise of pressure continues to increase, there is actually a decline in sensation—the pressure on the shoulder is becoming too fleeting for the nervous system fully to record it. The accompanying graph illustrates the principle. The rising part of the sensible-recoil curve represents the range over which cushioning principles and devices are most effective. The falling part is that over which sensible recoil can be reduced by faster-burning powders.

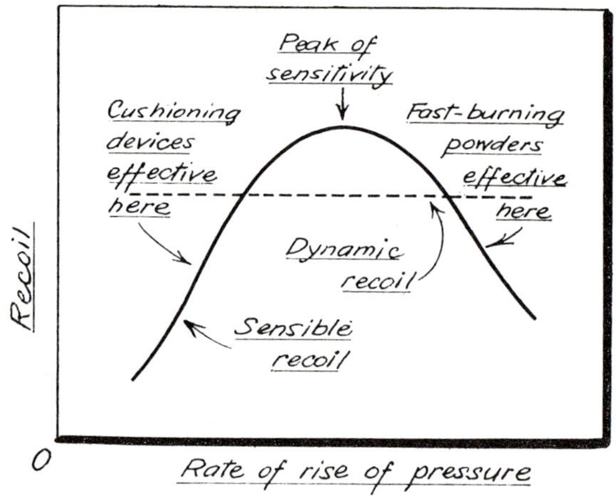

39. In a gun firing successive charges of the same weight and at the same velocity, the dynamic recoil will be constant, as indicated by the level dotted line, but the sensible recoil will vary with the rate of rise of pressure in the gun. There is a particular rate of rise which gives maximum sensible recoil, and this can be reduced either by increasing or reducing the rate of rise.

I submit that this explanation reconciles the conflicting evidence, accords with common sense and practical experience, and is probably capable of explaining all major anomalies arising in this connection.

Of course, it must not be forgotten that part of the effectiveness of the recoil-absorbing devices mentioned lies in the fact that they not only reduce the rate of rise of pressure transmitted to the shooter's shoulder, but also absorb more or less of the energy of the recoil. The reduction in sensible recoil claimed for the newer gas-operated automatics, such as the Winchester M1400 and the two-shot Armalite, is in all probability due to the same thing—the increased amount of energy absorbed in unlocking the latest rotating forms of breech-locking mechanism.

In pursuing these technical considerations, the importance of gun-fitting must not be overlooked. Sensible recoil can be painfully exaggerated by an ill-fitting gun—a fact that was forcibly brought home to me at a very early stage in my shooting career, when, because of the bruising I had suffered from a misfit stock, I became almost afraid to shoot. Conversely, a snugly fitting gun, tucked firmly into the shoulder and against the face, is the best first line of defence against recoil.

17 June 1965

more about recoil

In my preceding article, 'Searchlight on Recoil', I dealt with the principles concerned in this important aspect of the shoulder-gun. I dealt with recoil as measured by the ballistician, and as felt by the shooter—two different things, which I endeavoured to relate in terms that will not, so far as I am aware, be found in any text-book. Inevitably, there were several practical points emerging from these considerations which I was unable to go into for lack of space. I should like to do so now.

By way of recapitulation, the main points I made in the previous article were as follows:

1. Ballisticians measure recoil chiefly by the momentum (weight multiplied by velocity) of the recoiling gun
2. Shooters measure recoil by their feelings.
3. For a given recoil, as measured by a ballistician, the shooter's feeling of recoil can be significantly different in different circumstances.
4. The main things determining this difference are the fit of the gun and the steepness of the pressure wave transmitted to the shooter's shoulder—in other words, *the rate of rise of pressure*. This last, in turn, is chiefly decided by whether the powder is fast-burning or otherwise, and whether a rubber recoil-pad or the like is fitted.
5. For a given gun, recoiling with a given momentum, the feeling of recoil experienced by the shooter increases as the rate-of-rise of pressure is increased, *up to a certain point*—the peak of sensitivity. Beyond this point, sensation declines—the pressure on the shoulder becomes progressively too fleeting for the nervous system fully to

record it. In the limit, sensation would fail . . . death by the guillotine *is said* to be painless.

This last was my key point: it was an attempt to reconcile conflicting field evidence, which shows that recoil-sensation, or 'sensible recoil', can be reduced (*a*) by cushioning devices, proved by scientific measurement to smooth-out the rate of rise of pressure, and (*b*) by fast-burning powders, having precisely the opposite effect.

Puzzle of the Darne

I have already undertaken to try to explain how the light sensible recoil of the French sliding-breech guns of the Darne type fits into this picture. It is a thing I am asked from time to time, the latest occasion being in connection with a lightweight 12-bore of this kind. From this gun, weighing little over 6 lb., the owner fires ordinary $2\frac{3}{4}$-in. loads of $1\frac{1}{4}$ oz. of shot without inconvenience, he himself being a lightweight. Tested in a pendulum cradle, these guns register a recoil little different from an ordinary gun; and yet the makers have for many years offered them at weights below the normal for firing the charges concerned, and with the justification provided by users' testimony. Their light sensible recoil must, it seems, be accepted as a fact.

The explanation, I have no doubt, lies in their compressive breech-closure. In the ordinary 12-bore gun, the official clearances regulating the thickness of the cartridge rim, and the recess in the chamber provided for its accommodation, are such that, even when the gun is new, there may be a head-space of over 0·3 mm. or, say, sixteen-thousandths of an inch. Quite a rattle! The Darne, however, takes advantage of its powerful breech-closing and ejection facilities to employ a restricted chamber and a head-space that is slightly minus—in other words, the head of the cartridge has to be crushed to a minute degree in order to close the breech.

The effect here is that, in the Darne, the full gas pressure in the cartridge is immediately communicated to the standing breech, and thence to the butt-plate and the shooter's shoulder. In an ordinary gun, there is a delay of some micro-seconds while the cartridge and its metal head are expanding and filling the chamber and head-space. The final effect is that a given cartridge in this kind of gun will produce a greater rate of rise of pressure at the butt-plate—in other words, a steeper-fronted pressure wave—than it will in an ordinary gun, and will give less sensible recoil by the virtue of the process described in my previous article, and referred to under 5 above. For the same reasons, the recoil from a loose, rackety gun that has been tightened may appear much reduced.

An improved recoil pad?

The recoil pad, as I have said before, operates on the opposite side of the sensitivity peak by reducing the rate of rise of pressure communicated to the shooter's shoulder. But it also absorbs some of the *energy* of recoil. This is because it is not perfectly elastic. When it is squeezed and released, energy is absorbed in internal friction, and disappears from the recoil account.

I have thought that the recoil-pad could possibly be made more efficient if more use were made of it as an energy-absorber. The suggestion arising here is of a pad with an indiarubber outer shell of maximum elasticity, and an interior filling of some soft substance chosen for its high energy-absorbing quality.

A matter of weight

In the days when all guns were of the fixed-breech sort, a regular basis of compromise had been evolved between the gunmaker's need for the necessary weight of metal to ensure strength, the shooter's desire for lightness, and their common recognition of the need to limit recoil. Then, any added weight necessary to enable the shooter to withstand the recoil of heavier charges was represented by added strength built into the action and barrels.

Recoil was thus a gun's active and effective defence against abuse: if the shooter overloaded it, it punished him. Nowadays, however, not all guns possess this means of self-defence, whilst some have been unnaturally deprived of it. For example, an effective muzzle-brake, by reducing recoil, may tempt a shooter to increase his load. But the brake, though suppressing the danger signal, does nothing to fortify the gun, which may thus suffer accelerated deterioration, if no worse.

Again, in some self-loaders, sensible recoil is sufficiently modified by delayed action and energy-absorption within the mechanism to fail as a safeguard against overloading, especially if the weapon is fitted, not only with a muzzle-brake, but also with the passenger-weights for which accommodation is sometimes provided.

The passenger-weight principle may be regarded as pernicious. Any weight added to a gun should, I feel, belong to the gun functionally: it should make its due contribution to strength and endurance, and should be applied, as it can, without detriment to handling quality. The principle is most objectionable when it takes the form of a stock plugged with lead to render the recoil from a fine game gun endurable when it has been rechambered, and is used for firing heavier loads than those for which it was designed. This is rank abuse, for which a heavy price has to be paid in shortened life.

State of mind

It is a curious fact that the sensible recoil from a given gun-cartridge combination may be light and in every way acceptable in the course of sport, but objectionable, or even painful, when firing deliberately at a plate.

I think there may be several factors involved—gun mounting, distraction or concentration of attention, and consequent tenseness or relaxation of muscles. On the first point, I can only say that, however carefully I tuck my gun into my shoulder and against my face when I am firing deliberately at a mark, I am always likely to get an unpleasant blow on the cheekbone—a thing I never experience in the course of sport. This suggests that gun mounting, like many other actions, is not done so well when it is conscious and deliberate as it is when it is left to the care of the subconscious mind.

Again, the complete distraction of attention from the gun—and from oneself—and its concentration on a flying target would often be enough to inhibit any sensation of recoil from reaching the place where these things register. And lastly, I am fairly sure that, when one is about to take a deliberate shot, the recoil-resisting muscles are more tense than they are when shooting flying game.

The conclusion to be drawn from all this is that a man whose shooting is hesitant, introspective and deliberate is likely to feel more recoil from a given gun and cartridge than one whose style is free, extrovert and spontaneous.

5 August 1965

reduced recoil of automatics

A recoil-sufferer has asked if it is true that gas-operated shotguns recoil less than conventional guns, and if so, why. He expresses doubt, based on the consideration that Newton's law, that action and reaction are equal and opposite, surely knows no exceptions.

The short answer to the main question is that these weapons do indeed recoil less than conventional, fixed-breech guns, and that this involves no breach of Newton's law. The question, why they do, may perhaps be made clear in everyday language.

When an ordinary gun is fired, the force of the explosion acts forwards on the charge of shot and rearwards on the standing breech. This force acting to the rear is the only one involved in the question of recoil.

When a gas-operated automatic is fired, things are not so simple. Until the charge travelling up the barrel uncovers the gas port, the gun behaves like an ordinary gun. The breech is fixed, and the pressure acting on it causes it to start recoiling in the ordinary way. But when the gas port is uncovered, two fresh factors come into the picture. The high-pressure gas, acting on the piston in the cylinder, causes it to start moving. This movement unlocks the breech, which becomes free, so that the gas pressure acting on it, now very greatly reduced, is no longer effective in forcing the gun back. Since the piston is also free, and linked to the breech block, the gas pressure driving it to the rear similarly does nothing to accelerate the rearward motion of the gun.

But the gas pressure in the cylinder not only acts on the piston, it also acts forwards on the head of the cylinder; and since the head of the cylinder is a fixed part of the gun, this pressure tends to drive the whole gun forwards, and thus partly neutralizes the recoil.

So far, be it noted, we have said nothing to offend Newton.

Paying debts

But we must not forget that we have left the free breech-block and the piston travelling at high speed to the rear inside the gun. They are doing so against the action of a return spring, the back end of which is adding something to the recoil by the rearward pressure it exerts. What is more important is that the piston and the breech-block, when arrested, deal the receiver a hammer blow, and thus deliver up the kinetic energy, or energy of movement, that they acquired earlier in the proceedings. This makes a significant contribution to the velocity of recoil. It is indeed easy to prove mathematically that if these parts paid their energy debts in full, the final momentum of recoil of the gun would be exactly the same as that of a corresponding fixed-breech gun. But the debts are not paid in full: like some others, they suffer attrition—in this case by friction. All the movements of the internal parts described involve friction, particularly, perhaps, the unlocking of the breech and the impact of the breech-block on its buffer-stop; and the energy loss thus involved disappears from the energy of recoil. This finally relieves Newton of his watching brief.

Dynamic *v.* sensible recoil

In what I have said so far, I have been considering the dynamic recoil only—that is, the recoil measured in terms of momentum or kinetic energy. But the thing that matters in this context is the sensible recoil, or the recoil capable of being perceived by the senses of the shooter. Here we are on grounds where mathematical analysis fails; yet it can be said that even if there were no friction losses in the gun, so that it attained the same final momentum as its fixed-breech counterpart, it by no means follows that the sensible recoil would be the same. The initial retardation of the recoil, due to the pressure acting on the cylinder head, and its final acceleration, due to the hammer blow delivered by the moving parts, would undoubtedly give a different feeling. The hammer blow itself can be highly objectionable to some shooters, including myself, and may outweigh advantages otherwise arising.

But even if we are unable to interpret in terms of sensible recoil the claims made on behalf of these weapons ('55 per cent less kick') for the Remington M1100 and '10 per cent less than any other automatic' for the Winchester M1400) most shooters would no doubt concur in the results of a test I recently had carried out with the help of I.M.I., in which one of these guns, a Remington M58, was fired, first, with its gas port closed, so that it worked as a fixed-breech weapon, and then in its normal state as an automatic. Three independent shooters did not hesitate in stating that they felt more recoil when the breech-block was fixed than when it was free. But the recoil-sensitive man, and particularly the gun-headache sufferer, should proceed by personal trial of the gun of his choice.

30 July 1964

shotgun headspace and excessive recoil

My mental case-book on shotguns records many instances of allegedly excessive recoil. The symptoms may be bruising or headache or simply acute discomfort. The easiest cases to diagnose are those in which the shooter is using a load which is obviously too heavy in relation to the weight of his gun. Young aspirants firing Alphamax cartridges in ordinary game guns are the chief sufferers here. Other instances are attributable to unsuitable stocks which transfer the thrust of recoil to parts of the shooter's frame ill adapted to withstand it. Others again are more obscure, and it is of a special subdivision of these last that I now write. Four closely related cases have come up almost together, and another springs at once to mind.

Case 1 referred to a pre-war 12-bore game gun of normal weight which recoiled so viciously that the user found ten shots as much as he could stand. He used standard Grand Prix cartridges.

Case 2 arose in Ireland. The gun was a superior-grade Continental game gun firing standard Grand Prix or Trapshooting cartridges. Independent and experienced witnesses, not previously warned, concurred in the description, 'a good killer, but terrible recoil'.

Case 3, also in Ireland, appeared to conform substantially to the preceding.

Case 4 referred to a $2\frac{3}{4}$-in. 12-bore Italian over-and-under weighing 7 lb., but using only normal $2\frac{1}{2}$-in. trap cartridges. The user, an experienced shot, testified to painful recoil. ('I'm seldom pleased to get rid of any gun, but I was certainly glad to see the back of that one.')

Case 5 concerned an old, off-the-face 12-bore firing Grand Prix cartridges. The recoil was 'dreadful'.

The cause

In these cases, and innumerable others not on record, but in the same category, people are being hurt, and are naturally inclined to retaliate by blaming the nearest thing to hand. It may be the cartridges, or a particular gun, or all guns of a particular make. But in the cases I am dealing with, *it is always a particular gun that is to blame.* And this, I hasten to add, may be due to a condition it has acquired simply by wear and tear. It is the condition well known to riflemen as excessive headspace clearance.

In order that a gun may close on a particular cartridge, it is necessary, for manufacturing reasons, that there should be a clearance between the cartridge head and the standing breech. This is regulated by official tolerances, and the highest legitimate value I can get for a new 12-bore is for a minimum-rimmed Continental cartridge in a maximum-recessed English gun, thus:

Max. depth rim recess (British Rules of Proof, 1954)	·079 in.
Min. rim thickness (C.I.P. Specification)	·063 in.
Maximum clearance	·016 in.

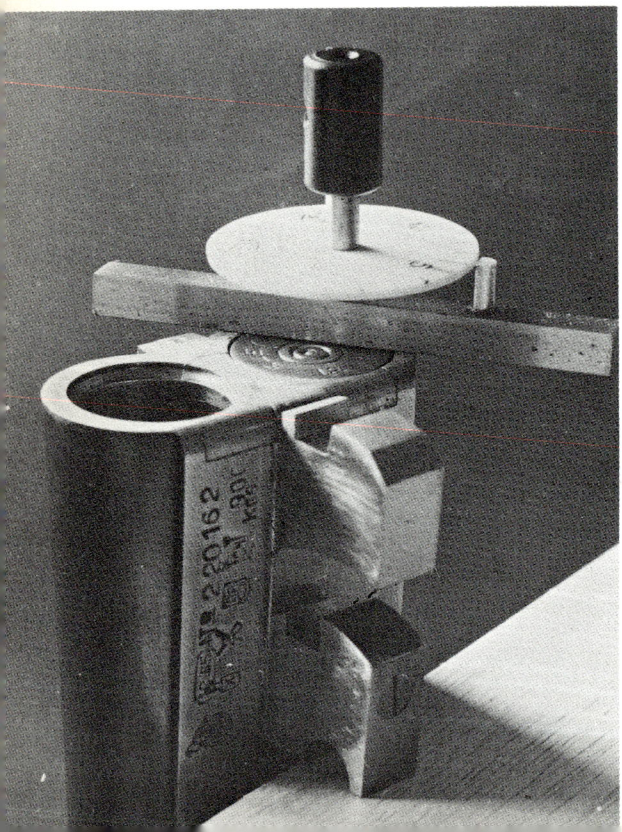

40. MEASURING SHOTGUN HEADSPACE CLEARANCE

The gun shown has a very small clearance and a correspondingly light feeling of recoil.

There are complications here which I have no space to go into, but this figure (sixteen-thousandths of an inch) can be taken as a fair guide.

When a gun is fired, the striker first pushes the cartridge forward as far as it will go into the chamber; and then, when the charge burns, the cartridge case is accelerated violently to the rear, acquiring kinetic energy in the process, which, subject to losses, it duly delivers up to the standing breech as an impact. *This kinetic energy, be it noted, is greatly in excess of what would have been contributed to the gun by the direct action of the pressure on the breech during the interval concerned.* In a rifle with dangerously large headspace, the cartridge case usually parts, but what comes back in this way may wreck the weapon. I have never heard of a shotgun being thus damaged, but there may be a very serious increase in recoil.

Temporary remedies

In the first Case, the cause of the violent recoil was diagnosed as excessive headspace by a gunsmith. I confirmed the reasonableness of this diagnosis and suggested that the shooter should test it by preparing some cartridges with metal-foil discs stuck on their heads so as to fill the headspace. He did this and duly reported, 'I stuck two discs of foil on the ends of ten cartridges with a standard load. The gun shut comfortably. I shot off all these cartridges in five minutes. I did not notice the recoil at all, and shot without any discomfort. Your prescription was perfect.'

In Case 2 also, a gunsmith found excessive headspace. In Cases 3 and 4, the 'exhibits' have been lost sight of, but in the latter it had been noticed that the cartridges 'seemed to rattle excessively' when the gun was closed. In Case 5, the shooter roughly tightened the gun himself. The owner from whom he had borrowed it subsequently volunteered the information that 'the gun seems to have no kick now'.

Measurements

I have already said that $\frac{16}{1000}$ in. may be taken, with some reserve, as the maximum headspace clearance normally to be expected in a new 12-bore gun firing British or Continental cartridges. But how actual clearances run in new guns and old, what constitutes excessive clearance and what can be done to provide a permanent cure when the existence of such clearance is established remain to be seen.

The following are clearances measured with the 12-bore guns and cartridges immediately available. All figures are thousandths of an inch.

Gun	*Cartridge*							
	British (Eley)		*American (Rem'ton)*		*Italian (Fiocchi)*		*Czech (S. & B.)*	
	R.	L.	R.	L.	R.	L.	R.	L.
Best English H.E. (70 yrs. old)	18*	10	16	8	25	17	15	9
Best English H.E. (20 yrs. old)	14	14	28	39	19	19	18	19
Med. quality Spanish H.E. (new)	10	9	17	17	12	12	16	16
Med. quality Spanish H.E. (new)	6	8	16	19	11	14	13	14

(* Obvious wear present)

None of these guns show any signs of excessive recoil with standard loads in any of the English or Continental cartridges named. (American cartridges have not been fired. The Spanish guns, and particularly the last, weighing only 6 lb., were remarked for their light recoil with English game cartridges before any headspaces were measured. The figures may provide the reason.

The cartridges show striking differences and some anomalies. For example, with the Remington cases, the old English gun shows a smaller clearance and the newer one a larger. It is evident that chamber diameter in relation to cartridge diameter, as determining how tightly the cartridge is held beneath the rim, is a big factor in determining headspace clearance. Gun and cartridge makers will have had some headaches over this.

Excessive clearance and cure

As to what constitutes excessive clearance, all I can say at the moment is that, as indicated, the Italian case loaded with a full $1\frac{1}{16}$ oz. of shot, and fired in the first gun, weighing 6 lb. 11 oz., gives no abnormal recoil. From this it would appear that even $\frac{25}{1000}$ in. is not excessive. But the shape of the pressure curve suggests that there may be a more-or-less critical value beyond which recoil increases very rapidly. There is some practical evidence in support of this, and I am hoping to come up with more information on the subject.

Where excessive recoil is established as being due to the cause discussed—and it must not be forgotten that there may be other causes—the conventional cure would be to reduce the barrels at the breech end, and to rejoint the gun so as to bring them back to the face. But I would like to suggest the unconventional, but much cheaper and easier, alternative of soldering two discs of shim steel to the standing breech. In the kind of thicknesses necessary, there should be no difficulty in clearing the opening arc, and for test purposes they could even be secured with Araldite.

15 December 1966

Section 15

SAFETY AND DANGER

'We will merely at present say on this head: be ever careful; always treat a gun as if it were loaded, whether you be in or out of doors, and learn to handle it with . . . absolute and unswerving caution.'

(The Badminton Library—*Shooting*)

the safety-catch fallacy

An acquaintance of mine, an experienced shot, recently had occasion to remonstrate with the owner of a loaded gun, which he was pointing straight at him, only to be assured that 'the safety catch on *my* gun is absolutely safe, old boy'. I gather that the offender thereupon received some necessary enlargement of his sporting education, of which, my acquaintance suggests, many others are in need. I am sure he is right, and that the ignorance of the man who so offended him is widespread, and is often shared by experienced shots, whose consideration for the safety of their companions in the field is quite unexceptionable. But this does not mean that they know what happens inside their guns when they put the safety catch on.

What *does* happen? Nothing more than that the triggers are bolted, so that they cannot be pulled. The gun does not become uncocked, as many of the older generation of sportsmen I knew in my youth used to believe; still less does it become unloaded. The internal hammers, in fact, remain poised over the cartridges, and are only prevented from falling by a little steel beck, or sear, resting in a shallow notch, or bent, in the hammer, a mere thumbnail thickness in depth. Nothing could be less justified than the display of the word 'Safe' in these circumstances. The gun is far from being safe: indeed, inasmuch as the indication is misleading, it is in some respects more dangerous than ever.

What, then, could go wrong? Several things. It does not necessarily follow that the triggers *are* securely bolted. If the bolting arrangements are out of adjustment, the gun is capable of responding to a hard pull on the trigger. Years ago, a young Hungarian woman killed her sister this way, when demonstrating the alleged safety of her safety catch—a horrid tragedy. Then again, unless the gun is a good sidelock, it is almost certain not to be fitted with intercepting safety sears. This means that it could be jarred off by a blow or a fall. It also means that any tiny particle of foreign matter lodging on the nose of the sear could prevent its engaging properly with the bent. In such event, the gun could go off spontaneously. So it could if the lockwork were not properly hardened, when the sear and/or the bent could wear and become rounded and incapable of effective engagement.

The best safety

It is these considerations that make me sceptical of the value of the practice, conscientiously followed by many highly experienced and competent sportsmen, of keeping the safety catch on, and only pushing it forward just as they are about to take a shot. If a man walked up his game with his finger crooked around the trigger, this might be a valuable precaution against an inadvertent pull, resulting, say, from a fall or even a stumble. But the kind of men who practise this particular drill are the last to crook their fingers around their triggers: except in act of firing, they invariably carry their trigger fingers in the right place—straight forward, and resting lightly on the front of the trigger guard. There seems to be no tendency in such case to pull the trigger inadvertently. I have many a time fallen with a gun on broken ground, but have never pulled a trigger unintentionally, or felt in the slightest danger of so doing. In such cases, I find, one clutches the small of the stock with a four-fingered grip and throws the gun forwards, in what is the safest possible way in the circumstances.

But still, it might be objected, the practice in question is a good one, if only regarded as an added precaution—something one does after obeying every other safety rule. I would not wish to be unreasonable, but I am afraid my objection remains. It rests on nothing more or less than the implication that a gun is safe when its safety catch is on, whereas in fact, as I have explained, it is nothing of the kind. At best, it is like a servant of doubtful loyalty—capable of useful work, but not to be trusted.

By contrast, standing in front of it on the tang of the action is the finest and most easily operated safety catch any gun could possibly have—the top lever. It is open to doubt if a gun needs any other. Press it and drop your barrels, and you *know* your gun is safe. What is scarcely less important, everybody else in sight knows it too. Even if there are cartridges still in the breech, they are as safe there as they would be in your pocket.

And in case any young shooter reading this should think that I am just being an old fusspot, I would say that I have been very near in my time, either physically or in spirit, to several shooting fatalities. They are worth a lot of trouble to avoid.

23 November 1962

another safety-catch fallacy

With the more or less simultaneous publication of Major Roderick Willett's attractive book on *Gun Safety* and a new edition of the B.F.S.S. *Gun Code*, the subject is evidently much in the air, and there are one or two aspects to which I feel bound to return.

In my article on hammer guns I dealt at some length with their safe manipulation. But beyond a reference to safe shooting with a pair of such guns, which I made to emphasize an incidental point, I said nothing about their handling in the field. This quickly got me involved in an argument as to whether hammer guns should be carried cocked when expecting game, or whether the act of cocking should be performed as the gun is brought to the shoulder. One shooter, the proud possessor of a pair of hammer Purdeys, advocated the latter procedure, which he admittedly demonstrated with impressive neatness. But this was in cold blood, and when taking an imaginary bird going conveniently straight ahead. It might be very different in practice, with a woodcock, say, calling for some really high-speed action, including, perhaps, a rapid change in the shooter's attitude. Then the thumb might well slip on the hammer and the gun go off . . . where?

My own preference—and practice—when walking up game with a hammer gun is to carry it fully cocked when expecting a shot, and at the 'high port', with the gun held diagonally across my chest, and the barrels pointed at the sky. I had the opportunity at the Game Fair of seeking the views of two or three shooters who were best qualified, I thought, to express an opinion on the subject. They agreed with me; and it was emphasized that, even if one could safely cock one lock when bringing the gun to the shoulder, one could hardly cock both.

Outdated delusion

In a recent issue of a distinguished contemporary, a no less distinguished soldier, moved, perhaps, by this pre-season solicitude for gun safety, wrote an article on the subject which was admirable for its conciseness and coverage. Yet it contains several references which stirred me more than a little. 'In walking up game,' said the author, 'the gun can safely be carried at the ready, but not at full cock. . . . Never carry a gun at full cock. The cocking of the gun should be automatic as the gun is put to the shoulder. This . . . is the practice of all shooters who can be classified as safe.' Again, when referring to shooting with a pair of guns, he says that 'guns should never be exchanged at full cock'.

The writer was, of course, not referring to hammer guns, and thus exposes himself to the suspicion of sharing a delusion that was common among elderly shooters in the faraway days of my youth—the delusion, I mean, that the operation of the safety catch of a hammerless gun cocks and uncocks the internal hammers. This is more than a delusion: it is a dangerous delusion, and no shooter who harbours it can be classified as truly safe. Hammerless guns, once loaded, are *always* fully cocked, and of necessity are carried and exchanged in that state. All the safety catch commonly does is to bolt the triggers, so as to prevent them from being inadvertently pulled, and it cannot be relied on to do even that with absolute infallibility, as many tragic accidents have proved. But even if it could, the internal hammers of the loaded gun remain poised over the strikers, and there is nothing in the safety catch to prevent them from falling in one or other of several possible contingencies. So a shooter whose self-esteem as a safe shot rests to any extent on the perfection of his safety-catch drill is deceiving himself. He is only guarding against what should be a negligible risk—the risk of inadvertently pulling a trigger. Even if one has a fall, and I have had many a fall when carrying a gun, there seems to be no risk of this provided one observes the more important drill of keeping the fingers right away from the triggers except in the act of shooting. All that then happens in case of a fall is that one involuntarily clutches the gun more tightly around the waist. For these reasons, I would certainly not condemn a man as an unsafe shot simply because he walked with his safety catch off when expecting a shot. He might be the safest shot going—the more so for harbouring no outdated delusions.

16 September 1967

impetuous gases

Not all hammers have heads of steel and shafts of ash. Water, for example, which is heavy and even more incompressible than steel, makes a first-class hammer in certain circumstances. When water, travelling along a pipe, is suddenly checked, it is capable of delivering such a violent blow to the valve, or whatever it may be that checked it, as to knock it clean off the end of the pipe. So much is common knowledge.

Gases, too, can act as hammers. Though so much lighter than water, they are more mobile, and may make up in speed and quickness off the mark what they lack in substance. When travelling at about the speed of sound, as they do in gun barrels, the gases generated by the burning of the powder are capable of exerting destructive pressures if checked in any way. As a broad indication of the sort of forces that may be set up, it may be said that the gas produced by an ordinary 12-bore charge of black powder, travelling at the speed of sound, or, say, 1,100 ft. per second, has a kinetic energy, or energy of movement, equivalent to that of an ordinary 7-lb. sledge hammer falling from a height of over 30 ft. Evidently, there is something here that needs treating with respect.

It may, in fact, be laid down as a general principle, of which all users of firearms should be aware, that *anything that checks, prevents or interferes with the orderly and progressive development of pressure in a gun, whether that pressure is exerted forward on the charge or backwards on the breech, is a source of potential danger.*

Several possibilities

There are several ways in which dangerous transient pressures can be set up in gun barrels. The most familiar is some sort of solid obstruction. This, it should be noted, need not be an airtight plug of mud or snow; any solid object will do, such as a piece of cleaning material or some part or component of a defective cartridge left behind in the barrel. When the charge meets the obstruction, it is checked, whereupon the propellent gases undergo a pile-up, and exert a local wave pressure which may be quite capable of bursting the barrel, or at least causing a ring-bulge, which is really the characteristic trademark of such a happening.

But it should be recognized, particularly by users of muzzle-loading weapons, that it is not necessary to have a foreign body in the barrel for a dangerous wave-pressure to be set up. The French pioneer investigator of this subject, Vieille, produced intense wave-pressures by merely allowing the powder gases a free run up the bore of a test barrel, which was closed at the end. This is the situation substantially reproduced when, by the repeated firing of one barrel only of a double muzzle-loading gun, the charge in the other barrel has been shifted up the bore by the recoil. The danger of firing a charge in this state will be appreciated by all who have ever done a naval gunnery course, and was well recognized in the days of the older weapon. It should not be under-rated, even though there are those who regard it as negligible. Many a muzzle-loader was, in fact, burst by its user's failure to resettle the charge in the unfired barrel, and the habit of re-ramming it every time was therefore strongly urged by the more knowing of the old-time practitioners.

Dangers of the 'free run'

In modern guns, with their self-contained ammunition, the foregoing risk is avoided, but others take its place. These are the dangerous breech-pressures that can arise from excessive head-space in guns and rifles. In guns that are 'off the face' or otherwise in a condition to allow the cartridge case a short free run before it comes up against the solid standing breech, a high, rearward-acting wave-pressure may be set up, sufficient to split open the cartridge rim, or even, in a bad case, to smash the bar of the action.

But it is in rifles that the dangers of excessive head-space are most pronounced, not only because of the higher pressures and stresses normally involved, but because the momentum of the heavier cartridge case (or what may be left of it), added to the wave-pressure of the gas, is a more significant factor. Head-space tolerances commonly run to no more than five or six thousandths of an inch, and a similar amount in excess may well give rise to dangerous conditions, sufficient even to wreck the rifle.

Danger of oily barrels

But while on the subject of rifles, I must not forget to mention a particular kind of barrel obstruction against which all rifle shooters should be on their guard. If a heavily oiled rifle barrel is fired without first wiping it out, the accumulating resistance of the oil swept forward by the bullet may be sufficient to cause a pile-up of the gases behind it, thus giving rise to a wave-pressure that may bulge the barrel.

24 September 1964

a deadly danger

There are certain stock dangers connected with guns and shooting which need to be ventilated and explained from time to time, not only for the sake of beginners and others who may possibly be unaware of them, but also to serve as a warning against carelessness on the part of those who should know better.

The particular danger in question arises from the inadvertent mixing of 12 and 20-bore cartridges, and was well brought out in an account of a hair-raising escape recently brought to my notice. It followed the classical form in all detail, except that the shooter concerned was providentially spared the normal penalty of his carelessness.

What usually happens is this: the shooter aims at a bird and pulls the trigger, only to hear the click of a misfire. On opening the gun, he finds the chamber empty. He then assumes either that he forgot to reload, or that, if in fact he did so, he must have tilted the gun on closing it and spilled the cartridge on the ground. Sometimes he is *certain* that he reloaded, and spends some time looking around for the missing cartridge, though he never finds it. So he reloads—and the next time he fires the barrel concerned, it bursts most horribly at the breech end, and perhaps gravely injures the unlucky sportsman.

The explanation is that the shooter had a 20-bore cartridge mixed up with his 12s, which he loaded, unnoticed, into his gun. Now, the dimensions of the smaller cartridge are such that it slips down the chamber until the brass head rests in the cone at the entrance to the bore proper. There it escapes notice, and offers no impediment to the 12-bore cartridge which the shooter, thinking the chamber empty, reloads on top of it. When he next fires, the 12-bore cartridge usually sets off the 20-bore, when nothing can save a burst—unless, indeed, the bar of the action is smashed clean across, as in the case of a gallant colonel a little while ago, who found himself, after a shot, which I guess was a noisy one, holding a gun which had been neatly divided in two.

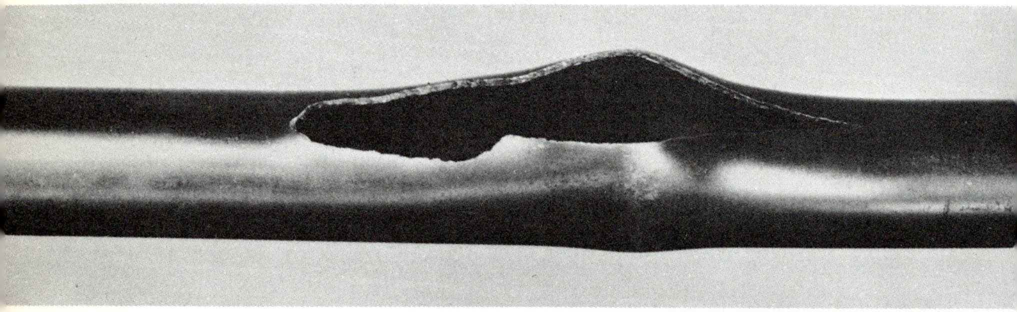

41. IMPETUOUS GASES AND A DEADLY DANGER

Above A barrel burst at the muzzle due to a plug of mud or snow. *Below* Accidental insertion of a 20-bore cartridge in front of a 12-bore caused this serious burst at the breech.

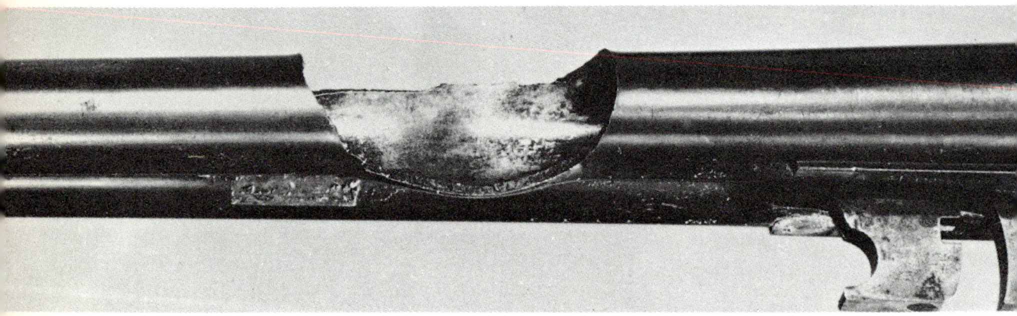

Lucky escapes

If the 20-bore cartridge escapes being fired by the 12, there is some possibility that the gun may not burst, though the only specific case of this that I know of concerned a Darne gun, the barrel of which swelled greatly but did not part. In the instance that prompted this article, the shooter was spared by having no occasion to fire his twice-loaded barrel. But he must have suffered a nasty shock when he emptied three cartridges instead of two out of his gun, for he understood quite well what *could* have happened. In two other cases I remember, the shooters escaped serious injury because the right-hand barrels were the ones involved—otherwise there would appear to be all the makings of a fatality every time this happens.

An insidious danger

There is no doubt that this is a particularly insidious danger: it seems capable of trapping the most experienced and careful shots. For my part, I find it hard to believe that any man of experience could confuse 12- and 20-bore cartridges when handled in cold blood. But then these things do not occur in cold blood: they are most likely to happen in the heat of a drive or the like, when excitement is running high and concentration is elsewhere. Besides, many men (myself included), when they have fired both barrels, like to take two cartridges and load them simultaneously into their guns—a neat and workmanlike-looking thing to do if done successfully, but offering a fatally easy chance for a 20-bore cartridge to get picked up undetected.

If, as recently related, a man can unknowingly load a tube of peppermints into his gun, the only way of reducing the 20-bore cartridge risk to vanishing point would appear to be to refuse to keep 12- and 20-bores in the same house. Nothing less is likely to serve in all contingencies.

Oil a danger

A tail-piece to this subject is provided by the case of a loader whom I watched cleaning his employer's guns. Having disposed of the barrels, he took a flat tin of oil fitted with a spout and proceeded to give the gun a good squirt of oil in and through every available joint and orifice, including the striker holes. Apart from the fact that the guns, if always treated in this manner, must have been sopping with oil to an offensive degree, the oiling of strikers can be positively dangerous. This was particularly so years ago when oils were much more prone to gumming than they are nowadays. A gummed-up striker is capable of firing the cartridge when the gun is in the act of being closed. This is most likely to happen in very cold weather, when I have known guns to misfire because the oil was frozen in the over-lubricated lockwork. Strikers, if oiled at all, should be oiled extremely sparingly.

And while we are on this subject, the possibility of a gun going off when it is being closed, whether through a gummed striker or otherwise, adds point to the maxim that the stock should always be raised to the barrels, and not the barrels to the stock.

9 September 1964

danger in case-length

It is clear from the letters I receive that one of the worries most afflicting thoughtful shooters—particularly those who have studied their Burrard—is the ammunition manufacturer's use of $2\frac{3}{4}$-in. cases in the crimp-closed cartridges provided for $2\frac{1}{2}$-in. chambered guns.

Some are concerned about the safety aspect of this practice; others are more worried about the allegedly bad effect on ballistics; whilst a few are suspicious that their interests are being sacrificed to the exigencies of production. I should have thought that all these doubts and misunderstandings had been cleared up by now, but this is evidently not the case, so I make no apology for returning to the subject.

On the safety aspect, Burrard is specific. In *The Modern Shotgun* he says, '. . . pressure is raised very considerably by using cartridges which are appreciably longer than those for which a gun is chambered. It is, for example, distinctly dangerous to fire $2\frac{3}{4}$-in. 12-bore cartridges in a gun chambered for the ordinary $2\frac{1}{2}$-in. cases.' And again, 'I have come across several instances of sportsmen abroad using $2\frac{3}{4}$-in. 12-bore cartridges in guns chambered for the ordinary $2\frac{1}{2}$-in. case, and when this has happened the gun has usually been damaged considerably.'

The remaining aspects were fairly put to me some time ago by a reader who reasoned thus: (1) excess case length is dangerous, *vide* Burrard; (2) $2\frac{3}{4}$-in. cased cartridges designed for use in $2\frac{1}{2}$-in.

chambers must therefore be 'watered down'; (3) if these watered-down cartridges are fired in a gun with $2\frac{3}{4}$ in. chambers, in which they can open up freely, they will of necessity give feeble ballistics. The reader concluded that good performance in $2\frac{3}{4}$-in. chambers was being sacrificed in the interests of standardization.

The real danger

Burrard leaves no doubt in his readers' minds that the danger in question arises from the inability of the longer case to open up properly in the shorter chamber, and the higher pressure generated by the constriction thus formed. *It cannot be too strongly emphasized that it is indeed dangerous, in general, to use cartridges whose unloaded case-length exceeds that of the chambers of the gun.*

But in the particular case cited by Burrard, the main danger arises, not from the constriction when the cartridge is fired, but from the fact that the longer-cased cartridges he had in mind invariably carried heavier loads; and heavier loads in a given gun, *using a given powder*, of necessity involve higher pressures. It is, in fact, pressure that causes the danger: no gun was ever burst or damaged by a cartridge case; and if advantage is taken of the range of powders with different burning characteristics, nowadays available to cartridge loaders, to design a cartridge for use in chambers shorter than the case length, the extra length of case by itself constitutes no danger. Nor, if the cartridge is correctly designed, need there be any falling off in ballistics when this longer-cased variety is fired in the longer chambers.

Proof of the pudding

To satisfy myself on this point, I arranged some years ago for a test to be carried out, in which cartridges from a production batch of Eley 12-bore *Grand Prix*, as sold for use in $2\frac{1}{2}$-in. chambered guns, but having $2\frac{3}{4}$-in. cases, were tested, first, in a $2\frac{1}{2}$-in. chambered pressure barrel, in order to check if the pressures and velocities were normal; and then in a $2\frac{3}{4}$-in. chambered barrel, to see if there had been any falling off. The test completely vindicated the cartridges concerned on both counts. As I briefly reported at the time, they gave notably consistent results within standard limits throughout; but as it is obvious that the bogey concerned is continually being resurrected, I now give the actual test figures in the accompanying table, in the hope that, in this more conspicuous form, they may attract the notice of those in need of the reassurance they provide.

Eley Grand Prix 12-bore crimp-closed cartridges ($1\frac{1}{16}$ oz. shot)
($2\frac{3}{4}$-inch cases, intended for $2\frac{1}{2}$-inch chambers)

$2\frac{1}{2}$-in. chambered barrel			$2\frac{3}{4}$-in. chambered barrel		
Pressure in tons per sq. in. at stated distance from breech		Velocity over 20 yds.	Pressure in tons per sq. in. at stated distance from breech		Velocity over 20 yds.
1 in.	6 in.	(ft./sec.)	1 in.	6 in.	(ft./sec.)
2·67	1·40	1082	2·65	1·44	1086
2·45	1·42	1078	2·59	1·46	1084
2·69	1·45	1096	2·40	1·37	1052
2·63	1·38	1057	2·61	1·42	1068
2·68	1·46	1079	2·76	1·42	1063
2·74	1·44	1068	2·77	1·52	1092
2·44	1·39	1055	2·82	1·40	1055
2·70	1·45	1076	2·66	1·44	1083
2·80	1·47	1093	2·72	1·48	1074
2·50	1·42	1080	2·48	1·40	1062
Av. 2·63	1·43	1076	2·65	1·44	1072

(Note: The designed velocity was 1070 in each case.)

29 October 1964

bursts

A week or two ago, I had a letter from a North Country doctor—a satisfied user of one of the better kind of Spanish guns—who had, it appeared, been made somewhat apprehensive about it by the ill-judged remarks of a friend, who assured him that these guns were inclined to burst. The implication, I take it, was that any Spanish gun was likely to burst with a normal charge—presumably because it was Spanish. A few years ago, when Spanish guns first invaded the British market in force, sweeping allegations of this sort were fairly common, but I thought that they had latterly been abandoned, along with other aspersions, equally sweeping and equally unjust, and often not entirely disinterested.

But this allegation of a bursting tendency is evidently still being made, and because of its insidious and disquieting character, it should be pinned down wherever met, not only in fairness to the guns concerned, but to reassure those like my correspondent whose pleasure in the use and possession of what may be a thoroughly sound weapon has been marred by a niggling distrust. I accordingly asked him to try to obtain chapter and verse from his friend, which he undertook to do; but I have heard nothing more, nor do I expect to do so. All the same, this incident makes me feel that the whole subject of bursts would be better for an airing.

A congenital tendency

It is well to recognize, and to bear always in mind, that *all* guns whether English or foreign, and whether of the cheapest or most expensive kind, have a powerful and innate tendency to burst. Further, that *any* gun can easily be provoked into bursting by a simple act of negligence. Further still, that *all* gunmakers with any length and breadth of experience will have had cases of their guns bursting. If, therefore, an English gunmaker were to point to a burst Spanish gun as exemplifying a perverse and mischievous tendency from which English guns are virtuously free, it would be an arrant piece of humbug. It would be indiscreet, too, for if Spanish gunmakers started exhibiting burst English guns they would not lack for distinguished examples. No; it would be more honest and more helpful to recognize the basic facts to which I have just drawn attention, and to consider what protection the shooter has against danger, and what he can do to preserve and extend it.

Proof

Recognition of the tendency of guns to burst, and of the need to protect the public from those made to inferior standards, resulted in most civilized countries making some form of proof compulsory. Here, we have been proving guns in London for three centuries, and in Birmingham for a century-and-a-half. Proof, I need hardly say, consists of subjecting the gun to the same kind of stresses as those to which it will be subjected in service, but on a higher scale. It is in short an over-stressing test, as commonly applied in engineering; and like all tests of this kind is not entirely free from the reproach of being potentially capable of starting flaws or weaknesses that would not otherwise exist. In the case of English gun proof, however, the incidence of this reproach is much diminished by the close and expert scrutiny to which every gun is subjected after the actual proof test. This scrutiny, or 'view', is regarded by our proof authorities as an essential part of the proving process, and is one that we undoubtedly carry out more rigorously than do some other countries. Spanish proof has been criticized here in the past for inefficient viewing, but never, so far as I am aware, for lack of rigour in the proof test itself; and I recall that when I was at the Spanish Proof House at Eibar a year or two ago, proof cartridges which I selected at random and personally tested were fully up to their nominal pressure.

No continuing guarantee

But it is obvious, though often overlooked, that however thoroughly it may be carried out, proof has strict limitations. It can afford no certain protection against improperly loaded cartridges, or cartridges that are not adapted to the gun; and it can safeguard the shooter only so long as the gun remains substantially in the condition as proved. Many guns have had their original margin of strength so far eroded by wear, abuse, neglect, loss of barrel metal, incompetent repair and the like as to be 'out of proof', and only the user's vigilance and common sense, aided perhaps by the advice of a competent gunsmith, can protect him from the dangers so arising.

Even with gun and cartridge in perfect order and accord, destructive pressure can easily be set up, sufficient to bulge or burst the barrel and seriously strain the action, or even smash it. So although such mishaps may not fall within the lifetime experience of the average shooting man, they are always lurking around the corner, and may well be dragged forward for examination.

Causes of failure

A gun may fail from some intrinsic weakness or external cause. Intrinsic weaknesses, whether arising from bad design; bad, incorrectly heat-treated or flawed material; or simply bad workmanship, are in every way likely to be exposed at proof. The number of cases in which proof itself may initiate a flaw, or in which there is incipient metallurgical deterioration of the kind known as age-hardening, hardly constitutes a recognizable hazard.

The only other causes worthy of present consideration are excessive pressure and/or some weakening of the gun in one or more of the ways I have already mentioned. Excessive pressure can arise from incorrectly loaded, defective or unsuitable cartridges, or from some obstruction in the bore, whereby the developing gases are either prevented from expanding or are checked in their course. Once the shot charge has got under way, *anything* that serves to check it will cause a pile-up of high-velocity gases behind it, giving rise to a localized 'wave-pressure'. This may well exceed the corresponding proof pressure and may bulge or burst the barrel.

The commonest causes of obstructional bulges and bursts are (1) the inadvertent loading of a 20-bore cartridge in front of a 12-bore; (2) plugs of mud or snow picked up in the muzzles; and (3) pieces of cleaning material left behind in the bore. One cannot emphasize too strongly the need to keep 12- and 20-bore cartridges rigidly apart; to make sure that no cartridges are used that are not designed for the gun (this may include certain non-British magnum kinds); and to check that bores are clear before starting shooting. This should be done as frequently thereafter as occasions arise on which any obstruction could have been picked up, or when any unfamiliar sound is heard on discharge, which may signal some part or component of a faulty cartridge left behind in the barrel.

Procedure

A man whose gun has burst has probably had at least a bad fright. He is likely to have suffered substantial damage to an article of value, or even its total loss. He is thus almost certain to be angry, and to be looking round for someone to blame, and from whom to claim compensation. He will also be legally recognizable as a biased witness, and his subsequent conduct should therefore be regulated by discretion. *The gun should on no account be cleaned*—to do so would arouse suspicion as being destructive of possible evidence. Ideally, it should be impounded on the spot by a credible witness, together with the remains of the cartridge and any others from the same batch, and, if possible, the carton. Together with these, it should then be sent to an independent authority—say, one of the proof houses—for examination and report. In the meantime, the gunmaker or retailer, or the ammunition manufacturer, or whoever it may be against whom the shooter considers he has a prospective claim, should be fully advised of the circumstances, so that he may inspect the gun, if he so desires, while it is in the custody of the independent authority. From such a basis, the ensuing battle—if it be a case for a battle—can be fairly joined.

24 March 1966

drachms and drams

A Canadian reader, who is taking up shooting with muzzle-loaders, and who wrote to me on a question of loads, rather made my scalp tingle by hinting at a doubt whether certain tabulated loads referred to Avoirdupois of Apothercaries' measure. *All* the tabulated loads I have ever seen, apart from those in metric quantities, are in avoirdupois measure. But the point here is that some writers (Burrard, for example) incorrectly label their powder charges as being so many 'drachms', whereas *the drachm is an apothecaries' unit, of rather more than twice the weight of the avoirdupois dram.* Further, if a conscientious reloader or, more particularly, a user of muzzle-loaders went to a chemist's shop and bought an apothecaries' balance for weighing out his charges, he would get with it a set of weights labelled 'drachms' which would weigh out double the charges intended by Burrard and others who incorrectly use this designation for the avoirdupois dram.

Of course, the reloader would quickly realize that there was something wrong from the sheer bulk of the charges so thrown, but not necessarily so the neophyte muzzle-loading man.

Our English weights and measures are, in all conscience, confusing enough on their own account, but at least the Weights and Measures Act of 1878, and an Order in Council made thereunder on August 14, 1879, make the point at issue perfectly clear. By that Act and Order, the fundamental British unit of weight is the avoirdupois pound—the Imperial Standard Pound—to which there are 16 ounces each of 16 *drams*, and also 7,000 grains. There are thus almost exactly $27\frac{1}{3}$ grains in a dram. But, by definition in the Order, a *drachm* is an apothecaries' unit of 60 grains—as I said, more than twice the weight of a dram.

In the circumstances, the safest thing is to work exclusively in *grains*. There is only one grain—the 7,000th part of a pound. But the spelling *drachm* should be emphatically dropped when avoirdupois weights are under consideration.

25 February 1965

Section 16

CARE OF GUNS

'Further, should he wish all this to be done well, let him do it himself; and, so doing, his gun will be dearer to him for the trouble it costs him, unless he be idle indeed.'

(Blaine—*Encyclopaedia of Rural Sports*)

after a wet day

The other day I had a most enjoyable afternoon's snipe shooting on some of the undrained culm measures of North Devon—starvation farm land, but congenial to the little longbills. But the weather was not kind to us, for it rained so hard that we got comically wet, including our three volunteer beaters of what we have learned to regard as the tougher sex.

Gun cleaning would, I knew, be a major operation that night; and when in due course I got the side-locks off, there was indeed an astonishing amount of water. It seemed to have penetrated freely everywhere, even where the close-fitting wood and metalwork might have been expected to ensure a water-tight joint. At one time this used to puzzle me, but now I believe I understand how it happens. I have noticed that under rainy conditions, the more cartridges one fires in the course of the day, the more water finds its way inside the gun. This, I am sure, has little to do with the frequency with which the gun has been opened for loading. Rather it is due to the water being impacted by the shock of firing and thereby scattered and sprayed into all sorts of crevices and corners into which it would otherwise scarcely penetrate. The moral of this is that a gun needs more attention after a heavy day in the rain than it does after a light one.

I may reasonably be asked, as in fact I often have been, what is my drill on these occasions? My first line of defence, since rust builds so much more easily on rust than it does on bright surfaces, is to make sure there is no initial rust anywhere on my guns. If I buy one second-hand, I have it stripped and any rust thoroughly polished out. Then I see that every part of all the internal surfaces is protected with a very thin film of vaseline. I apply this by mixing vaseline with petrol to make a water-thin oil, which, by capillary action, runs instantly into every crevice and between all closely fitted surfaces. When the petrol evaporates, which it does very quickly, all surfaces are left with their thin, unbroken vaseline film.

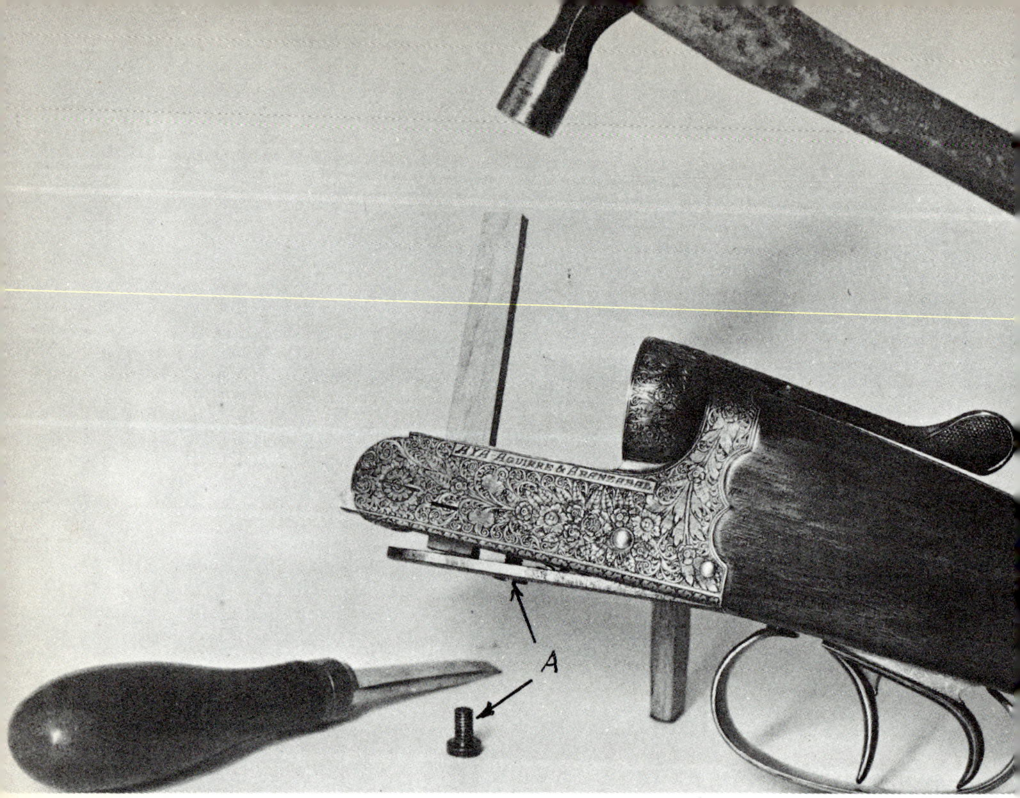

42 CARE OF GUNS
Only by removing the bottom plate of a boxlock gun can access be obtained to the essential mechanism for cleaning, drying and lubrication. Remove screw *A* and tap out the plate by a small piece of wood inserted in the forward action slot.
Note that in some Continental guns the bottom plate is in one piece with the trigger plate, and cannot be removed in the manner shown.

Mopping up

After a day out in heavy rain, I take the locks off, and shake out, tap out and mop up all the water I can. I find ordinary cotton pipe-cleaners useful for pursuing odd globules of water and absorbing them. Then I put the locks on folded newspaper on the top of an anthracite stove, so that they get fairly warm without being hot. There is no danger to the temper of the springs in this treatment, and I do not hesitate to leave the locks there all night. In the morning, I re-oil them while they are still warm.

As for the stock with the action attached, I first give it a good shaking, or, rather, swinging, so as to fling out any loose water by centrifugal action. Then I mop up any visible water with my pipe-cleaners, which, by the way, should be damp and not oily if they are to do their job. I remember under the lever and between the triggers, and I do not fail to clear out the slots for the cocking dogs, if any. Then I either leave the stock overnight in its well-ventilated, lockless state on the mantelpiece above the same anthracite stove, where, in my case, it seems to get ideally warm in a dry atmosphere; or I put it in an airing cupboard, with the action bar resting on the expansion pipe, where the action seems to get rather warmer than it does on the mantelpiece, but the stock not so warm. In either case, I feel quite happy in the morning to put things together again, after having lightly re-oiled the parts of the action requiring it.

I have forgotten to mention the fore-end, but I do not forget to look after it: it gets the same treatment as the stock. The barrels are easy, but one must not forget to take out the extractor, and mop out the holes, because there is always water there.

If I have been using a box-lock gun, I cannot, of course, remove the locks; but I do remove the cover-plate under the action, both to chase out any visible water and to ventilate the interior. Otherwise I proceed as previously described.

My methods may not be scientific: I make no use of any chemical oils or proprietary mixtures, but I have been treating my guns in this way for longer than I care to remember; yet, on the comparatively rare occasions when they are completely stripped, there is never any rusting. As for the stocks, I use one part of turpentine to three parts of boiled linseed oil, applied sparingly and well rubbed in. I always use the 'artist's' quality, so as to avoid the synthetic substitutes, which are decidedly inferior.

If I have been out on the tideway, I wash off salt spray and salt mud with soapy water—hot for the barrels and lukewarm for the woodwork, applied with a nailbrush. *Never* wipe a gun with an oily rag while it still has any salt deposit on it. Wash away the salt first, should be the golden rule.

21 December 1962

treating a gunstock

I have several times explained to enquirers the way to give a gunstock the so-called London oil finish. The process is long and takes much of my limited space to describe; and so it was a relief to be asked by a young wildfowler how to preserve the shiny, varnished finish of his new Continental gun. I accordingly recommended a modern synthetic resin varnish, and in so doing appear to have shocked at least one eminent gunmaker. But I am unrepentant: if anyone positively likes a glittery, varnished finish to his gunstock (which I myself emphatically do not), I can imagine nothing better than what I recommended. Many years ago, I experimented with a formaldehyde resin varnish, duly matted, on a wildfowling gun, and found it remarkably durable and resistant to scratches, as well as being quite unaffected by rain and salt water. Since then I believe these varnishes have undergone considerable improvement, and if only it were possible to apply them without detriment to patina, they might yet make the best possible finish for a stock. In the meantime, the oil finish remains the best way to preserve and bring out the beauty of a fine, figured stock, and so I will repeat it as it was explained to me by a professional.

The oil finish

First remove all old finish with a varnish remover. Remove scratches by scraping or sandpapering. Remove dents by pressing a wet cloth on the place with a hot iron (I use an electric soldering iron and a strip of wet felt). Finish with the finest cabinet-maker's sandpaper followed by fine steel wool.

The stock must then be 'clansed' to raise the grain. Wet it and dry it quickly over a gas ring; then rub it well down with steel wool. Repeat several times. Next apply a good dark filler, and set the stock aside. When the filler has thoroughly hardened, rub it down with the steel wool to a fine surface.

The stock should then be swabbed with hand-hot linseed oil, to which has been added (away from flame) one part of turpentine to three of oil. I use the 'artist's' quality. When the stock will absorb no more, set it aside for a few days, then repeat, and set aside for ten days or so.

Next make a buff stick by sticking a strip of felt to a flat piece of wood, and buff the stock with this, using fine pumice powder and water. Finally rub the stock by hand with boiled linseed oil, or three parts of oil to one of turpentine, using very little oil and much elbow-grease. Repeat this last process indefinitely. *If the stock is of a quality to respond to the treatment,* the result will be a glorious finish of great depth and lasting quality, bringing out the figure and grain of the wood to perfection . . . and (it has to be said) making it so beautiful that it is a shame to take it out. That is why, for my own part, I content myself with a less rigorous version of the process. I think nothing looks worse in the field than a man with a gun which he has to keep polishing with a silk handkerchief.

17 October 1963